GENDER AND SPACE IN BRITISH LITERATURE, 1660–1820

Between 1660 and 1820, Great Britain experienced significant structural transformations in class, politics, economy, print, and writing that produced new and varied spaces and with them, new and reconfigured concepts of gender. In mapping the relationship between gender and space in British literature of the period, this collection defines, charts, and explores new cartographies, both geographic and figurative. The contributors take up a variety of genres and discursive frameworks from this period, including poetry, the early novel, letters, and laboratory notebooks written by authors ranging from Aphra Behn, Hortense Mancini, and Isaac Newton to Frances Burney and Germaine de Stael. Arranged in three groups, Inside, Outside, and Borderlands, the essays conduct targeted literary analysis and explore the changing relationship between gender and different kinds of spaces in the long eighteenth century. In addition, a set of essays on Charlotte Smith's novels and a set of essays on natural philosophy offer case studies for exploring issues of gender and space within larger fields, such as an author's oeuvre or a particular discourse. Taken together, the essays demonstrate space's agency as a complement to historical change as they explore how literature delineates the gendered redefinition, occupation, negotiation, inscription, and creation of new spaces, crucially contributing to the construction of new cartographies in eighteenth- and early nineteenth-century England.

British Literature in Context in the Long Eighteenth Century

Series Editor: Jack Lynch, Rutgers University, Newark, USA

This series aims to promote original scholarship on the intersection of British literature and history in the long eighteenth century, from the Restoration through the first generation of the Romantic era.

Both "literature" and "history" are broadly conceived. Literature might include not only canonical novels, poems, and plays but also essays, life-writing, and belles lettres of all sorts, by both major and minor authors. History might include not only traditional political and social history but also the history of the book, the history of science, the history of religion, the history of scholarship, and the history of sexuality, as well as broader questions of historiography and periodization.

The series editor invites proposals for both monographs and collections taking a wide range of approaches. Contributions should be interdisciplinary but always grounded in sound historical research; the authoritative is always preferred to the merely trendy. All contributions should be written so as to be accessible to the widest possible audience, and should seek to make lasting contributions to the field.

Gender and Space in British Literature, 1660–1820

Edited by

MONA NARAIN
Texas Christian University, USA

and

KAREN GEVIRTZ
Seton Hall University, USA

ASHGATE

Published by
Ashgate Publishing Limited
Wey Court East
Union Road
Farnham
Surrey, GU9 7PT
England

Ashgate Publishing Company
110 Cherry Street
Suite 3-1
Burlington, VT 05401-3818
USA

www.ashgate.com

British Library Cataloguing in Publication Data
A catalogue record for this book is available from the British Library

The Library of Congress has cataloged the printed edition as follows:
Gender and Space in British Literature, 1660–1820 / edited by Mona Narain and Karen Gevirtz.
   pages cm. — (British Literature in Context in the Long Eighteenth Century)
   Includes bibliographical references and index.
   ISBN 978-1-4724-1508-0 (hardcover: alk. paper) — ISBN 978-1-4724-1509-7 (ebook) — ISBN 978-1-4724-1510-3 (epub)
   1. English literature—History and criticism. 2. Space and time in literature. 3. Gender identity in literature. 4. Personal space in literature. I. Narain, Mona, editor of compilation. II. Gevirtz, Karen Bloom, 1969– editor of compilation.
   PR149.S75G46 2014
   820.9'38—dc23

                                                                                    2013020329

ISBN: 9781472415080 (hbk)
ISBN: 9781472415097 (ebk – PDF)
ISBN: 9781472415103 (ebk – ePUB)

Printed and bound in Great Britain by
TJ International Ltd, Padstow, Cornwall.

*For Peter and Stephen, Tanushri, Naomi, and Ben
and for our families*

Contents

Notes on Contributors

Courtney B. Beggs is a visiting lecturer at Bridgewater State University. Her scholarship focuses on literature and culture of the long eighteenth century. Her current research explores representations of motherhood in British fiction and cultural imagination. It draws attention to the material and narrative history of women and female characters who challenge the dominant ideology of maternity in this period.

Pamela Cheek is associate professor of French at the University of New Mexico. Her book *Sexual Antipodes: Enlightenment Globalization and the Placing of Sex* was published by Stanford University Press in 2003. She is currently working on a study of relationships among late eighteenth-century women writers in Europe and Britain entitled *The Gender of Cosmopolitanism, 1747–1815*.

Mary Crone-Romanovski is assistant professor of eighteenth-century British literature at Florida Gulf Coast University. Her research focuses on space in eighteenth-century British novels. Her contribution to this collection, on gardens in amatory fiction, is taken from a larger project demonstrating the centrality of different architectural spaces and their accumulated literary and cultural meanings to the emergence of the novel as a genre.

Ambereen Dadabhoy is currently a visiting assistant professor at Harvey Mudd College in Claremont, California and formerly a lecturer in the Humanities at Boğaziçi University in Istanbul. Her scholarship addresses the intersection of gender and race in literature of the early modern period and the long eighteenth century. Dr. Dadabhoy's most recent work examines the construction of Ottoman imperial praxis in English texts.

Karen Gevirtz is associate professor of English and co-director of the Women and Gender Studies Program at Seton Hall University. Her book *Life After Death: Widows and the English Novel, Defoe to Austen* was published by the University of Delaware Press in 2005. She has published on women authors from Aphra Behn to Jane Austen, and is the executive president of the Aphra Behn Society for Women and the Arts, 1660–1830.

Aleksondra Hultquist is associate investigator at the ARC Centre of Excellence for History of Emotion at the University of Melbourne. She specializes in British prose fiction and concepts of desire particularly in the work of women writers. She has published articles on Eliza Haywood and is finishing her monograph on amatory fiction. She has held academic positions in Australia and America and is managing editor of *ABO: An Interactive Journal for Women in the Arts, 1640–1830*.

Jeong-Oh Kim is a visiting scholar at Vanderbilt University. His essay in this collection on Anne Finch's construction of the estate as political space is part of a larger scholarly interest in geography and literature. Dr. Kim has published on space in poetry and the novel and has presented at conferences in North America, Europe, and Asia. He is the recipient of a Mellon Foundation summer fellowship.

Zoe Kinsley is senior lecturer at Liverpool Hope University. Her monograph *Women Writing the Home Tour, 1682–1812* was published by Ashgate in 2008, and she coedited *Mapping Liminalities: Thresholds in Cultural and Literary Texts* (published by Peter Lang in 2007) with Lucy Kay, Terry Phillips, and Alan Roughley. In addition, Dr. Kinsley has published an extensive collection of articles and essays on eighteenth- and nineteenth-century travel writing. She is co-founder and organizer of the annual Liverpool Travel Seminar.

Heather A. Ladd is assistant professor of English at the University of Lethbridge. Her research focuses on the representation of authors and booksellers in eighteenth-century literature, and she has presented her work at national and international conferences. She has held fellowships at Chawton House and the Lewis Walpole Library at Yale University.

Kristine Larsen is professor of physics and astronomy at Central Connecticut State University. She has published extensively on the history of these disciplines in journals and edited collections, with a focus on women astronomers and physicists. Her biography of Stephen Hawking (Greenwood Press, 2005) has been translated into three languages and was reissued in 2007 by Prometheus Press.

Laura Miller is assistant professor of English at the University of West Georgia, and specializes in late seventeenth-century British literature, print history, and natural philosophy, particularly Isaac Newton. She has published on these topics in *Studies in Eighteenth-Century Culture* and the collection *Sex and Death in the Eighteenth Century* (Routledge, 2013).

Mona Narain is associate professor of English, director of graduate studies, and an affiliated faculty member of the Women's Studies program at Texas Christian University. She has published on women authors of the eighteenth century and the intersections of gender and space in journals such as *ELH*, *Studies in Romanticism*, and *SEL*. She has coedited a special issue of *JEMCS* on postcolonial revisions of early modern writing and is currently working on early modern spaces, eastern travel narratives about the west, and colonial discourse.

Kathleen M. Oliver is associate professor of English at the University of Central Florida. Her monograph *Samuel Richardson, Dress, and Discourse* was published by Palgrave Macmillan in 2008. In addition to extensive contributions on Richardson, Dr. Oliver has published on authors including Frances Sheridan, Daniel Defoe, and Sarah Fielding in journals and collections, including *Masters* *of the Marketplace: British Women Novelists of the 1750s*, edited by Susan Carlile (Lehigh University Press, 2011). She received the Emilie du Chatelet Award for Independent Scholarship, awarded by the Women's Caucus of the American Society for Eighteenth-Century Studies, in 2002.

Laura L. Runge is professor of English at the University of South Florida. She is the author of *Teaching with the Norton Anthology of Literature by Women* (Norton, 2007), *Gender and Language in British Literary Criticism, 1660–1790* (Cambridge, 1997), and numerous articles and essays. She edited *Texts from the Querelle 1641–1701* (Ashgate, 2006) and an edition of Clara Reeve's *Old English Baron* and Horace Walpole's *Castle of Otranto* (College Publishing, 2002). She also coedited *Producing the Eighteenth-Century Book: Writers and Publishers in England, 1650–1800* with Pat Rogers (University of Delaware Press, 2009) and the *Instructor's Guide for the Norton Anthology of English Literature* with Sondra Archimedes and Elizabeth Fowler (Norton, 2007). Dr. Runge is the editor of *ABO: An Interactive Journal for Women in the Arts, 1640–1830.*

Acknowledgements

The editors would like to thank Laura L. Runge, whose idea for a panel on "Women Writing Time and Space" at the 2009 Aphra Behn Society biannual conference at Cumberland University was the catalyst for this collection. They would also like to thank the Muzeum Narodowe w Warszawie, Poland, for permission to use a photographic image of Georg Friedrich Kersting's (1785–1847) painting *Hafcierka*, for the cover image of the book and Eliza Kasprzyk, Specialist, Digital Documents Department of the Muzeum Narodowe w Warszawie for her assistance.

Mona Narain would like to thank Dr. Andrew Schoolmaster, Dean, College of Liberal Arts, the English Department and Dr. Karen Steele, Chair of the English Department at Texas Christian University for generously providing funding for the production of this book. She also thanks Ms. Laura Steinbach, Reference Librarian at Texas Christian University for assistance in locating a cover image for the book, Jennifer Bauer-Krueger and Carrie Tippen for research assistance, Mark Filus for library assistance, and Alexandria Gomez for typing assistance. Travel for research for the collection was supported in part by a grant from the TCU Research and Creative Activities Fund.

Karen Gevirtz would like to thank Dr. Larry Robinson, Provost at Seton Hall University, for granting a sabbatical to facilitate the completion of this collection. She would also like to thank the English Department for supporting her sabbatical; Dr. Mary Balkun, chair of the English Department at Seton Hall University, for the generous funding that made additional travel in support of this collection possible, and Theo Grayer, her research assistant.

Together, we would like to express our deep gratitude to Ann Donahue, our editor at Ashgate, for her generous support and enthusiasm for the project from the very beginning.

Introduction

What does attending to questions about "space" and "place" add to our understanding of the construction of gender and its role in eighteenth-century Britain as viewed through the lens of literature?

To answer this question, the essays in *Gender and Space in British Literature, 1660–1820* bring the axis of gender to the forefront in considerations of the concept of space and place in eighteenth- and early nineteenth-century British literary texts of various genres, reading them from a spatial perspective to examine textual representations of gendered practices of the time period. Such a generic, methodological, and chronological scope enables an investigation of larger issues involving the interaction of space, genre, and gender during the long eighteenth century while supporting the exploration of specific texts, authors, and themes at the same time. Readers will find essays that analyze how spaces and places, ranging from material spaces such as Surinam, Jamaica, country houses, gardens, labyrinths, and seacoasts to abstract spaces such as borders and scientific discourse, produce certain kinds of hybrid subjectivities and power dynamics. Collectively, the essays show how the intellectual landscape of the eighteenth century was spatially mapped in a gendered way by writers through the means of important topoi such as exile, redemption, nature, and science.

As part of this project, this collection expands notions of space and gender, complicating the conceptualization of their relationship with each other and with literature. One of our central claims is that space itself is conceptualized in gendered terms in the eighteenth and early nineteenth centuries, not just lived and represented through gendered demarcations. Consequently, contributors reference the familiar apparatus of geography such as material maps, cartographical charts, the historical production of spaces and places, architecture, and abstract intellectual structures of science, alchemy, and nature, although their essays hardly comprise an exhaustive survey of different spaces. Rather, the essays focus on the textual representation and construction of space; in Diana Fuss's words, they "challenge the too easy bifurcation between the literal and figurative space reinforced by the separate disciplines of architecture and literature," delineating how each discourse of space was shaped by the other.[1]

Similarly, through this collection we call for a reevaluation and reconceptualization of the connections between space and gender. We abandon the traditional binary bifurcations in conceiving the logic of space, such as purely masculine or feminine, as purely restrictive or libratory for a certain gender: for example, the semi-public garden as threatening to women, or the much-used

---

[1] Diana Fuss, *The Sense of an Interior: Four Writers and the Rooms that Shaped Them* (New York: Routledge, 2004), 4.

separate spheres theory of the public and private. As a result, although used extensively in this volume, the terms "public" and "private" are invoked with an awareness of the ways in which they are largely a product of historically specific ideological constructions of the nineteenth century. When used in premodern and eighteenth-century contexts, the paradigm has to be differently described and deployed.[2] Consequently, many of our contributors deploy these terms to show how we can understand them better through the questions that the terms provoke in the context of this period. In this regard, the contributors follow the lead of recent postcolonial scholars who interrogate the binary spaces established by earlier writers, whether they are challenging the "hub-spoke" construction of an empire and its periphery or the "empire-Other" opposition, or advocating a polyphonic cosmopolitanism in eighteenth-century British literature.[3]

Our collection's complex sense of space interacts with a similarly nuanced view of gender, and of how text constructs both it and space. As much as gender is an abstract concept, it is also a lived reality with concrete forms and different manifestations in different spaces. Gender is the real as well as the imaginary locale of identity construction and social demarcation fashioned through the discrete interaction with various topoi and geographic locations. The late seventeenth through early nineteenth centuries were a crucial transition period for the development of modern notions of identity and subjectivity.[4] Consequently, in this collection, "gender" is not code for "female" as it so often is; rather, "gender"

---

[2]   Amanda Vickery, "Golden Age to Separate Spheres? A Review of the Categories and Chronologies of English Women's History," *The Historical Journal* 36, no. 2 (June 1993): 383, 400–401. Vickery also historicizes the emergence of the categories of "public" and "private" by tracing them in the writing of English historians, and discusses the ideological attraction of the separate spheres theory for modern scholars.

[3]   Alan Mikhail, "An Irrigated Empire: The View from Ottoman Fayyum," *International Journal of Middle East Studies* 42 (2010): 569–90; Pheng Cheah, Bruce Robbins, and the Social Text Collective, *Cosmopolitics: Thinking and Feeling beyond the Nation* (Minneapolis: University of Minnesota Press, 1998); Laura J. Rosenthal, "Eliza Haywood: Discrepant Cosmopolitanism and the Persistence of Romance," special issue, *Nineteenth-Century Gender Studies* 3, no. 2 (2007), http://linksource.ebsco.com.ezproxy. shu.edu/FullText.aspx?linkout=http%3a%2f%2 fatoz.ebsco.com%2flink.asp%3fid%3d105 06%26rid%3d1206065. See also, for example, Christine Daniels and Michael V. Kennedy, eds., *Negotiated Empires: Centers and Peripheries in the Americas, 1500–1820* (New York: Routledge, 2002); Lisa Lowe, *Critical Terrains: French and British Orientalisms* (Ithaca: Cornell University Press, 1991); Billie Melman, *Women's Orients: English Women and the Middle East, 1718–1918* (Ann Arbor: The University of Michigan Press, 1992).

[4]   See, for example, Timothy J. Reiss, *Mirages of the Selfe: Patterns of Personhood in Ancient and Early Modern Europe* (Stanford: Stanford University Press, 2003); Charles Taylor, *Sources of the Self: The Making of the Modern Identity* (Cambridge, MA: Harvard University Press, 1989); Roy Porter, *Flesh in the Age of Reason* (New York: W. W. Norton, 2003); Dror Wahrman, *The Making of the Modern Self: Identity and Culture in Eighteenth-Century England* (New Haven: Yale University Press, 2004); Linda Colley, *Britons: Forging the Nation, 1707–1789* (New Haven: Yale University Press, 1992).

encompasses both masculinity and femininity. Following Karen Harvey's study on gender and sexual constructions in the eighteenth century, our collection contends that embodiment's connection with space is a useful way of understanding how bodies and spaces were conceived in structural ways in eighteenth-century writing. Bodies and spaces were inextricably linked in imaginative depictions, showing bodies as space and bodies in space, and both were "shaped by geographical knowledge and its modes of expression."[5] This collection thus triangulates the relationship between space, gender, and literature, recognizing how these forces combine to enable the literary to shape the lived.

Lastly, the essays in this collection expand our understanding of how literature as a force contributes to these developments in imagining space and gender. This investigation has been taken up productively but in a limited fashion so far, primarily in examinations of specific genres, such as utopian literature and travel narratives.[6] Following the challenge implicit in Lawrence Klein's statement that "a more precise account of gender in relation to publicity and privacy can be

---

[5]   Karen Harvey, *Reading Sex in the Eighteenth-Century: Bodies and Gender in English Erotic Culture* (Cambridge: Cambridge University Press, 2004), 174–75.

[6]   See for example, Nicole Pohl and Brenda Tooley, eds., *Gender and Utopia in the Eighteenth Century: Essays in English and French Utopian Writing* (Burlington, VT: Ashgate, 2007); Pamela Cheek, *Sexual Antipodes: Enlightenment Globalization and the Placing of Sex* (Stanford: Stanford University Press, 2003); Katherine Turner, *British Travel Writers in Europe, 1750–1800: Authorship, Gender, and National Identity* (Burlington, VT: Ashgate, 2002); Susan Lamb, *Bringing Travel Home to England: Tourism, Gender, and Imaginative Literature in the Eighteenth Century* (Newark, DE: University of Delaware Press, 2009); Sharon Harrow, *Adventures in Domesticity: Gender and Colonial Adulteration in Eighteenth-Century British Literature* (New York: AMS Press, 2004); Kathleen Wilson, *The Island Race: Englishness, Empire, and Gender in the Eighteenth Century* (London: Routledge, 2003); Felicity Nussbaum, ed., *The Global Eighteenth Century* (Baltimore: The Johns Hopkins University Press, 2003); Maria Hanna Makowiecka, *The Theme of "Departure" in Women's Travel Narratives, 1600–1900: Taking Leave from Oneself* (Lewiston, NY: The Edwin Mellen Press, 2007); Lizabeth Paravisini-Gebert and Ivette Romero-Cesareo, eds., *Women at Sea: Travel Writing and the Limits of Caribbean Discourse* (New York: Palgrave Macmillan, 2001); Rosenthal, "Eliza Haywood"; and Chloe Chard, "Women Who Transmute into Tourist Attractions: Spectator and Spectacle on the Grand Tour," in *Romantic Geographies: Discourses of Travel, 1775–1844*, ed. Amanda Gilroy (Manchester: Manchester University Press, 2000), 109–26. Although concerned with a later period, Catherine Hall's *Civilising Subjects: Metropole and Colony in the English Imagination, 1830–1867* (Cambridge: Polity Press, 2002) also makes a valuable contribution to this discussion. It is perhaps worth noting with Fatima Vieira that utopia narratives get their structural foundation from travel narratives, suggesting a potentially rich investigation of gender and generic concerns. Fatima Vieira, "The Concept of Utopia," in *The Cambridge Companion to Utopian Literature*, ed. Gregory Claes (Cambridge: Cambridge University Press, 2010), 7.

achieved by closer examination of both space and *language*,"[7] our collection takes one more step back, to look at the interaction of genre and literature with notions of gender and space. While drawing on spatial theory, however, our approach is not purely theoretical; rather, the essays in this collection recognize that literature and cultural concepts are grounded in historicity. Our approach to the notion of demarcated and gendered spatial logic in particular, therefore, is that categories such as private/domestic and public, or metropole and colony, although useful conceptually for scholars, were rarely an exclusive material reality for eighteenth- and early nineteenth-century British men and women.

Critical Framework

Gender and Space in British Literature has its origins in the geographical turn in literary studies that has energized the study of literature in the last decade and a half. This approach considers how space and place interacted with history, time, language, and culture to produce specific social and aesthetic formulations, such as gender, which construct literature and are in turn constructed by and represented in literary texts. Since Raymond Williams, and particularly vigorously since the early 1990s, theorists have been arguing that "space" is constructed in whole or in part by and through ideology. Space as a category of analysis provides the opportunity to make new, intricate discoveries and models to understand the situatedness of discourse. As critics and cultural geographers including Mary Pat Brady, Peter Jackson, Linda McDowell, Doreen Massey, and Gillian Rose have argued, such discoveries allow us to add an additional dimension to our temporal and historical understanding of literature.[8]

The terms "space" and "place" are not interchangeable, although they are closely related, and the politics of each zone can be similar or even, at times, the same. In this collection, the term "space" refers to a geographical, material area; "place" is an area delineated by the convergence of the material, the ideological, and memory. The essays demonstrate how historicizing space is as important as theorizing space. Each essay studies and provides a snapshot of discrete histories of eighteenth-century spaces. Additionally, this collection is an effort to provide a literary and historical framework for abstract theories of space by grounding

---

[7]   Lawrence Klein, "Gender and the Public/Private Distinction in the Eighteenth Century: Some Questions about Evidence and Analytical Procedure," *Eighteenth-Century Studies* 29, no.1 (1995): 99, original emphasis.

[8]   See, for example, Mary Pat Brady, *Extinct Lands, Temporal Geographies: Chicana Literature and the Urgency of Space* (Durham: Duke University Press, 2002); Peter Jackson, *Maps of Meaning: An Introduction to Cultural Geography* (London: Routledge, 1992); Linda McDowell, *Gender, Identity and Place: Understanding Feminist Geographies* (Minneapolis: University of Minnesota Press, 1999). See also Allan Pred, "Place as Historically Contingent Process: Structuration and the Time-Geography of Becoming Places," *Annals of the Association of American Geographers* 74, no. 2 (1984): 279.

them in specificities. Thus, questions about the relationship among these forces—material, ideological, theoretical—are transcendent in the sense that they are always worth posing, and historically bounded in the sense that they are answered differently at different times.

These questions are particularly pressing when they mark, catalyze, or signal a moment of transition, as they do in the shift into modernity during the late seventeenth through early nineteenth centuries. For example, Henri Lefebvre has historicized the emergence of new kinds of spaces in the early modern western world that arose with the rise of capitalism, such as urban centers, where the demarcation between "private" and "public" created new divisions of spatiality.[9] Some of the key transitions critical to the eighteenth century were historical changes, like the emerging marks of capitalism on geography: large demographic shifts from rural to urban centers; the linkage of distant geographical locations through the flow of power, money, and print; the changing borders and peripheries of nations and societies due to war; architectural shifts in interiors of houses; and the way individuals constructed and inhabited new and old spaces with changing proximity. In fact, Michel Foucault inaugurated inquiries into the relationship between space and modernity when he argued that modernity is separated from the premodern by a singular concern with space, and his insistence on space as an analytical category for modernity has been critical to the spatial turn in early modern literary studies.[10] Although his method pioneered the fusion of theory and historicity, much work remains to be done in the exploration of aspects of history and modernity as they have to do with space and place. In particular, we need to study the emergence of historically specific modern phenomena from the period between 1660 and 1820, such as the appearance of new, hybrid identities formulated in new locations not extant before in time or space due to these large historical transitions. Some of this discussion may be found among historians, such as the debate on the relationship between economic theory, political party, and the spaces of empire waged in the Winter 2012 issue of *The William and Mary*

---

9   Henri Lefebvre, *The Production of Space*, trans. Donald Nicholson-Smith (Malden: Blackwell, 1991), 53–59.

10   Michel Foucault, "Of Other Spaces," *Diacritics* 16, no.1 (Spring 1986): 22. Edward Soja discusses the foundational contributions of Michel Foucault to theories of space and the interdisciplinary value of Foucault's formulations. He writes, "Foucault focused our attention on another spatiality of social life, an 'external space', the actually lived (and socially produced) space of sites and the relations between them." Edward Soja, *Postmodern Geographies: The Reassertion of Space in Critical Social Theory* (New York: Verso, 1989), 17. Similarly, Peter Jackson argues that a Foucauldian approach to analyzing systems of power "provide[s] tools for knowing the forms of power that underpin discourses of prisons, madness, sexuality, and other topics" that are sensitive to the role of historical context. Peter Jackson, "Why I am a Foucauldian," *SOJOURN: Journal of Social Issues in Southeast Asia* 21, no. 1 (2006): 115, 114.

Quarterly, but literary scholars have not been as forward to engage these issues.[11] The essays in this collection begin this project, examining the ways in which identity and space and/or place mutually construct each other and, in so doing, create a dynamic in which modernity itself can be and is constructed, as well.

Central to our purpose, then, is the idea that during the late seventeenth through early nineteenth centuries, identity and space or place enjoyed a dialectic relationship: neither came first and each informed the construction of the other. Building on the ideas of the eighteenth-century public and private spheres and the "republic of letters" proposed by Jurgen Habermas in *The Structural Transformation of the Public Sphere* and importantly critiqued and modified by his successors,[12] this collection shows how these realms in this period enabled the emergence of particular kinds of spaces, from the coffeehouse to the Royal Society to the salon, and with them, different ways of being or imagining what it is to be a particular kind of person. The new space of capitalist print culture, for example, generated the metaphoric "room" that allowed women writers to publish.

The expression of what Gaston Bachelard called the "spatial imaginary" in literature is a particularly fertile ground for understanding how space and identity are constitutive, and mutually constitutive, forces.[13] In recent years, scholars studying the early modern world, especially the long eighteenth century, have productively employed these concepts to understand the interaction of time and space, of subjectivities and places and the aesthetics of borders and locations. This interdisciplinary work has revealed how concrete locations interact with the imaginary in a vital, ongoing dialogue within texts. So far, however, the issue of gender and space or place has not been explored in a sustained manner that merges a theoretical and historiographical understanding. While there has been crucial

---

[11]   The William and Mary Quarterly 69, no. 1 (January 2012), http://www.jstor.org/stable/10.5309/willmaryquar.69.1.FM.

[12]   See for example, Lefebvre, *The Production of Space*; Seyla Benhabib, "Models of Public Space: Hannah Arendt, the Liberal Tradition, and Jurgen Habermas," in *Habermas and the Public Sphere*, ed. Craig Calhoun (Cambridge, MA: MIT Press, 1999), 73–98; Nancy Fraser, "Rethinking the Public Sphere: A contribution to the critique of Actually Existing Democracy," in Calhoun, *Habermas*, 109–42; and Joan Landes, *Women and the Public Sphere in the Age of the French Revolution* (Ithaca: Cornell University Press, 1988).

[13]   Gaston Bachelard, *The Poetics of Space* (New York: Orion, 1964). See also, for example, Edward Soja's *Postmodern Geographies*. For a discussion of key theoretical contributors to this methodology see Mike Crang and Nigel Thrift, eds., *Thinking Space* (New York: Routledge, 2000) and Phil Hubbard, Rob Kitchin, and Gill Valentine, eds., *Key Thinkers on Space and Place*, 2nd ed. (Thousand Oaks: Sage Publications, 2004). For an early examination of the spatial dimensions of literature, see the collection of essays, Margaret R. Higonnet and Joan Templeton, eds., *Reconfigured Spheres: Feminist Explorations of Literary Space* (Amherst: University of Massachusetts Press, 1994).

work theorizing space and gender, a consistent historical understanding of either category has not been a focus of this work.[14]

Similarly, although studies of the British eighteenth century using space as an analytical category have begun to appear, they do not yet fully account for gender. Daniel Brewer's groundbreaking essay "Lights in Space" (2004) and longer studies such as Cynthia Wall's *The Literary and Cultural Spaces of Restoration London* (1998), Miles Ogborn's *Spaces of Modernity: London's Geographies, 1680–1780* (1998), and Ogborn and Charles Withers's recent and important collection *Georgian Geographies* (2004) recognize the eighteenth century as an important spatial and temporal location in which to interrogate how new forms of physical connections, material locations, intellectual landscapes, and representational practices converged and were transformed, but as yet, gender remains essentially uninvestigated. Amanda Flather's *Gender and Space in Early Modern England* (2007) most closely approaches this task, but Flather's excellent study leaves unregarded the larger question that concerns us: how does the interaction between gender and space or place not only construct gender, but also, and crucially, construct and gender space and place in modernity?[15]

The essays in this collection answer this question using different methodologies and apply them to a variety of genres, but they separately and together maintain that the period's cultural imagination produced or modified ideas about identity, as well as about specific identity, that went on to shape spaces and places that were material, psychological, and/or ideological. For example, the relationship among the literary, ideological, and material spaces of empire was central to the formation of new places being labeled as "home" or "colony," and to the identities of those who went on to inhabit them or traveled among them. These new roles in new

---

[14] Some of the most important early feminist interventions that provide a sustained theorization of the space from the point of view of gender include Beatriz Colomina's edited collection, *Sexuality and Space* (New York: Princeton Architectural Press, 1992); Daphne Spain's *Gendered Spaces* (Chapel Hill: University of North Carolina Press, 1992); Gillian Rose's *Feminism and Geography: the Limits of Geographical Knowledge* (Minneapolis: University of Minnesota Press, 1993); Doreen Massey's *Space, Place and Gender* (Minneapolis: University of Minnesota Press, 1994); Dolores Hayden's *The Power of Place* (Cambridge, MA: MIT Press, 1995); Kathleen Kirby's *Indifferent Boundaries: Spatial Concepts of Human Subjectivity* (New York: Guilford Press, 1996); Linda McDowell and Jenny Sharp's edited collection *Space, Gender, Knowledge: Readings in Feminist Geography* (New York: J. Wiley, 1997); and Linda McDowell's *Gender, Identity and Place*.

[15] Daniel Brewer, "Lights in Space," *Eighteenth-Century Studies* 37, no. 2 (Winter 2004): 171–86; Cynthia Wall, *The Literary and Cultural Spaces of Restoration London* (New York: Cambridge University Press, 1998); Miles Ogborn, *Spaces of Modernity: London's Geographies, 1680–1780* (New York: Guilford Press, 1998); Miles Ogborn and Charles Withers, eds., *Georgian Geographies: Essays on Space, Place and Landscape in the Eighteenth Century* (Manchester: Manchester University Press, 2004); Amanda Flather, *Gender and Space in Early Modern England* (Woodbridge, UK: Boydell Press, 2007).

places include colonial or slave identities that were produced in far-off locations on the edges of a nascent empire, such as British-controlled Surinam or Jamaica, and identities of exile, formed in the places and spaces created by the Napoleonic wars. European colonialism's appropriation of geography, culture, and memory had led to contemporary exiles and to the dis-placement and dis-location of (post) colonial identities.[16] Exile is always and already a condition of the (post)colonial subject emerging simultaneously with the conception and narration of modern nation states.[17] Extending insights into later periods offered by Edward Said, Homi Babha, and Gayatri Spivak, essays in our collection describe eighteenth-century conditions of exile as Britain's geographical borders shifted due to wars and territorial acquisitions during this time. Peter Hitchcock has argued that the history of transnationalism is much longer than the term itself. Our collection demonstrates that when we insert considerations of the space of narration and form itself, we bring the local sharply into focus to understand cultural differences within narratives. This focus on the local, we argue, makes visible differences of gender as well: women and men experience exile differently and inhabit different spaces at home and abroad in different ways.[18] Local history and different places define the meaning of exile in different ways. Whether it is the Caribbean or Europe or the wild seacoast, as Hultquist's, Cheek's, and Kingsley's essays in this collection reveal, exile has a Janus face. Exile could mean travel to freedom, away from long-rooted negative identities for English women to the "new" colony of Jamaica; a return to an exilic "home" of wartime Britain or France as a place of melancholic loss; or living on the ambivalent margins of patriarchal society

---

[16]   Edward Said, "Reflections on Exile," in *Reflections on Exile and Other Essays* (Cambridge, MA: Harvard University Press, 2000), 174–75. See also Said's *Orientalism* (New York: Pantheon, 1978) and *Out of Place* (New York: Vintage, 1999); Homi Bhabha and W. J. T. Mitchell, eds., *Edward Said: Continuing the Conversation*, (Chicago: Chicago University Press, 2005); John D. Barbour, "Edward Said and the Space of Exile," *Literature & Theology* 21, no. 3 (September 2007): 293–301; Mark Muhannad Ayyash, "Edward Said: Writing in Exile," *Comparative Studies of South Asia, Africa and the Middle East* 30, no. 1 (2010): 107–18. See Philip Major, ed., *Literatures of Exile in the English Revolution and Its Aftermath, 1640–1690* (Burlington, VT: Ashgate, 2010) for a historical and literary assessment of exile in the seventeenth century.

[17]   Homi Bhabha, ed., *Nation and Narration* (New York: Routledge, 1990); Gayatri Charkravorty Spivak, *A Critique of Postcolonial Reason* (Cambridge, MA: Harvard University Press, 1997). Daniel Carey and Lynn Festa have argued that the "incorporation of postcolonial theory into the field of eighteenth-century studies has helped to illuminate … the uneven development of early modern categories of gender, race, and nation; it has opened up new avenues to critique the omissions and aspirations of Enlightenment thought." Daniel Carey and Lynn Festa, "Introduction, Some Answers to the Question: What is Postcolonial Enlightenment?" in *The Postcolonial Enlightenment: Eighteenth-Century Colonialism and Postcolonial Theory*, ed. Daniel Carey and Lynn Festa (Oxford: Oxford University Press, 2009), 3.

[18]   Peter Hitchcock, *The Long Space: Transnationalism and Postcolonial Form* (Stanford, CA: Stanford University Press, 2010), 8–9.

on the remote coastlines of the country—locations of both expulsion and self-actualization for women.

We have divided the essays into three sections: Outside, Borderlands, and Inside. Throughout the collection, the authors explore the definitions and limitations of these spatial concepts as they were deployed or challenged in literature during the period between 1660 and 1820. While we intend the groupings to provide structure and an easy way to recognize the affinities of these essays, we also urge our readers not to be constrained by them. As this collection should suggest, spatial divisions can and should be recognized and challenged for the constructs that they are. There are any number of overlaps, cross-pollinations, and interinanimations between and among essays in different groups. We hope our readers, therefore, will move through and across the spaces of this collection, following ideas, texts, authors, and methods as their interests and the work of our contributors suggest. These groupings are aids to conceptualization, nothing more; it would sadden us to think they had limited our readers' opportunities to see the depth and complexity of the individual essays or of the field as these essays shape it.

Outside

The essays in this first section show the recurring interest in how "outside" as a space, as a place, and as a state are constituted. Building on Benedict Anderson's insight in *Imagined Communities* that nationality is constructed within material space but through imaginative acts of aggregation, Peter Jackson points out in *Maps of Meaning* that there is a significant "territorial dimension of local ideological struggles." "Places are made through power relations which construct the rules which define boundaries," Linda McDowell explains. "These boundaries are both social and spatial—they define who belongs in a place and who may be excluded, as well as the location or site of the experience."[19] For the authors discussed in this section, whether "outside" refers to a space outside certain boundaries or a particular place, it acts as a site of in-betweenness and "dis"placement,[20] a potent topos for eighteenth-century writers as the expansion of the geographical boundaries of the globe made far-flung colonial locations, such as seventeenth-

---

[19] Benedict Anderson, *Imagined Communities: Reflections on the Origin and Spread of Nationalism* (New York: Verso, 2006); Jackson, *Maps of Meaning*, 73; McDowell, *Gender, Identity and Place*, 4.

[20] See Homi Bhabha's theorization of (post)colonial hybridity as a product of global trade and travel and colonial/imperial expansion, a historical phenomenon first experienced in the eighteenth century in Britain. Both the colonizer and the colonized experience this displacement. See also Gloria Anzaldua and Cherrie Moraga's deployment of borderlands as a material metaphor for the dispossessed Chicana/o identities in several of their works; see, for example, their edited collection *This Bridge Called My Back: Writings by Radical Women of Color* (New York: Kitchen Table, Women of Color Press, 1983).

century South America and the Caribbean, locations where people went willingly or unwillingly when home was inhospitable.

Laura Runge's essay, "Constructing Place in *Oroonoko*," sets the terms for the discussion of "outside" as well as for the collection as a whole. Behn's record of human experience of disparate, far-flung locations, and the process of attaching meaning to them for readers who had never been there, reveals place-making's literary, cultural, political, and ideological importance: "Place," Runge argues, is a "geographical location invested with meaning in a context of power" within larger concepts of space. Runge's reading highlights the late seventeenth-century stakes in defining places as outside. Innovatively reading Behn's novella, which connected the Atlantic to Europe for Restoration readers through print and memory, she peels back the layered connotations of these places recorded for history in the novella and its subsequent adaptations. Runge complicates the concept of the metropole and colony by situating Behn's novella within the context of the Dutch acquisition of Surinam. Runge argues that Behn is as concerned about the relationship between the English and Dutch, and their early competition as colonizers in South America, as she is in depicting the colonization of Surinam and the slave trade. Uncovering these layered meanings, Runge offers today's readers—students and scholars— insights on how to relate to the past and to the places delineated in the novel.

The rest of the essays in this section take up aspects introduced by Runge in her lead-off contribution. The recurring conflation of being outside as being in exile, a social state often defined by a geographical location, raises for writers not only the ideology of political, social, religious, and physical inclusion, but also the ideology of political, social, religious, and material identity. Aleksondra Hultquist addresses constructions of exile and the implications of those notions of exile and exilic spaces for gender. Hultquist complicates the conventional view that in the eighteenth-century British imagination, Jamaica was a literal and symbolic physical and literary repository for admirable colonial ambition (for men) or disgraceful sexual immorality (for women). If, as Jon May contends, "for those in a position of considerable cultural and economic power, it would seem possible to construct a markedly bounded, and thus reactionary, sense of place through a particular vision of those global connections understood as articulated in an ethnically diverse area,"[21] Hultquist's analysis of Eliza Haywood's and Delarivier Manley's handling of Jamaica shows the challenges and possibilities for people who do not occupy such a position. Drawing on the concept of the metropole, she shows how women authors like Haywood and Manley rewrote these associations, using Jamaica to give women the same social and economic refashioning that Jamaica offered men, thereby inverting Jamaica's function as a sign of moral irredeemability to render the island a force instead for moral recuperation. Women who are initially exiled to Jamaica become cosmopolitans

---

[21]   Jon May, "Globalization and the Politics of Place: Place and Identity in an Inner London Neighbourhood," *Transactions of the Institute of British Geographers*, New Series 21, no. 1 (1996): 196.

who occupy various subject positions simultaneously, as citizens of both the metropole and the colony—subject positions that would have been unavailable to them had they continued to live in England. In this sense, exile becomes the condition for a cosmopolitan identity. Material Jamaica itself is less important, Hultquist demonstrates, than the space that "Jamaica" occupies in the cultural imagination. The dynamic among the construction of the spaces that are Jamaica, England, and "woman" (both virtuous and vicious) was more contested than has been thought, requiring a reconceptualization of the progress of imperialism in the British imagination and in the British literary imagination.

Like the authors in Hultquist's essay, Lady Mary Wortley Montagu uses place to establish but also to interrogate constructions of gender. Following Mary Louise Pratt's notion of the "contact zone," a region of imperial space in which the "spatial and temporal copresence of subjects previously separated by geographic and historical disjuncture" is characterized by "copresence, interaction, interlocking understandings and practices,"[22] Ambereen Dadabhoy demonstrates how Montagu's letters transform normally established, delineated spaces—national space, domestic space, and especially the physical space staked out by clothing, notably the veil in Muslim countries—into sites of intersection and therefore reorganization or reconstruction. Consequently, while Montagu is sometimes linked with other female travelers of the eighteenth and early nineteenth centuries, such as Lady Hester Stanhope and especially Lady Elizabeth Craven, Dadabhoy's analysis challenges this association by showing how Montagu, unlike the others, is interested in the permeability of identity.[23] For Montagu, the act of traveling, of moving further and further outside, becomes a metaphor: through her letters, catalyzed by physical travel, Montagu travels through and reconstitutes the places which she encounters, thus reconstituting the associations which those places possess for her English audience. This redefinition of place in turn becomes

---

[22]   Mary Louise Pratt, *Imperial Eyes: Travel Writing and Transculturation* (New York: Routledge, 1992), 6–7.

[23]   For discussions of Montagu and Craven, see, for example, Donna Landry, "Horsy and Persistently Queer: Imperialism, Feminism and Bestiality," *Textual Practice* 15, no. 3 (2001): 467–85; Donna Landry, "Love Me, Love My Turkey Book: Letters and Turkish Travelogues in Early Modern England," in *Epistolary Histories: Letters, Fiction, Culture*, ed. Amanda Gilroy and W. M. Verhoeven (Charlottesville: The University Press of Virginia, 2000), 51–71; and Melman, *Women's Orients*. Primarily discussed by Joyceans because of her connections to Molly Bloom, Lady Hester Stanhope has been an object of biographical interest recently, boasting three biographies since 2006: Lorna Gibb's *Lady Hester, Queen of the East* (London: Faber & Faber, 2006); a reissued edition of Joan Haslip's 1934 *Lady Hester Stanhope: The Extraordinary Life of the "Queen of the Desert"* (Charleston, SC: The History Press, 2006); and Kirsten Ellis's *Star of the Morning: The Extraordinary Life of Lady Hester Stanhope* (New York: HarperCollins, 2008). For discussions of Lady Hester in the context of Joyce's *Ulysses*, see, for example, Michael H. Begnal, "Molly Bloom and Lady Hester Stanhope," in *Joyce and Popular Culture*, ed. R. B. Kershner (Gainesville: University Press of Florida, 1996), 64–73.

a redefinition of the identities to which place contributes. Ultimately, Dadabhoy argues, by reconceptualizing spaces that define through inclusion and exclusion into spaces that define by combination and intersection, Montagu does not simply self-fashion herself, but also refashions the more general identities—foreigner, English woman, writer, and so forth—constituted by such spaces.

The last essay in this section, Kristine Larsen's "Margaret Bryan and Jane Marcet: Making Space for 'Space' in British Women's Science Writing, 1797–1819," takes up the many aspects of the term "space." Larsen points out that "space" and its discipline, astronomy, were constituted by gendering a range of spaces, from the viewing end of the telescope to the observatory to the Royal Society to the cosmos itself. Gendering these spaces, Larsen points out, was interrelated with the gendering of astronomy's textual genres, its generic space, during this period. Larsen's essay concludes by pointing out the continued importance of this exclusion for women, well into the twenty-first century, as the control of observatories and other scientific places limit women's access to science's discursive spaces: the space of the profession, the space of its genres, and to astronomical space itself. Thus "outside" for Larsen, Dadabhoy, Hultquist, and Runge becomes necessarily contestable space and place.

Borderlands

"Women have a history of reading and writing in the interstices of masculine culture," Caren Kaplan observes as she discusses the displacement of marginality.[24] These interstices are the material, imaginary, and metaphorical as well as ideological margins and borders of patriarchal cultural terrains. In the section entitled "Borderlands," our contributors discuss how the representation of space was used to render permeable or unstable the space and the gender associations that it constructed and was constructed by. The essays in this section investigate ways in which eighteenth- and early nineteenth-century writers tested, deconstructed, and sometimes reconstructed the spaces in which notions of gender and notions of space collide or combine.

Using a variety of seemingly definite spaces—the house, the seashore, the garden—Pamela Cheek, Zoë Kinsley, and Courtney B. Beggs expand upon the idea that women authors rendered permeable, or exposed the permeability of, spaces crucial to the self-fashioning of individual as well as national identity during this period. Pamela Cheek explores the difference between cosmopolitanism, as a self-selected decision to be a citizen of the world and a refusal to belong to one nation, and exile as expulsion from a nation in her essay on Frances Burney and Germaine de Staël. Although increased travel and territorial acquisitions opened new geographies for exploration to eighteenth-century European women, Cheek

---

[24]   Caren Kaplan, "Deterritorializations: The Rewriting of Home and Exile in Western Feminist Discourse," in "The Nature and Context of Minority Discourse," special issue, *Cultural Critique* 6 (Spring 1987): 187.

makes the perceptive observation that eighteenth-century European women were ultimately "exiles *avant la lettre*," because they could claim neither citizenship nor nationality. As Cheek shows, the nation as home is rendered even more unfamiliar and uncanny as borders close for the protagonists of Fanny Burney's and Germaine Staël's novels after the French Revolution. For Burney's and de Staël's self-exiled heroines, borders are fluid but the uncanny nature of displacement makes displacement a psychic and material inevitability—often a location of the modern self. Cheek examines the biographical details of Burney and Staël's personal relationship and the writers' "own wanderings and exile with an analysis of their heroines'" exiles and travels. Both Burney and Staël, she argues, stretch the novel's spatial form and its narrative boundaries in an attempt to capture this self's displacement.

Zoë Kinsley explores the spaces of eighteenth-century borders and the margins of cartography and human psychology as depicted in Charlotte Smith's work. Kinsley shows how Charlotte Smith, a writer uncommonly aware of the spatiality of gender, used the ocean's coastline in her poems and novels as an interstitial dwelling as well as a metaphoric representation of the interstices in which women marginalized from society live. While in the eighteenth century coastlines were important demarcations of national territories, such as between warring Britain and France, they were also spaces beginning to be carefully charted by surveyors and naval cartographers for legible, legal specificity. Kinsley's essay shows instead that coastlines are the metaphoric and real places that exiled women inhabit, the no man's land of expulsion. Through a close reading of Smith's *The Young Philosopher*, Kingsley persuasively demonstrates how Smith imagined the coast as a suitable and fertile site for the formation of eighteenth-century feminine identity and, simultaneously, its erasure. Ultimately, Kingsley finds, Smith rejected "pinning" down the British coast as a location simply of leisure, pleasure, and national boundary, much as she rejected the consignment of women to prescribed, socially sanctioned identities, instead leaving readers with the image and concept of the coast and feminine selfhood as spaces where varied possibilities could be realized.

Courtney Beggs's essay on Hortense Mancini, Duchess of Mazarin demonstrates how Mancini self-consciously rendered seemingly stable material and literary spaces unstable in order to remake the literal and discursive spaces to which she was assigned or to which she sought to lay claim. Beggs demonstrates how Mancini's liminal position in the Stuart court, as a French immigrant fleeing her husband's power, yet a favorite of the king, gave the duchess opportunities to rewrite herself out of her victim status and use the space of the salon to empower herself. In Mancini's project, even poetry becomes a borderland as she uses verse to cross between different countries, roles, and social positions, thus rendering poetry itself a no (wo)man's land. The three essays in this section reveal how writers deployed and rewrote material spaces to metaphorically and productively stretch genre, narration, and language in order to capture the fluidity of gendered self-representation and identification.

Inside

The five essays of this section—two pairs bridged by a single essay—expose how the notion of "inside" space involves several closely related meanings. The first pair of essays in this section consider "inside" in the sense of enclosed but outdoor spaces. In the hands of early novelists such as Eliza Haywood and Mary Davys, as Mary Crone-Romanovski contends, the public spaces of the garden, which also paradoxically enclose private spots, allow heroines a freedom to appropriate both interior and exterior spaces which they can use to assert their desires and agency. Crone-Romanovski demonstrates how these writers of amatory fiction used the narrative possibilities of the garden to extend women characters' ability to enact that which was not possible within the house, such as a forbidden erotic encounter, or in the public sphere, such as the expression of feminine agency against patriarchy or the expression of reason and discourse on women's part. As Crone-Romanovski shows, eighteenth-century transitions in garden design and the garden's changing cultural meaning at the time became transgressive instruments in the hands of amatory fiction writers. Similarly, Jeong-oh Kim argues that the poet Anne Finch uses the seclusion of the private country house as a public pulpit, and her country landscape as the location for political arguments after she was sent to the country by a displeased monarch. The specifically spatial genre of poetry, Kim contends, was an important means for Finch to overcome the exclusion from the public space of the court. Finch's reimagination of the purpose of the spaces of the country house and the genre of pastoral poetry for engagement rather than romantic isolation transforms both the material and the imaginative location. The immediate orientation might seem different: Finch's move to redefine the estate is both highly political and profoundly personal, while Haywood and Davys are making more socially oriented claims. Nevertheless, these essays share an important subtext, pointing out implicitly but crucially how the paradox of enclosed natural spaces—used to give the feeling of being outside and yet deliberately hemmed about—offers authors like Finch, Haywood, and Davys the opportunity to explore the paradox of genre and gender.

Laura Miller's essay provides a transition between the two pairs of essays in this section. Extending the insights of scholars such as Steven Shapin, Simon Shaffer, and Philip Carter into sociability and early science, Miller considers the ways in which what has come to be considered "scientific space," the laboratory, is not simply work space but also social space for men. As Charles W. J. Withers explains, "The fact that the nature of science is conditioned by place, is *produced through place* as practice rather than simply *in place* is of greater significance …. Understanding science's claims to knowledge is thus a matter of understanding its mobility, of travel between places not just epistemic practice in place."[25] Like Crone-Romanovski and Kim, Miller recognizes ways in which activities, as well

---

[25]   Charles W. J. Withers, "Place and the 'Spatial Turn' in Geography and in History," *Journal of the History of Ideas* 70, no. 4 (2009): 653, original emphasis.

as the textual vocabulary and structures used for those activities, delineate and value space. Pushing beyond the conventional "gentleman's club" idea, Miller labels the laboratory "alchemical space" rather than "scientific space," based not only on the point that it was alchemy rather than science that was practiced in these places, but also on the notion that the practices and relationships themselves were alchemical. Like alchemy, with its mixed identity as a practice of knowledge and a practice of faith, these male, domestic spaces themselves possessed and fostered a mixed or liminal identity, fostering as they did social behaviors and relationships that permitted a more mixed sexual identity for the men, such as Isaac Newton, who occupied them.

The second pair of essays in this section addresses works by Charlotte Smith, a writer clearly sensitive to the interrelationships among gender, space and place, and ideology. Heather Ladd's study of domestic spaces in Smith's *The Banished Man* expands the material and ideological elements of "home" to include empire and the idea of the nation as home. As Ladd demonstrates, Smith's novel reveals how space can be made liminal by events, and how such space in turn renders all identity liminal: "Contested spaces translate into contested selves and an emphasis on gender as it is spatially defined and destabilized," Ladd writes. "Smith highlights problems of space as a personal as well as national issue, space being intimately connected to the gendered self as it is conceived and charted from the inside and the outside." This essay suggests that anxieties about porous domestic boundaries could also be read as anxieties about porous gender and national boundaries, as the contest for empire that played out on the physical battlefields of Europe and the symbolic battlefields of Britain had profound implications for gender as well as for the notion of home itself.

Kathleen Oliver's analysis of Charlotte Smith's novel *Emmeline* narrows the investigation of spaces in Smith's work to focus on Smith's interrogation of domesticity. Smith depicts "home" as a perilous rather than a safe domestic location for women. In Oliver's reading, Smith's novel exposes the problems of gendering the home female, because a home was also a house and therefore traditionally the property of men. For Smith, spaces carved out by females and the feminine shelter of nature—traditionally unsafe, public locations such as forests, hard-to-reach islands, and female households—instead provide a place for women, even though in ideological conceptions of space, home was the place for women. As the last essay of the collection, Oliver's analysis of Charlotte Smith's emphatic redefinition of the traditional domestic space of the house as not the place for women, and Smith's rewriting, instead, of the natural world as the "room" that women could make their own, signals a profound acknowledgment of the gendered nature of eighteenth-century spaces and their active restructuring and reconceptualization in literature. Furthermore, the last pair—Ladd's and Oliver's essays—serve as a case study, particularly when Kinsley's essay from the "Borderlands" section is added. All the essays of this collection provide insights into specific authors, texts, or issues, just as the groups of essays offer ways of considering different models and functions of space. The cluster of essays addressing Charlotte Smith's work provides another way to apply space theory to literature, considering how space operates within the work of specific authors or within particular genres.

As the essays in this collection suggest, the subject of space in the long eighteenth century and the early decades of the nineteenth century is full of possibilities. These essays offer their own valuable insights into the specific works they examine, as well as into the larger subject of space and literature during this period: they also, if we might borrow a metaphor from our topic, present hints of vistas yet before us. We hope that the space outlined by our contributors will serve as a borderland, a zone of transition and opportunity.

PART I
Outside

Chapter 1
Constructing Place in *Oroonoko*

Laura L. Runge

Aphra Behn's popular narrative *Oroonoko* is an important example of place-making by an early modern female author. Speaking from the largely invisible space of London, the narrator tells the story of an African prince and his beloved Imoinda, who are traded as slaves to the British colonial outpost in Surinam in the 1650s or '60s. Behn repeatedly—if not always precisely—situates her tale in a specific place and time, and details exotic locales for the consumption of a Restoration audience. Unlike news accounts and some travel narratives of that era, however, *Oroonoko* is not time-bound. The story is reprinted, translated, and adapted throughout the eighteenth century and, after a lull in the nineteenth century, continues to receive widespread readership and interest.[1] It is a hybrid text that is at once heroic fiction and travel narrative, memoir and political allegory, and its complexity and inconsistencies draw the reader back again and again to try to make sense of its details. Discussions of *Oroonoko* over time have variously analyzed its relationship to travel narratives, America, and imperialist complicity, generally seeking a way to understand the narrative's truth claims.[2] This is understandable, given the improbability of the tale and the controversial moral issues at stake in narrating a story of slavery and colonialism. I would like to shift the focus away from measuring truth claims—be they geographical, narrative, or ideological—

---

[1] Mary Ann O'Donnell, *An Annotated Bibliography of Primary and Secondary Sources*, 2nd ed. (Burlington, VT: Ashgate, 2004).

[2] For example, George Guffey, "Aphra Behn's Occasion and Accomplishment," in *Two English Novelists: Aphra Behn and Anthony Trollope: papers read at a Clark Library Seminar*, May 11, 1974 (Los Angeles: William Andrews Clark Memorial Library, 1975), 1–41; Percy Adams, *Travel Literature and the Evolution of the Novel* (Lexington: University Press of Kentucky, 1983); William C. Spengemann, "The Earliest American Novel: Aphra Behn's *Oroonoko*," *Nineteenth-Century Fiction* 38, no. 4 (1984): 384–414; Stephanie Athey and Daniel Cooper Alarcon, "Oroonoko's Gendered Economies of Honor/ Horror: Reframing Colonial Discourse Studies in the Americas," *American Literature* 65, no. 3 (September 1993): 415–43; rpt. in *Subjects and Citizens: Nation, Race and Gender from Oroonoko to Anita Hill*, ed. Michael Moon and Cathy N. Davidson (Durham: Duke University Press, 1995), 27–55; Margaret Ferguson, "Juggling the Categories of Race, Class and Gender: Aphra Behn's *Oroonoko*," *Women's Studies* 19 (1991): 159–81; Laura Brown, *Ends of Empire: Women and Ideology in Early Eighteenth-Century English Literature* (Ithaca: Cornell University Press, 1993); Srinivas Aravamudan, *Tropicopolitans: Colonialism and Agency, 1688–1804* (Durham: Duke University Press, 1999).

which, however valuable, ultimately limit our understanding of the story in a binary way. Instead, I want to see what meaning opens up when we investigate the story as a component of early modern place-making. This essay reads *Oroonoko* as a self-conscious and imaginative construction of place circulating in the Atlantic Enlightenment in order to better understand both the meaning of the text and the text's meaning in its world.

Charles J. Withers's description of the Atlantic Enlightenment as a viable intellectual tradition in connection with the European Enlightenments is useful for considering the meaning of Behn's story. Withers envisions "a sense of the Enlightenment not as static, something fixed in space by national boundaries, but as something dynamic, a matter of enlarging knowledge about the world in ways that involved the production, reception and mobility of ideas and artefacts over land and sea."[3] Rather than seeing the Atlantic region, which includes Africa and the Caribbean, as an empty space or a destination for Europeans, Withers emphasizes the importance of movement—"of people, of ideas, of books to name but a few"—across and through the space of the Atlantic region. Furthermore, he calls for a "consideration of different scales, the differential impact of European ideas on the communities on the Atlantic's margins and the varying impact of the Atlantic 'new' upon the European mind."[4] According to Withers and Ogborn, the triangle trade in the Atlantic and the East India Company in the Pacific stimulated an increase in trade in the late seventeenth century that created a need to know the world, and in response a series of different forms of writing on geography appeared: "There was a huge market for printed texts and images fed by a vast range of products. Many of these were dubious in their credibility, either outdated, plagiarized, or simply fictional … . Geographical knowledge was produced for many reasons, and its forms and contents exceeded the boundaries of imperial power."[5] Behn's "True History" of the Royal Slave clearly participates in this generation of geographical knowledge. I am not suggesting, however, that the information in Behn's text is limited to geography or a conventional sense of geography as a place on a map. As Adrienne Rich reminds us, "a place on a map is also a place in history," and the value that accrues to a place is a product of human construction.[6] If we read *Oroonoko* as a product, and part of the process, of exchange that characterizes the Atlantic Enlightenment, we recognize that the narrative records—or imagines—a specific transactional place in history that

---

[3]   Charles W. J. Withers, "Where Was the Atlantic Enlightenment?—Questions of Geography," in *The Atlantic Enlightenment*, ed. Susan Manning and Francis Cogliano (Aldershot: Ashgate, 2008), 37.

[4]   Ibid., 42.

[5]   Miles Ogborn and Charles W. J. Withers, "Travel, Trade, and Empire: Knowing Other Places, 1660–1800," in *A Concise Companion to The Restoration and Eighteenth Century*, ed. Cynthia Wall (Malden, MA: Blackwell, 2005) 19.

[6]   Adrienne Rich, *Blood Bread and Poetry: Selected Prose 1979–1985* (New York: Norton, 1986), 27, quoted in Kate Chedgzoy, *Women's Writing in the British Atlantic World: Memory, Place and History, 1550–1700* (Cambridge: Cambridge University Press, 2007), 2.

might otherwise be erased. Moreover, we see the novel as a complex vehicle for the importation of ideas from the Atlantic, such as the gendered and racial impact of colonialism, a transfer that ultimately has far-reaching implications for the abolitionist movement in England.

Borrowing from the discipline of human geography, "place" can be understood as a geographical location invested with meaning in a context of power, and most geographers link place to human meaning and experience. Place is both human product and consumption; it is also a way of being, rootedness and authenticity, as in concepts of home or "my place."[7] Concerns over the compression of time and space, as witnessed by global commerce, travel, and digital communications, have led geographers to conceive of place as always in process and never complete. Memory and cultural productions, such as literature, play fundamental roles in this continuing process of construction of meaning in place. While geographers have looked to literature for source material in analyzing regions, people, and places, early conversations between the disciplines tend to read literature for representations of landscape or phenomenological description of regions.[8] More recent theories of place as historical process, with layers of interactions and reiterated practices, suggest a more constitutive role for literary productions like *Oroonoko*.[9]

By attending to the ways in which a Restoration text constructs place, we foreground more than setting. Indeed, seeing "place" as always in process, literature becomes a part of the cultural production of meaning in place, and as such provides access to analyzing the power dynamics that structure space, as well as the ways of knowing and being that belong to the humans in place. Literature offers a profound and detailed interaction between the author and the geographical location that potentially yields enormous information about the historical process of making a place; moreover, the act of reading this literature becomes a reiterated practice that is also constitutive of place. Thus the construction of place can be understood productively on at least two levels: within the Restoration text itself and in the contemporary interpretation of the text in the classroom. In Lawrence Buell's phenomenology of subjective place-attachment, imagining place can be equally important to attachment as being in place. People can form attachments to place based entirely on imagining, from folklore and nursery rhymes to favorite novels. The fact that the imaginer does not actually see the place "hardly lessens the intensity of such storied or imagined places to induce longing and loyalty, and in some cases even to influence national behavior and the course of world

---

[7]   Tim Cresswell, *Place: A Short Introduction* (Malden, MA: Blackwell, 2004), 12.

[8]   See Douglas C. D. Pocock, *Humanistic Geography and Literature: Essays on the Experience of Place* (London: Croom Helm, 1981), and Roberto M. Dainotto, *Place in Literature: Regions, Cultures, Communities* (Ithaca: Cornell University Press, 2000).

[9]   Cresswell, *Place*, 82. See also Allan Pred, "Place as Historically Contingent Process: Structuration and the Time-Geography of Becoming Places," *Annals of the Association of American Geographers* 74, no. 2 (1984): 279–97, and Lucy Lippard, *The Lure of the Local: Senses of Place in a Multicentered Society* (New York: New Press, 1997).

affairs."[10] This has obvious implications for theorizing the impact of literature of place, in that a work like *Oroonoko*, which constructs exotic locales for an urban audience, might foster an attachment to places and peoples unseen. Indeed, Behn's narrative proved to be immensely popular both in its written form and, perhaps more influentially, in the stage adaptations of Thomas Southerne as well as the 1999 version by 'Biyi Bandele. Given this, the details of the text's place-construction merit attention.[11]

My argument proceeds by first establishing how *Oroonoko* constructs place within the text. The construction of London, though essential, is largely assumed by direct appeals to the audience or comparisons with Surinam. Behn's construction of Coramantien demonstrates clearly how the London-centric view of the author affects the representation of early modern Africa. More attention is given to the construction of Surinam as a place, which is organized around Behn's repeated references to the Dutch. England's commercial rival, Holland, takes over the colony from England in 1667, which is after the timing of events in the tale and long before she writes it in 1688. Thus the Surinam constructed in *Oroonoko* is already part of the past, but the text obsesses about the consequences of it as a transactional place in history. Behn conjures the imagined place of Surinam as a space contested by these European powers and, in the process, articulates a nostalgic nationalism on the eve of the Glorious Revolution, when the Dutch William of Orange takes the English throne. The five textual examples in which Behn invokes the Dutch demonstrate how memory constructs place in specifically ideological contexts, raising issues about gender and writing. The text not only conveys the conflicting ways that European countries disrupt and recreate colonized spaces, but also, importantly, it demonstrates the impact of the Atlantic on European culture. The last section explores how *Oroonoko* the book imports ideas about slavery, class, and gender into popular stage adaptations, primarily Southerne's, thereby making *Oroonoko* a cultural production that continues the process of constructing the meaning of Surinam. Behn's novel becomes a product and part of the process of exchange that characterizes the Atlantic Enlightenment.

*****

In *Oroonoko*, Behn describes in detail—and with more accuracy than is her wont—the colony of Surinam and her habitation on the plantation of St. John's Hill, some 30 miles up the Surinam river.[12] Surinam is the most visible place in Behn's narrative, but it is not the only place in the novel. The narrative constructs

---

[10]   Lawrence Buell, *The Future of Environmental Criticism: Environmental Crisis and Literary Imagination* (Malden, MA: Blackwell, 2005), 73.

[11]   Thomas Southerne, *Oroonoko: A Tragedy* (1696), in *The Works of Thomas Southerne*, ed. Robert Jordan and Harold Love, vol. 2 (Oxford: Clarendon Press, 1988); 'Biyi Bandele, *Aphra Behn's* Oroonoko*: In a New Adaptation* (Oxford: Amber Lane Press, 1999).

[12]   Janet Todd, *The Secret Life of Aphra Behn* (London: Pandora, 2000), 48.

essentially three places: Surinam, the colony lost to the Dutch, Coramantien, the birthplace of Oroonoko and a historical portal for the commercial slave trade, and London, the transparent place from which the narrator speaks.

The text is marked by references to "here," a place that is transparent in the Lefebvrean sense in that it is largely unseen by the narrator and her audience, except as the foundational identity and lens through which to view the other.[13] The narrative positions readers squarely within an English worldview, comparing a grove of citrus trees to the length of the mall at St. James and persuading them of the size of the Amazon by saying it is "almost as broad as the river Thames."[14] Given that the Amazon is the widest river in the world, such claims only make sense as part of the proliferation of geographical knowledge—true and false— that characterized the Atlantic Enlightenment. Through Behn, Surinam and its products become a feature of London cosmopolitanism. She mentions a native-made feather garment of variegated colors presented to her in Surinam: "I gave 'em to the King's Theatre, and it was the Dress of the *Indian Queen*, infinitely admir'd by Persons of Quality."[15] Behn self-consciously renders *Oroonoko* itself as a product for this jaded audience in a way parallel to the Amerindian headdress. In the second paragraph, for example, she claims that she will abbreviate Oroonoko's story for the reader's sake, omitting "a thousand little Accidents of his Life, which however pleasant to us [in Surinam], where History was scarce, and Adventures very rare; yet might prove tedious and heavy to my Reader, in a World where he finds Diversions for every Minute, new and strange."[16] She presents London as the urban space of continual novelty and her reader as one who avidly consumes this entertainment. The transfer of meaningful items—the set of feathers or the "true history" of Oroonoko—illustrates a relationship between Surinam and London that is not merely commercial or political, though it is both. The narrator's presence in Surinam, after all, results directly from the British administration of the colony; she tells us that her father, who died on the voyage over, was intended to be "Lieutenant-General of six and thirty islands besides the continent of Surinam."[17] She returns to London and writes this story over two decades later. Just as the narrator's presence as the daughter of a colonial administrator altered the meaning of the place rendered in *Oroonoko*, so, too, does the narrator, altered by her time in Surinam, contribute to the cultural meaning of London through the transfer of items, not least of which is the text itself.

The first half of the novel takes place in the setting of Coramantien, or Kormantse, on the early modern Gold Coast and the Fante region of Africa. The transfer of people from Coramantien carries far greater historical and narrative

---

[13]   Henri Lefebvre, *The Production of Space*, trans. Donald Nicholson-Smith (Malden, MA: Blackwell, 1991).

[14]   Aphra Behn, *Oroonoko: An Authoritative Text, Historical Backgrounds, Criticism*, ed. Joanna Lipking (New York: Norton, 1997), 51.

[15]   Ibid., 9.

[16]   Ibid., 8.

[17]   Ibid., 43.

significance than the American feathers that grace the London stage. Behn's text is one of the earliest representations in English fiction of the slave trade, and her attitude toward and complicity in the colonial subjugation of African slaves has been widely canvassed.[18] I follow Adam Beach in taking seriously Behn's geographical knowledge of Africa and allowing her narrative details credence in conveying an early modern Eurocentric understanding of African slavery.[19] By attending to the work of West African scholars who analyze early modern African nations as sophisticated agents with complex systems of intra-African slave trade, Beach demonstrates how one can separate *Oroonoko*'s apparent support of "honorable" slavery from its critique of the colonial slave trade. While Behn's presentation of "heroic" or "chivalric" slavery depends upon a glossing over of historical details regarding Oroonoko's and Imoinda's involvement in slavery in Coramantien, the text demonstrates a certain awareness of the non-heroic system of trade that existed in West Africa at the time. For example, Beach argues, the heroic mode of slavery ostensibly celebrated by Oroonoko—and hence Behn—suggests that only soldiers taken in war are sold as slaves from Africa's coast, but Oroonoko himself arrives with women and children, and the women and children he meets in St. John's, the narrator claims, were mainly sold into slavery by Oroonoko. *Oroonoko* confuses the condition of slavery, which is alienated from kin, property, and identity, with the state a slave maintains, which could be free of labor. That Behn can raise criticism of slavery without condemning wholesale the condition of slavery arises in part from her Eurocentric view, which fails to envision an Africa of agency and sophistication. Thus we need to read critically the representation of the slave systems on the Gold Coast, even while we take seriously the details Behn represents. Similarly, the construction of place in the Coramantien section suffers from a Eurocentric stereotyping. Unlike the purportedly autobiographical account of the Surinam section, the Coramantien story is second-hand narrative: "I was my self an Eye-Witness to a great part, of what you will find here set down; and what I cou'd not be Witness of, I receiv'd from the Mouth of the chief Actor in this History, the Hero himself."[20] Adopting the rhetoric of the heroic romances popular at the time, the evocation of Coramantien is in many ways resistant to the historical and ideological type of analysis which the descriptions of Surinam and London readily permit. The remainder of this section, therefore, focuses on Surinam.

Behn punctuates the second half of her tale with five references to the Dutch takeover of Surinam. These references situate the author and immediate reading audience in a geopolitical relationship to the setting of the story. She writes of this Caribbean land as a former colony, one valued in her memory though undervalued by Charles II and his ministers: "had his late Majesty, of sacred Memory, but

---

[18]   Wiley Sypher, *Guinea's Captive Kings: British Anti-Slavery Literature of the Eighteenth Century* (1942) (New York: Octagon, 1969); Athey and Alarcon, "Oroonoko's Gendered Economies"; Ferguson, "Juggling"; Aravamudan, *Tropicopolitans*.

[19]   Adam Beach, "Behn's Oroonoko, The Gold Coast, and Slavery in the Early-Modern Atlantic World," *Studies in Eighteenth-Century Culture* 39 (2010): 209–27.

[20]   Behn, *Oroonoko*, 8.

seen and known what a vast and charming World he had been Master of in that Continent, he would never have parted so Easily with it to the Dutch."[21] Present-day students of the novel know from history (or footnotes) that after the Dutch attacked the English colony of Surinam in 1667, Charles II ceded the land to the Dutch with the Treaty of Breda; in that treaty the English gained New York. Given the current place value of New York, present-day readers in the United States can hardly share Behn's chagrin over the trade of Surinam, a smaller region within Guiana, later Dutch Guyana, and now Suriname. Yet, Behn's desire for the land of Surinam and lament over its loss are insistent. The story is shaped by the narrator's complex and reiterated relationship to that place. In part, these repeated imaginings of the Dutch takeover convey the threat of the imminent Dutch takeover of the British throne and so create a political context for its audience in 1688.[22] But because of their specificity and, indeed, the representation of excessive violence, the historical or political asides do significant work in constructing an idea of place. In doing so, these references also reinforce a sense of the Englishness of her story, a nationalist impulse that, according to Kate Chedgzoy, is unusual for seventeenth-century women writers.

Chedgzoy reads *Oroonoko* through an anthropological lens as an example of "memory work done in the field," yielding a narrative of "history and testimony as well as memory."[23] While the evocation of memory historicizes and testifies to the author's experience, it also functions powerfully in place-making. According to Tim Cresswell, memory and place seem inevitably intertwined. David Harvey explains: "Places do not come with some memories attached as i[f] by nature but rather they are the contested terrain of competing definitions."[24] In Behn's retrospective memory, Dutch colonization threatens the erasure of the English memory of Surinam and her hero. Behn's narrative takes pains to undo this Dutch formation of place. For example, the narrator recounts the English renaming of Oroonoko as a significant act, obscured by the depredations of the Dutch:

> I ought to tell you, that the *Christians* never buy any slaves but they give 'em some Name of their own, their native ones being likely very barbarous, and hard to pronounce; so that Mr. *Trefry* gave *Oroonoko* that of *Caesar*; which Name will live in that Country as long as that (scarce more) glorious one of the great *Roman*; for 'tis most evident he wanted no part of the Personal Courage of that *Caesar*, and acted things as memorable, had they been done in some part of the World replenish'd with People and Historians that might have given him his due. But his Misfortune was, to fall in an obscure World, that afforded only a

---

[21] Ibid., 43.

[22] See, for example, Richard Kroll, "'Tales of Love and Gallantry': The Politics of *Oroonoko*," *Huntington Library Quarterly* 67, no. 4 (2004): 573–605, http://www.jstor.org. ezproxy.lib.usf.edu/stable/3817945.

[23] Chedgzoy, *Women's Writing*, 172.

[24] David Harvey, *Justice, Nature and the Geography of Difference* (Cambridge, MA: Blackwell, 1996), 309, quoted in Cresswell, *Place*, 62.

Female Pen to celebrate his Fame; though I doubt not but it had liv'd from others
Endeavors, if the *Dutch*, who, immediately after his Time, took that Country,
had not kill'd, banish'd, and dispers'd all those that were capable of giving the
World this great Man's Life much better than I have done.[25]

The passage represents a series of contestations over the meaning of place,
between African and European, male and female, and English and Dutch. The
"obscure World," Surinam, is not a place "replenish'd with People and Historians,"
a categorical doubling that speaks to the text's site as a contested place; some
"people" simply inhabit space, while others concern themselves with historicizing
and hence preserving meaning in place. The passage ends with a jumbled rationale
for her work of recording what she calls "Fame." The narrator speculates that in an
act of purgation, the Dutch eliminated all legitimate historians, which we can infer
would have been educated British males. Her minimizing of "only a Female pen"
reconstructs the gendered politics of place, a stratification probably shared by both
British Surinam and her London audience. Behn's allusion to classical history,
represented by the colonist's use of Caesar's name and "fame," as well as her
later reading of Plutarch's *Lives of the Romans* to Oroonoko/Caesar, invokes an
elite, European, and masculine tradition. Dutch political sovereignty and violence,
then, ultimately deprive Oroonoko of his place in official history. Behn's narrative
of Surinam offers an unauthorized construction of place that contests the Dutch
power of erasure and the British dismissal of female history.

Without proper historians, Surinam is, nonetheless, a place replenished
with history in the actions of "people and" slaves. The very act of renaming
Oroonoko demonstrates the imposition of the imported language and religion of
the colonizers whose power orders the place. Recognizing how her character's
name memorializes the clash of competing cultures, Behn suggests that memory
of Oroonoko/Caesar depends upon who names him. Caesar, the slave, nearly slips
through the record of British history, but Behn remembers Oroonoko. Naming in
place is a gesture of power and value. In this passage, she claims that the name
of Oroonoko/Caesar will live in Surinam almost as long as that of the Roman, a
construction of memory that links the local to European civilization and conquest
through Oroonoko. Behn records the erasure of Oroonoko's African identity, but in
the same gesture she restores the trace of his African character to history. Ironically,
she gives life to his hybrid name—not in Surinam, perhaps, but in London. Behn's
textual construction of Surinam contests the Dutch-imposed silence on the figure
of Oroonoko and claims his story as part of British heritage.

Behn often represents England's loss of Surinam as a loss *to* Surinam, an
assumption consistent with emerging ideas of British nationalism. Importantly,
in *Oroonoko*, England competes with Holland rather than the native people of
Surinam for national supremacy. Instead, Behn positions the native people as
more or less in collusion with the British, with one notable exception: "About

---

[25]   Behn, *Oroonoko*, 36.

this time we were in many mortal Fears, about some Disputes the English had with the Indians; so that we cou'd scarce trust our selves, without great Numbers, to go to any Indian towns, or Place, where they abode; for fear they shou'd fall upon us, as they did immediately after my coming away."[26] Whereas elsewhere in the text, Behn mingles peaceably with natives, this passage suggests that the Amerindian people resist colonial imposition in place and aggressively claim space for themselves. The potential for violent reprisal constrains the narrator's movement in place and destabilizes the very notion of a British colony.

She immediately restores the idea of British paternalism through contrast to the later behavior of the Dutch: "[I]t was in the possession of the Dutch, who us'd 'em not so civilly as the English; so that they cut in pieces all they cou'd take, getting into Houses, and hanging up the Mother, and all her Children about her; and cut a Footman, I left behind me, all in Joynts, and nail'd him to Trees."[27] She uses the rather unbelievable claim that British civility engendered good will only to underscore the stereotypical contrast between her countrymen and the boorish Dutch. While she imagines the bloody violence of the Indians, this passage is essentially about the wrongful occupation of place by the Dutch. Interestingly, Behn records that the extent of the massacre reaches the domestic front. The Indians violate a European construct of domestic space, which always encloses the feminine within the protection of male power. By disrupting the domestic, the native people challenge the patriarchal authority of the Dutch colonial culture, which is ironically what Behn achieves in writing Oroonoko's history.

The language of this passage constructs a paradigm wherein the prized English stewardship gives way to Dutch cruelty and greed, a theme she reprises in the episode about the arrival of gold-bearing natives. Behn describes her interaction with a non-local tribe of Amerindians who had traveled down from the mountains and offered themselves as guides. "And because all the Country was mad to be going on this Golden Adventure," the governor, who was not on location, ordered by letter that the visiting natives be retained and that guards be set at the mouth of the river until his arrival. Behn concludes: "But we going off for England before the Project was further prosecuted, and the Governour being drown'd in a Hurricane, either the Design dy'd, or the Dutch have the Advantage of it: And 'tis to be bemoan'd what his Majesty lost by losing that part of America."[28] The governor recognizes the value of the natives' knowledge of place and takes measures to exploit it for his advantage. His lack of success, Behn suggests, is a matter of fate intervening with his untimely death. Yet the passage conveys a sense of place in time, recognizing that even though the narrator leaves for England, the land, with its various tribes of people, dramatic weather, and potential stores of gold, goes on. What endures is also the economic value of place, now enjoyed by the Dutch. As in previous references to the Dutch, Behn expresses bitterness at

---

[26]   Ibid., 47.

[27]   Ibid.

[28]   Ibid., 51.

the idea of their succeeding to the English possession, and this prompts a second lament over Charles II's negotiations.

Other than this pattern of lament, this extraordinarily detailed passage has no purpose in the larger narrative, but her extended treatment of the El Dorado myth is more interesting with respect to present day place-making. It suggests the way a cultural production contributes to the meaning of a place through accretion over time. With this passage, Behn situates *Oroonoko* in a line of Western texts that reiterate the El Dorado myth, the foundational legend that brought European explorers to the Caribbean and South American lands. The myth originates in English with Sir Walter Ralegh's attempts to discover the fabled city or mountains of gold. The El Dorado myth is not, of course, confined to Surinam, but in fact speaks to a widespread European desire to explore and exploit the untapped value of exotic regions, and it becomes, according to Janet Todd, an overdetermined, "constant discursive reality" for the Caribbean.[29] Recently, Shona N. Jackson, following Antonio Benítez-Rojo, argues that the El Dorado myth is alive and well in this region and continues to be deployed in the post-independence campaigns for developing Guyana's hinterland: "[D]espite its shift from being re-presented in white-settler, colonialist narratives to postcolonial, nationalist narratives, Guyana's interior continued to be endlessly yielding for both material and cultural production."[30] Behn's description of the gold event connects the reader to the present-day region of the text, forming a layer of the cultural production of place in time. Current Caribbean studies of the environment, like Jackson's, invite students to consider the implications of this reiterated early modern European construction.

In the final reference to the Dutch takeover of Surinam, Behn reverses her prejudice and allows them to serve a bit of poetic justice. Her animus at the end of the tale is rather directed to the English colonists, who vote unanimously to hang Oroonoko. In language very similar to her treatment of the leaders of Virginia in *The Widow Ranter*, Behn criticizes the ruling class of the English colony, "who (not to disgrace them, or Burlesque the government there) consisted of such notorious Villains as Newgate never transported, and possibly originally were such, who understood neither the Laws of God or Man; and had no sort of Principles to make 'em worthy the Name of Men. ... (Some of 'em were afterwards hanged when the Dutch took possession of the place, others sent off in chains)."[31] The collapsing of time in this passage suggests that Oroonoko's death marks the end of English rule

---

[29]   Todd notes that "Sir Walter Ralegh landed in the mouth of the Oroonoko in 1616. See his *Discoverie of the large, rich and beautiful Empyre of Guiana, with a Relation of the great and Golden citie of Mano (which the Spanyards call El Dorado) ... Performed in the yeare 1595 (London, 1596) and Sir Walter Ralegh's apology for his last voyage to Guiana*" (*Secret Life*, 448n1).

[30]   Shona N. Jackson, "Subjection and Resistance in the Transformation of Guyana's Mytho-Colonial Landscape," in *Caribbean Literature and the Environment: Between Nature and Culture*, ed. Elizabeth M. DeLoughrey, Renee K. Gosson, and George B. Handley (Charlottesville: University of Virginia Press, 2005), 85.

[31]   Behn, *Oroonoko*, 59.

in Surinam, and the villainous colonists who condemn Oroonoko are punished for their cruelty. Here Dutch ruthlessness appears justified and mild in contrast to the behavior of the criminal English colonists. The critical tone and sarcasm of this passage sounds more like voices from Behn's plays and critical prefaces than the likable narrator of *Oroonoko*. It is the voice of social criticism. She envisions a London audience with her reference to Newgate, and she draws the colonial experience closer to London by narrating the disastrous outcome of transporting English criminals to build new English places abroad.

As a cultural production of sustained popularity, *Oroonoko* imports the Atlantic "new" into London, making it a differently informed place. The impact of a text in the early modern period is generally estimated by the number of editions, the sizes of the print runs (if available), and references in the diaries and letters of eighteenth-century readers. The impact of *Oroonoko* can also be measured by the number of its adaptations, in particular the popular stage versions. Written by other people, these different versions of *Oroonoko* provide a sense of what survives, and hence makes an impact, and what gets left out. Southerne's stage adaptation, first produced in 1695, met with incredible success and, according to its editors, Robert Jordan and Harold Love, became "one of the most frequently performed works in the eighteenth-century theatre."[32] In his dedication to the Duke of Devonshire, Southerne calls attention to his debt to Behn for the story while he appropriates the character of Oroonoko for himself: "Whatever happen'd to [Oroonoko] at *Surinam*, he has mended his Condition in *England*. He was born here under Your Grace's Influence; and that has carried his Fortune farther into the World, than all the Poetical Stars that I could have sollicited for his Success."[33] Southerne plays upon the idea of a reverse form of transportation, where the colonial subject comes to England to improve his condition. He lends credence to the veracity of Behn's story by suggesting that hers was created in Surinam, though it was written, published, and disseminated in London. His Oroonoko, in contrast, clearly exists in England—on the London stage, to be exact. His birth in London is due in large part to the actor, Mr. Verbruggen, whom the Duke recommended. With his transportation Oroonoko "mends his condition," a phrase that calls to mind the condition of slavery while it softens the implications; in his capacity as a stage slave, Oroonoko is primarily a vehicle for tragic sympathy and one that was astonishingly popular. The gruesome violence of Behn's story is wholly transformed or omitted. Southerne claims that through the Duke's influence, Oroonoko now enjoys worldwide fame rather than the ignominy of slavery or the substandard history of a female pen.

Southerne's dedication constructs Oroonoko himself as an object of movement in the Atlantic Enlightenment, significantly not as a slave but as the synecdoche whereby *Oroonoko* becomes a book and then a play: "he has mended his condition in England." This is only a slight textual remove from his becoming a stand-in

---

[32]   Jordan and Love, eds., *Works of Thomas Southerne*, 91.
[33]   Southerne, *Oroonoko: A Tragedy*, 102.

for all slaves in later literature. The relationship between Behn's violent hero and Southerne's sentimental re-creation suggests a crucial link in what Withers calls the "impact of the Atlantic 'new' upon the European mind." By the end of the century, Oroonoko becomes an icon for the abolition of slavery, as demonstrated in Hannah More's 1788 poem, "The Slave Trade": "No individual griefs my bosom melt, / For millions feel what Oronoko felt."[34] This tracing provides an example of how an Enlightenment idea travels across the Atlantic and influences—dramatically—a European place and the course of history.

Interestingly, very little of the contested place narrative that Behn constructs gets included in Southerne's work. As Suvir Kaul notes, Behn's version of *Oroonoko* "is much less able (than its adaptations) ... to repress the violence that defines the Caribbean plantation economy whose culture it engages."[35] Instead, the major discussion of place comes through the displacement of the two English sisters in the invented comic subplot. Lucy and Charlotte Welldon, in a trajectory that reverses that of Southerne's *Oroonoko*, sail to Surinam to improve their condition by getting husbands. The very opening scene creates a symmetry between the Welldon sisters and the London audience by dramatizing the move to an exotic locale:

> *Luc.* What will this come to? What can it end in? You have persuaded me to leave dear *England*, and dearer *London*, the place of the World most worth living in, to follow you a Husband-hunting in *America*: I thought Husbands grew in these Plantations.[36]

Charlotte quickly challenges the notion of "dearer London" by reminding her sister that the amours that once made London dear no longer exist. The play thus opens with an extended satire on the jaded and conspicuously unfair marriage market in London, setting up the parallel between marriage and slavery that links the comic and tragic plots. It renders the exotic space familiar by overlaying the London culture.

It is probably not surprising that much of the place discussion in Behn, which represents colonial violence and slaughter, is domesticated and displaced onto a comic subplot. In performance the stage itself is palpably a place with real bodies in the same space as the audience. Kaul argues that Southerne's adaptation "finds in the cadences of heroic verse a language for the redemption of the brutality and ugliness of slavery and the slave trade."[37] The generic constraints of heroic tragedy lead Southerne to omit aspects of Behn's narrative—particularly the fascination

---

[34]   Hannah More, "The Slave Trade" (London, 1788), 55–56, http://www.brycchancarey.com/slavery/morepoems.htm.

[35]   Suvir Kaul, "Reading Literary Symptoms: Colonial Pathologies and the *Oroonoko* Fictions of Behn, Southerne, and Hawkesworth," *Eighteenth-Century Life* 18, no. 3 (November 1994): 81.

[36]   Southerne, *Oroonoko: A Tragedy*, 107.

[37]   Kaul, "Reading Literary Symptoms," 80.

with bodily mutilation—that referenced the excessive violence of what Mary Louise Pratt calls the "contact zone."[38] Oroonoko becomes both less complex and more heroic in Southerne's adaptation; he is no longer solely responsible for the death of (now white) Imoinda, who holds the dagger with him as he stabs her, and he kills both the captain of the slave ship and the governor who attempts to rape Imoinda before killing himself. Southerne "glosses over [Behn's] text's colonial coordinates and contemporaneity in favor of a much more assimilable account of great human, that is, transcultural tragedy."[39] The colonial particulars of Behn's text are absent in Southerne's stage adapation, but as Kaul, Laura Rosenthal, and Joyce Macdonald discuss, the economic and social violence of the colonial governance in Surinam manifests to a lesser degree in the comic subplot.[40] Charlotte, in drag, negotiates for her sister's marriage in terms that baldly compare marriage and slavery: "This is your Market for Slaves," she tells the captain who has brought Oroonoko to Surinam. "My Sister is a Free Woman, and must not be dispos'd of in publick."[41] She will, however, be disposed of in private. Charlotte's success lies in swindling the stereotypically lascivious Widow Lackitt by marrying her son and fortune to Lucy, as well as managing to secure for herself a financially advantageous marriage with a hint of companionate desire. In terms of place, the comic Surinam is rendered like the London stage: a place of disguise, cross-dressing, and intrigue.

William Congreve's epilogue to the play further confuses the construction of place in London and Surinam by highlighting the comparison between the jaded lovers of the London audience and the faithful love of Imoinda:

> Then bless your Stars, you happy London Wives,
> Who love at large, each day, yet keep your lives:
> Nor envy poor Imoinda's doating blindness,
> Who thought her Husband kill'd her out of kindness.
> Death with a Husband ne'er had shewn such Charms,
> Had she once dy'd within a Lover's Arms.
> Her error was from ignorance proceeding:
> Poor Soul! she wanted some of our Town Breeding.[42]

Congreve's epilogue compares the playgoers of Covent Garden to the women of Surinam, specifically Imoinda, highlighting the moral laxity not of the colony but

---

[38] Mary Louise Pratt, *Imperial Eyes: Travel Writing and Transculturation* (London: Routledge, 1992).

[39] Kaul, "Reading Literary Symptoms," 89.

[40] Laura Rosenthal, "Owning *Oroonoko*: Behn, Southerne and the Contingencies of Property," *Renaissance Drama* N.s. 23 (1992): 25–58; see also Joyce Macdonald, *Women and Race in Early Modern Texts* (Cambridge: Cambridge University Press, 2002), esp. chap. 5, "Race, Women, and the Sentimental in Thomas Southerne's *Oroonoko*."

[41] Southerne, *Oroonoko: A Tragedy*, 116.

[42] Ibid., 180.

of London and the sophisticated wives who would not die for love. Southerne appears to be addressing the same cosmopolitan audience as Behn, though with different objectives. Whereas Behn treats her story as an exotic product introduced to London, Congreve metaphorically transports the audience to a domesticated Surinam. Similarly, Southerne simplifies the representation of place in the play and presumably accommodates the emotional needs of his audience by reducing and aestheticizing colonial violence, minimizing the cultural hybridity by virtually erasing the natives, and avoiding altogether discussion of the status of Surinam as a colony. He finds the contestation of gender in the form of female choice in marriage an acceptable substitute for Behn's harsher depiction of national and colonial conflict.

Significantly, John Hawkesworth's 1759 adaptation eliminates the subplot and replaces the gendered conflict with the contest between good and bad governance.[43] Intriguingly, 'Biyi Bandele's 1999 version, which adapts Hawkesworth, reverses the Eurocentric construction of place in Behn with the addition of an entire half set in Africa. In Elizabeth Kowaleski Wallace's view, "While part 1 of Bandele's *Oroonoko* offers a distinct construction of Africa, part 2 evokes nowhere in particular. … [N]o effort is made to evoke the geographic specificity of the British seventeenth-century slave system."[44] Through its stage adaptations we can trace how Behn's text sets in motion a discourse that constructs a global England and a negotiation of place that is reiterated with dramatic changes from the seventeenth century to the twentieth.

*****

Studying the construction of place in *Oroonoko* demonstrates how a cultural production of the late seventeenth century has relevance in our world today. As literature goes, *Oroonoko* offers an extremely rich and detailed interaction between author and location, only a fraction of which has been highlighted here. Lucy Lippard's understanding of contemporary mobility underscores the infinite potential of place-making in an already-hybrid locality: "Each time we enter a new place, we become one of the ingredients of an existing hybridity, which is really what all 'local places' consist of. By entering that hybrid, we change it; and in each situation we may play a different role."[45] While Lippard describes contemporary experience, Withers's emphasis on movement in the Atlantic Enlightenment suggests that we might see direct parallels between the early modern experience of globalization and our own. Behn, Oroonoko, and Imoinda travel across the Atlantic and change the place of Surinam, creating the history we know as *Oroonoko*.

---

[43]   Kaul, "Reading Literary Symptoms," 91.

[44]   Elizabeth Kowaleski Wallace, "Transnationalism and Performance in 'Biyi Bandele's *Oroonoko*," *PMLA* 119, no. 2 (March 2004): 275.

[45]   Lippard, *Lure of the Local*, 5–6.

Chapter 2
Creole Space:
Jamaica, Fallen Women,
and British Literature

Aleksondra Hultquist

Eighteenth-century Jamaica was a space of contradiction. As the wealthiest British colony in the eighteenth century, it was both central to British society and on the outskirts of civilization. It was a space where fecundity was contrasted by a particularly deadly slave labor system, where a lush landscape was frequently devastated by hurricanes, earthquakes, floods, and fires, and where the ever-increasing population of immigrants and slaves was decimated by recurrent pestilence. Male characters in British texts often make trips to Jamaica to repair depleted fortunes and prove their mettle (pirates become Governor General; yeoman farmers become land- and slave-owning planters); but for women, the trip to Jamaica is more likely coded as punishment. Eighteenth-century literature is replete with threats of removal to Jamaica for those women who have fallen on morally dubious times. Jonathan Swift's titular "Beautiful Young Nymph," for instance, has the nightmare of being transported to Jamaica without the indulgence of a wealthy suitor. Lady Mellasin in Haywood's *Betsy Thoughtless* is paid to move to Jamaica, where she hopes to profit from the flexible morality of the island. Sally Godfrey in Samuel Richardson's *Pamela* makes the decision to escape from her past, abandoning her bastard child and removing to Jamaica, where she passes as a young widow. It is possible to read this pattern as sending the damned to a damned place as a way to preserve the metropole; Felicity Nussbaum has examined the morally lax space of the torrid zones, such as Jamaica, for their "otherness" and the ways in which they help to define English honor and gentility through dishonor and ungentleness.[1] But as with any space so saturated with contradiction, Jamaica can sometimes allow certain women to regain their moral standing, just as masculine characters regain their financial or social prominence. Sometimes Jamaica is a space that recuperates the fallen female.

This chapter examines the power of Jamaica as a creolized space—a place in which several contradicting realities exist—to argue that such a space can be read as socially and morally redemptive, a locale with the power to allow female

---

[1] See Felicity Nussbaum, *Torrid Zones: Maternity, Sexuality, and Empire in Eighteenth-Century English Narratives* (Baltimore: The Johns Hopkins University Press, 1995).

characters to remake themselves. Critics have argued that "excess" women of the empire (like Swift's Nymph, Lady Mellasin, and Sally Godfrey) were "exported" to places like Jamaica because their economic un-productivity caused them to be intolerable dependants on the state.[2] But reading these and other texts through the lens of the creolized space of Jamaica provides a more complex understanding of what these characters mean to the larger empire, allowing us to read Jamaica as recuperative to women. Though the most common literary trope for fallen women characters exiled to Jamaica reads as punitive, such removal from the British homeland allows a conditional remaking, which is only possible in Jamaica's creolized space. The excess women of empire's intimate knowledge of patriarchal irresponsibility causes a refocused gaze in Jamaica, turning a scrutinizing eye back upon British soil. Such knowledge combined with Jamaica's creolized space can allow fallen women to recuperate their losses, provided they do not return to the metropole.

Creole Space

The defining social feature of Jamaican society from the mid-1700s onward was creolism, a blending of British, Caribbean, and African cultures, which produced a specific type of worldview originating in the British West Indies, especially in Jamaica. Several excellent studies exist about the economic, political, and social consequences of creole Jamaica as its sugar-producing capabilities and plantocracy society burgeoned in the mid-eighteenth century.[3] Edward Braithwaite's study is

---

[2]   See, especially, ibid. and Laura Rosenthal, "Eliza Haywood: Discrepant Cosmopolitanism and the Persistence of Romance," *Nineteenth-Century Gender Studies* 3, no. 2 (2007), www.ncgsjournal.com/issue32/rosenthal.htm.

[3]   See, especially Edward Brathwaite, *The Development of Creole Society in Jamaica 1770–1820* (Oxford: Clarendon, 1971), and Michael Craton, "Reluctant Creoles: The Planters' World in the British West Indies," in *Strangers Within the Realm: Cultural Margins of the First British Empire*, ed. Bernard Bailyn and Philip D. Morgan (Chapel Hill, NC: University of North Carolina Press, 1991), 314–62, both of which concentrate specifically on social aspects and consequences of Jamaican creolism and make extended arguments about the eighteenth century in particular. Kathleen Wilson provides an excellent summary of the social world of Jamaica in the mid-eighteenth century in *The Island Race: Englishness, Empire, and Gender in the Eighteenth Century* (London: Routledge, 2003), 146–58. Philip D. Morgan's "The Caribbean Islands in Atlantic Context, circa 1500–1800," in *The Global Eighteenth Century*, ed. Felicity Nussbaum (Baltimore: The Johns Hopkins University Press, 2003), 52–64, provides a general overview of the Caribbean context in the early modern period. Kathleen E. A. Monteith and Glen Richards, eds., *Jamaica in Slavery and Freedom: History, Heritage and Culture* (Barbados: University of the West Indies Press, 2002) focuses specifically on slavery to cultural development. Catherine Hall, *Civilising Subjects: Metropole and Colony in the English Imagination, 1830–1867* (Cambridge: Polity Press, 2002) focuses her study after 1830, but has a useful summary about eighteenth-century Jamaican cultural contexts.

especially illuminating in terms of the intricacies and definition of creolism and what was at stake in a culture founded on blended contradictions. He argues that "the single most important factor in the development of Jamaican society was not the imported influence of the Mother Country or the local administrative activity of the white élite, but a cultural action—material, psychological and spiritual— based upon the stimulus/response of individuals within the society to their environment and—as white/black, culturally discrete groups—to each other."[4] In this context, creolism is a specific culture brought about by the tensions between the Caribbean context on the one hand and the metropole on the other. While to the metropole, the creole context offers binaries such as master/slave, white/black, Christian/heathen, true creolism rests in the ways in which these binaries are collapsed in Jamaica itself. This collapse often manifests in the creole tendency to shape Caribbean reality into a kind of uncanny British world away from home, an inclination evident in the way the British colonists understood their landscape, art, and social structure.

Edward Long's *History of Jamaica* (1774) is one of the most frequently cited sources for embodying Jamaican creolism. While his work has caused him to be (justly) touted as the "father of racism" for his panicked and prejudiced descriptions of slaves on the island, the text is valuable in how it illuminates the tensions and anxieties that produced the contradicting ideas at the heart of Jamaica's creole culture.[5] Long's *History* is a justification for the planters' lifestyle, an advertisement for the profitable and increasingly genteel life of the plantocracy, and a description of the sometimes inelegant ways in which the multiple cultures of the island created a civilization that was simultaneously recognizably British, deeply unfamiliar to the metropole, and more English than England. Elizabeth A. Bohls and Kay Dian Kriz have both argued for the way in which creolized space in Jamaica produces an uncanny English space through landscape and painting.[6] Bohls contends that throughout Long's description of Jamaica as the perfect English landscape, there is a persistent underlying anxiety that Jamaica's Britishness is somehow overdetermined—in its attempts to be seen as cultured, civilized, and desirable as a space, it becomes uncanny and inauthentic. Palm trees

---

[4] Brathwaite, *Development of Creole Society*, 296.

[5] In the eighteenth century, the term "creole" was generally used for anyone not of island origin born there, and most often refers to the planters and merchants, white "British" men and women. The descendants of both African slaves and British colonists were considered "creole" regardless of their racial heritage. The implication of "hybrid" or "blending" or even "mixed race" in "creole" is a more recent phenomenon; see Brathwaite, *Development of Creole Society*, xiv–xv.

[6] See Elizabeth A. Bohls, "The Gentleman Planter and the Metropole: Long's *History of Jamaica* (1774)," in *The Country and the City Revisited: England and the Politics of Culture, 1550–1850*, ed. Gerald MacLean, Donna Landry, and Joseph P. War (Cambridge: Cambridge University Press, 1999), 180–96, and Kay Dian Kriz, "Marketing Mulatresses in the Paintings and Prints of Agostino Brunias," in Nussbaum, *The Global Eighteenth Century*, 195–210.

will emerge from these seeming georgic landscapes, slaves (or at least people of color) will labor in the margins—creolization occurs despite (and in direct response to) the arguments for authentic Britishness. Similarly, Kay reads portraits of mulatto mistresses as creating a creolized domestic space: mulattoes display wealth and sophistication and perform the housewifely duties, as do the white women in Britain. However, both aspects are tinged with physical racial markers that would make the domestic pointedly creolized. Less than purely white skin, black slaves/servants, and tropical backgrounds offer a view of British wealth that is mixed, overdetermined, and distinctly Jamaican in its representation.

Creole space was fashioned not only by its relation to Britishness, but also by its geographical position. Living in the torrid zones, Jamaica's inhabitants were thought to be especially prone to moral and physical changes caused by the heat of the subtropical climate. Long suggests that being creolized referred not merely to one's culture and morals, but to one's very constitution. He saw such creolization in the physical features and pallor of Britons who were born on the island. Their eye sockets were deeper, for instance, and even the very movement of creole men reflected differences wrought on them by climate: "The effect of climate is not only remarkable in the structure of their eyes, but likewise in the extraordinary freedom and suppleness of their joints, which enable them to move with ease, and give them a surprising agility, as well as gracefulness in dancing."[7] Indeed, the eighteenth-century concept of race itself had more to do with geographic space than genetic origin.[8] While the climate couldn't "change" race (and Long understood that it could not), there is a persistent link between climate and physical characteristics as well as behavioral actions. Creole men's emotions, for instance, are linked to the meteorological conditions of the area and the men are "liable to sudden transports of anger; but these fits, like hurricanes, though violent when they last, are soon over and subside into a calm."[9] The environment was also thought to induce lethargy, short tempers, fierce loyalties, and sexual appetite. Tropical climates supposedly promoted laziness, reducing productivity (and white women's reproductivity) and encouraging dissipated habits such as afternoon naps, heavy drinking, extended hours sitting at table, and excessive bathing. This indulgence extended to sexual attitudes as well, as Felicity Nussbaum has shown: "In [Scottish Enlightenment formulations] hot climates produce sexual desire … . Warmer climates naturally intensify the amount of sexual activity and consequently produce a larger population that freely indulges its libidinous energy."[10] Even if a woman had been properly domestic in the cooler climates, tropical climates would produce

---

[7]   Edward Long, *The History of Jamaica. Or, General Survey of the Antient and Modern State of that Island*. Vol. 2 (London, 1774), 261–62, Eighteenth Century Collections Online, http://find.galegroup.com.ezp.lib.unimelb.edu.au/ecco/.

[8]   See Roxann Wheeler, *The Complexion of Race: Categories of Difference in Eighteenth-Century British Culture* (Philadelphia: University of Pennsylvania Press, 2000).

[9]   Long, *History*, 265.

[10]   Nussbaum, *Torrid Zones*, 8.

especially libidinous activities. Sexuality and gender themselves become creolized in such configurations, mixing good British tendencies to industry, temperate behavior, and sexual continence with the rapacious and equally "natural" (tropical) tendencies to profligacy, indolence, and luxurious waste. Long commented that "few are more irreproachable in their actions than the Creole women ... . And, if we consider how forcibly the warmth of this climate must co-operate with natural instinct to rouze the passions, we ought to regard chastity here as no mean effort of female fortitude."[11] Long allows the creole women flexibility in their morality due to the climate of the Jamaican landscape. He even goes so far as to excuse any unexceptionable sexual behavior due to the climate and emphasizes their fortitude in chastity, rather than their sexuality—not only are these women "irreproachable in their actions," but if they are blameable, their moral lapses ought to be excused because of how strongly the climate affects them. Again, the uncanny domestic emerges as Long suggests that in their creolism, these women are stronger and better than native British women, who have only standards of chastity to live up to—creole women must be doubly strong if they are to live up to British principles of chastity in a virile and dangerous Jamaican climate. In the eighteenth-century understanding, morals stood little chance in this atmosphere—the only hope was to remove women from the area in the expectation that any damage could be reversed before it became permanent. As soon as one could, one was encouraged to go "home" to the British island and run the estate from there, and if possible, never bring his female relatives there at all.[12]

Perhaps the most defining feature of the creole culture was its sexual promiscuity (as compared to English sexual behavior) and the offspring which resulted from that promiscuity. This was the issue most commented on by British visitors to the island, and the feature that is most often associated with any woman who came in contact with creolized culture. As Catherine Hall has succinctly claimed, by the end of the eighteenth century, "England was for families, Jamaica was for sex."[13] This lack of virtue advertised itself in the mixed-race offspring that came to dominate the culture of the island in the mid-eighteenth century. Michael Craton has argued that "The most absolute form of creole syncresis occurred ... in sexual intercourse. All commentators touched on the subject of miscegenation, varying only in the degree of their delicacy and ignorance, and it was in fact in the long run, a more potent shaping factor on West Indian society than planter

---

[11]   Long, *History*, 283.

[12]   This attitude of real or perceived impermanence produced a phenomenon known as absenteeism, which is thought to significantly contribute to the creole culture in Jamaica. See Kenneth Morgan, *The Bright-Meyler Papers: A Bristol West-Indian Connection 1732–1837* (Oxford: Oxford University Press, 2007), 81; Trevor Burnard, "Passengers Only: The Extent and Significance of Absenteeism in Eighteenth-Century Jamaica," *Atlantic Studies*, 1 (2004): 181–83; and Clare Taylor, "The Journal of an Absentee Proprietor, Nathanial Phillips of Slebech," *Journal of Caribbean History* XVIII (1984): 67–82.

[13]   Hall, *Civilising Subjects*, 72.

absenteeism."[14] Through sexual intercourse, races and classes mixed, cultures and values mixed, and a creolized culture rose, one with specific understandings attached to its sexuality—the more mixed, the less pure, physically and morally. The collapse of the binaries set out by the metropole was attributed to sex itself.

By definition, creolized space cannot be pure—it must be hybrid, fluid, changing, and altering, and that concept is very much at stake when thinking about the ways in which Jamaica as a space infects British purity—and how it became a repository of impurity. Creole women were often referred to in positive terms, such as in Long's comments that they are

> lively, of good natural genius, frank, affable, polite, generous, humane, and charitable ... . They are faithful in their attachments; hearty in their friendships; and fond, to a fault, of their children. …They are temperate and abstemious in their diet, rarely drinking any other liquor than water. They are remarkably expert at their needle, and indeed every other female occupation taught them; religious in their lives and sentiments; and chaste without prudery in their conversation.[15]

Despite lapses in behavior brought about by climate, they are unexceptionable. Those women who are transplanted, transported, or tricked to Jamaica are read quite differently, not as beauties made languid by climate, but as fallen women without morality, shipped to the edge of empire, bringing their profligate habits with them, thereby preserving the sexual morality of the metropole. John Oldmixon, in the mid-1740s, noted that "of late years, it has been customary for young Women, who are fallen into Disgrace in England, or are ill-used by their Parents, to transport themselves thither, and, as they say, Try their fortunes."[16] Such women trying to better their fate are most often represented in eighteenth-century texts. Jamaica's creolized space offers them the opportunity to "rehabilitate" because of its creolization—not because of its Britishness.

Women and Jamaican Space

The typical Jamaican fallen-woman story emphasizes the fallen fortunes of the colonists, the devastating effect of the climate and position of the colony, women's inability to repair past wrongs, and the probability of their falling deeper into profligacy and ruin. In his travelogue *A Trip to Jamaica*, Edward Ward describes the lot he finds himself with on a ship en route to Jamaica in 1698: "We had one *Cherubimical Lass*, who, I fear, had *Lost her Self*, two more, of the same *Gender*, who had lost their *Husbands*; two *Parsons* who had lost their *Livings*; three

---

[14]   Craton, "Reluctant Creoles," 355.

[15]   Long, *History*, 280.

[16]   John Oldmixon, *The British Empire in America*, Vol. 1 (London 1741). Eighteenth Century Collections Online, http://find.galegroup.com.ezp.lib.unimelb.edu.au/ecco/, quoted in Wilson, *Island Race*, 144. Oldmixon's context is colonial Virginia.

Broken Tradesman, who had lost their *Credit*; and several, like me, that had lost their *Wits*; … all going with one Design, to patch up their *Decay'd Fortunes*."[17] This motley crew is characteristic of the cultural understanding of Jamaica on the British side of the Atlantic. Potentially, Jamaica was a space where one could recover losses of every sort—and while some did, most did not. Life was harsh in eighteenth-century Jamaica and the company sordid. Women, in particular, were more likely to be of dubious character than men. While a man might be shipped to Jamaica because he was in the army or because he was looking for business opportunities or because he was a second son, women who found themselves there were likely to be more desperate. This caused a particular brand of sexuality to be written into Jamaican creolized space through the problems which resulted from women who were removed from the center of the empire. The women who were being sent there were already (supposedly) on the verge of sexual explosion: fallen daughters, promiscuous wives, prostitutes, women with no other place to go.[18] As Nussbaum has argued, the pressures of empire consumed men from the mother country (as soldiers, sailors, colonists, and convicts) and left women to contend with disrupted family units, falling back on prostitution and child abandonment as resources for their survival.[19] London was overrun with thieves, and transportation was one way to deal with the social problems of a London overpopulated with the wrong kind of children of empire.

Transportation was meant to take care of as many excess women of empire as possible.[20] However, while much is implied about convict transportation to

---

[17]   Edward Ward, "A Trip to Jamaica," rpt. in *Caribbeana: An Anthology of English Literature of the West Indies 1657–1777*, ed. Thomas W. Krise (Chicago: University of Chicago Press, 1999), 83.

[18]   Prostitutes and fallen women living and working in Jamaica were more likely to be considered flawed in basic human character than victims of social pressures, and thus unable to be rehabilitated. For a complete understanding of the figure of the prostitute in eighteenth-century Britain, see Laura J. Rosenthal, *Infamous Commerce: Prostitution in Eighteenth-Century British Literature and Culture* (Ithaca: Cornell University Press, 2006).

[19]   Nussbaum, *Torrid Zones*, 26. Rosenthal has also explored these issues as a problem of "Women in Excess" in "Eliza Haywood," par. 8–17.

[20]   There are several excellent studies on transportation and the early modern justice system. A. Roger Ekirch's *Bound for America: The Transportation of British Convicts to the Colonies 1718–1775* (Oxford: Clarendon, 1987) is invaluable for information about the kinds of convicts that went to the colonies and how they fared once there. Farley Grubb's "The Transatlantic Market for British Convict Labor," *Journal of Economic History* 60, no. 1 (2000): 94–122, addresses the economics of colonial transportation. For gendered perspectives on crime and punishment in the eighteenth century, see J. M. Beattie, "The Criminality of Women in Eighteenth-Century England," *Journal of Social History* 8, no. 4. (1975): 80–116; Deirdre Palk, *Gender Crime and Judicial Discretion, 1780–1830* (Woodbridge: Boydell Press, 2006); and Kirsten T. Saxton, *Narratives of Women and Murder in England, 1680–1760: Deadly Plots* (Burlington, VT: Ashgate, 2009). Special thanks to Deborah Welham for historical perspectives on transportation.

Jamaica, the reality is that few convicts were shipped there at all, and statistically even fewer could have been women.[21] The idea that cast-off prostitutes from London's streets were unceremoniously dumped onto Jamaican shores is more cultural legend than historical reality (prostitution was never a transportable offense, for instance). But as cultural legend, it had a great influence on the representations of British women in Jamaica. It explained the kind of behavior that newly arrived women were expected to exhibit and the types of morals to which they were thought to be subjected. The infectious nature of Jamaica's space was assumed. Ward describes the men as looking as though they had only recently come from prison, and says that the women

> are such who have been *Scandalous* in *England* to the utmost degre, either
> *Transported* by the *State*, or led by their *Vicious Inclinations*, where they may be
> *Wicked* without *Shame*, and *Whore* without *Punishment* … *Swearing, Drinking*,
> and *Obscene Talk* are the principal Qualifications that render them acceptable to
> *Male Conversation*.[22]

In Ward's account, the British women are wicked within and without—they have come from the most corrupt classes in the metropole, either sentenced to transportation or inclined to seek out such a place because their tastes have led them to a place where they may be evil without fear of social ostracism—those who are wicked by necessity or by choice are placed under the same rubric. Once they are among Jamaican ruffians there is no need to better themselves, as drinking and swearing are more sought after than, say, fine needlepoint or harp playing. Modesty itself is read as overrated and would be ridiculed if (by some shock of social or divine pressure) such modesty actually occurred. Such accounts of women became folded into the fictional understanding of women. *The Jamaica Lady*, a 1719 work of fiction by William Pittis based on Edward Ward's accounts, describes the anxieties of excessive women.[23] Any British woman in Jamaica was suspect; when a woman presented herself to a sea captain for a passage back to England, the captain treated her sceptically: he "enquir'd how she came into that cursed Country; for he said none but mad People and Fools, when possess'd of a plentiful Fortune, or even a moderate Competency in *England*, in Paradice, would leave it, to go to *Jamaica*, the Sink of Sin, and Receptacle of all manner of Vices: A Place so intolerably hot and suffocating, that he swore there was only a brown

---

[21]   African slaves were more valuable to import and easier to offload than convicts, and women convicts were particularly undesirable as workers due to their "weaker" constitutions and their reproductive tendencies. For an extended argument regarding convict transportation to Jamaica, see Ekirch, *Bound for America*, 137–41.

[22]   Ward, "A Trip to Jamaica," 78–92, 91–92.

[23]   [William Pittis], *The Jamaica Lady: or, the life of Bavia. Containing an account of her intrigues, cheats, amours in England, Jamaica, and the Royal Navy.* London [1720]. Eighteenth Century Collections Online, http://find.galegroup.com.ezp.lib.unimelb.edu.au/ecco/, 45.

Paper betwixt it and Hell."[24] In the captain's account, proximity to Jamaica is cause enough to inquire about a woman's situation—if there were any reason at all to not be in Jamaica, but to stay in the homeland, she would. In such a social arrangement, only bad character or harsh fortune could bring someone so close to Hell.

There is no redemptive, reproductive, or productive power in Jamaica at all in *The Jamaica Lady*. Corruption breeds corruption in generations: cast-off mistresses bear illegitimate, prostitute children. It is not the place for women to make a fortune as much as it is the place to try to avoid the worst of the localizing infection while one remains there. The ship's doctor, Pharmaceuticus, is concerned for his wife, who has taken on bad habits while on the island. When she is accused of adultery on the England-bound ship,

> that he thought was not so much the Fault of the Woman as of the Climate, believing 'twas not her natural Inclination, but that cursed malevolent Planet which predominates in that Island, and so changes the Constitution of its inhabitants ... [It is] impossible for a Woman to live at Jamaica and preserve her Virtue.[25]

Interestingly, in this text Jamaica's position in the cosmos, in addition to the climate, has corruptive power over the doctor's wife. In some ways this is an even more haunting spectre—were Jamaica's climate to change, its astrological position would still render it a corrosive environment, one from which the person must be removed in order to effect a cure—if, indeed, it is not too late. She is in Jamaica long enough that her entire humoral nature is radically altered.[26] Not only is returning to England unlikely to have a redemptive affect on his wife, but also it looms as a hazard; the wife threatens to infect the rest of England in an almost vampiric manner, by tainted blood, with her Jamaican disease of profligacy. With such desperate possibilities in the tropical Jamaican air and the creolized social setting, transportation was effective in moving such women out of sight of the motherland, but never meant as rehabilitative.

Another fictional account of corrupted women going to a place of corruption—with no implied redemption—exists in Haywood's *The History of Miss Betsy Thoughtless*. In this unfolding of events, Lady Mellasin and her daughter Flora's moral, financial, and legal failings cause a voluntary/forced exile to Jamaica, a place chosen because of its reputation as a place of luxury, opulence, and moral flexibility. Haywood's characters imagine their transportation as a way to successfully continue with perfidious behavior. When Lady Mellasin Goodman loses hope of gaining anything from her husband's death, she appeals to his heir, who provides for her on the condition that she "retire forthwith, and pass the

---

[24]   Ibid., 10–11.

[25]   Ibid., 35.

[26]   Ibid., 36.

whole remainder of your days in some remote part of the kingdom."[27] Though Lady Mellasin is happy to leave London, where she cannot afford her pleasures or expect to be accepted in society after her infamous behavior, she can fix on a place no closer to London than Jamaica, which has a reputation for sumptuousness; she has heard that the "inhabitants thought of little else, but how to divert themselves in the best manner the country afforded; and that they were not too strict in their notions, either as to honor or religion;—that reputation was a thing little regarded among them;—so that in case the occasion that had brought her thither should happen to be discovered, she would not find herself in the less estimation."[28] Though this arrangement satisfies Lady Mellasin and her dead husband's heir, Flora's meditations on those things she lacks echoes Ward's list of losses: she is "—without reputation,—without friends,—without money,—there was no remedy but to share her mother's fortune."[29] Haywood arranges their affairs in London, ships them to Jamaica, and never mentions them again; and she uses the shorthand of Jamaica to insinuate a possible outcome: Lady Mellasin will be as opulent, pleasure-seeking, and opportunistic as she was in London, and she will likely die soon. Lady Mellasin's understanding that Jamaicans are not overly scrupulous or zealously religious provides suggestions about what kinds of moral loopholes she hopes to use to exploit the gaieties of court and capitol at less expense with the more liberal thinkers in Jamaica.

In spite of these fictional examples of damned women sent to a damned place, there exists also an implied redeemable power of the colonies to remake sexually corrupted women, and there is value in asking how such discrepant understandings could coexist. Despite the quagmire that women removed to Jamaica seem to be stuck in (corruption breeding generations of corruption and threatening to corrupt the metropole), there are also stories of recuperation associated with Jamaica. For male characters, such restorative stories are connected with production— the making and remaking of fortunes based on sugar and slaves. Fictively, those who return from the island successfully usually do so because they have become rich, and their wealth allows freer social acceptance and mobility—or at least the promise of such. Some critics have argued that it is legitimate reproduction on a woman's part that allows her to achieve "domestic redemption"—prostitutes can become mothers with legitimate and productive children, as Moll Flanders seems to accomplish, and adulterers can beget legitimate and wealthy heirs.[30] But (re)productivity is not the only possible outcome of recuperation. As Kathleen Wilson has noted, Jamaica was a "Janus-faced," hybridized culture.[31] Because this social space was created from a blending of cultures, it, in effect, created

---

[27]   Eliza Haywood, *The History of Miss Betsy Thoughtless*, ed. Christina Blouch (Peterborough: Broadview, 1998), 522.

[28]   Ibid., 522–23.

[29]   Ibid., 523.

[30]   Rosenthal, "Eliza Haywood," par. 11.

[31]   Wilson, *Island Race*, 129, 131.

moral loopholes and social possibilities which certainly distracted from dubious pasts, if it did not erase them altogether. Jamaica's wealth and creole structure made it possible to purchase the fiction and performance of British respectability and allowed women to preserve what they knew.

The Rehabilitative Power of Creole Space

Edward Said has noted that "Robinson Crusoe is virtually unthinkable without the colonizing mission that permits him to create a new world of his own in the distant reaches of the African, Pacific, and Atlantic wilderness."[32] Laura Rosenthal has rightly supplemented that "Equally unthinkable, we might add, would be Sally Godfrey with no West Indian colony in which to find redemption."[33] Indeed, it is not difficult to find a reference in a work of eighteenth-century British fiction that mentions Jamaica and the dubious, profitable, hybrid importance of its creole space. In addition to the texts I have cited above in Defoe, Swift, Haywood, and Richardson, there are references to Jamaica and its moral infectiousness in several novels of the long eighteenth century. Sarah Scott's *Sir George Ellison* (1766) represents Jamaica as profitable and corruptive, with Sir George both benefiting from the place as well as rehabilitating it himself. Jamaica, in Elizabeth Inchbald's *Belinda* (1801), is a dishonest space, one that ruins Victor, Belinda's suitor, before he leaves the island.[34] In Amelia Opie's *Adeline Mowbray* (1805), Jamaica becomes the bankroll for Adeline and her subsequent child when she reluctantly marries Berrendale, and it also provides the means for her freedom from that disappointing and soul-crushing marriage.

More often than not, the women who go to Jamaica do so out of desperation (fleeing from vanquished prospects or reputations) or expectation (as opportunists ready to make the most of what they have learned about the moral and social dubiousness of ill-behaved patriarchs). While such recuperation is not a given in eighteenth-century literature when it comes to female characters, there are examples of the colonies functioning for women as they do for men, as a space in which money and reputation can be rebuilt and fostered, though men can bring their wealth back to the metropole and women cannot without serious social disruption. Sally Godfrey is an example of the ways in which women could possibly find moral redemption. Yet such an example, though Rosenthal seems to treat it as the norm, is in fact quite rare. More often, Jamaica is read as further corrupting or—in the case of creole characters like *Belinda's* Victor—a kind of latent infection that rears its head in debauched bouts of gambling and excessive emotion. However, when redemptive examples manifest, they can do so because of the creole cultural context. In such a context, white, "lost" women could play the overdetermined

---

[32] Edward Said, *Culture and Imperialism* (New York: Knopf, 1993), 75.

[33] Rosenthal, "Eliza Haywood," par. 7.

[34] See, for instance, Tim Watson, *Caribbean Culture and British Fiction in the Atlantic World, 1780–1870* (Cambridge: Cambridge University Press, 2008), 37–49.

British female role—an effect similar to Long's overdetermined Jamaican/English countryside descriptions or Brunais' uncanny domestic space. Because of this context, Jamaica has the power to change some transported women due to its social flexibility and pecuniary profitability, which then act on female characters to rehabilitate them. They become uncanny domestic models, they send wealth back to England, they erase their faults—but only if they remain in Jamaica. Creole space is thus also a means to refine and cultivate the morally or socially corrupt. Through the right marriage, the right social stepping, the right accumulation of wealth, the right depiction of British gentility, women in Jamaica can reestablish themselves, because of their whiteness, their Britishness, within the context of creolism. The clearest literary example of moral rehabilitation in Jamaica is that of Sally Godfrey in Samuel Richardson's *Pamela* (1741).[35]

Seduced, impregnated, and abandoned by Mr. B., Sally Godfrey goes to Jamaica in self-imposed exile mostly to avoid further interaction with him. She is concerned "for her past Fault";[36] she still has a great affection for Mr. B., and the distance will remove her from temptation. Once in Jamaica she marries, "passing, to her Husband, for a young widow,"[37] and is rich enough to send gifts to her illegitimate daughter, the most interesting being "a little Negro Boy, of about ten years old, as a present, to wait on her."[38] While Sally claims to go to avoid further "faults" with Mr. B. and dissipate the shame brought on her herself, her daughter, and her family, Pamela reads Sally's removal as both sacrificial and redemptive: sacrificial because Sally abdicates her chance at motherhood (her daughter falls under the morally sound care of Pamela herself), redemptive because she has the good sense to stay away, preventing further fault and avoiding corrupting her daughter. In *Pamela*, Jamaica's creole space obfuscates just enough truth and provides enough distance to rehabilitate Sally—she is "well and happily marry'd,"[39] wealthy, and, conveniently for everyone, out of the way. In passing for a widow, she passes for a virtuous woman; she will not return to England, but remains exiled in Jamaica, and "her present Happiness is the Result of [God's] gracious Providence, blessing her Penitence and Reformation."[40]

Sally Godfrey offers a striking case of absolute Jamaican rehabilitation, partly because she remains there. For most British women characters sent to Jamaica, however, redemption is possible but never unconditional. Much of this "creole" rehabilitation depends on the fallen woman's never returning to the metropole, as she knows too much and threatens to expose the perfidy of the patriarchy. In both

---

[35]   One historical example of Jamaica recuperation is that of Teresa Constantia Phillips. See especially Wilson, *Island Race.*

[36]   Samuel Richardson, *Pamela*, ed. Thomas Keymer and Alice Wakley (Oxford: Oxford University Press, 2001), 483.

[37]   Ibid., 482.

[38]   Ibid., 486.

[39]   Ibid., 482.

[40]   Ibid., 483.

Sophia Lee's *The Recess* and Delarivier Manley's "The Physician's Stratagem," a knowing woman is redeemed by performing respectability in Jamaica, but the knowledge that she sends back to the metropole explodes the illusory stability of the metropole. Both characters use the rehabilitative power of the creolized space to critique the very social system that forced them to Jamaica. Where financially redeemed men bring wealth back to the metropole, knowledgeable women bring back their information and can substitute one kind of knowledge (immorality) for another (exculpatory). They turn the gaze from the island back to the metropole, critiquing it from a distance and collapsing the neat binary that transportation to Jamaica is meant to uphold.

The short Jamaica episode in Lee's *The Recess* is a decidedly uncanny story of a rehabilitated British woman, simultaneously recognizable and destabilizing. In this particular character's story there is the forced exile of a fallen woman, Mrs. Colville. When she bears an illegitimate child, she gets sent to Jamaica with an uncle who "used every means to prevail on her to marry Mr. Colville (a settler whose plantations joined his, and who was a passenger on board the same vessel) without acquainting him with her situation."[41] The Jamaican planter takes on the honorable Englishman guise here, especially when she confesses to a second pregnancy and he decides to marry her anyway. Acting as the perfect British patriarch, Mr. Colville takes on the beautiful, charming noblewoman, carrying her off, like a knight, to his country estate. Uncannily, she is pregnant with another man's child, he is of a lower social standing than she, and the estate is in the tropics rather than being an English manor. The erring mother can repair her fortunes in Jamaica by marrying a planter and creating a new family with him. Her behavior is unexceptionable once she becomes Mrs. Colville. She fulfils her role as the perfect English mother and wife to Mr. Colville, running his plantation, bearing him children, and thus atoning for her past; she claims, "it seemed as if the sincerity of my conduct had cancelled its errors."[42] Mrs. Colville's rehabilitation can only occur out of sight of the metropole, where her reputation does not seem to matter as much as her behavior as an English gentlewoman. But again it is a creolized, uncanny representation of British life: her children by this legalized, sanctified marriage do not live, leaving her only heirs the illegitimate ones by Lord Scrope. Maintenance of this fiction of familial British happiness is of the utmost importance. This tenuous representation of British life is revealed as a hybrid—not a natural family, but a stepfamily; not a creole birth, but an illegitimate British birth.

In this plotline the mother's performance of Britishness in the creole space, and the attempt to remake that Britishness, allow her a redemptive place in which to heal from her early, sexualized past. However, exile is necessary for Mrs. Colville's redemption—she states she cannot return, "for never, in respect to my husband's

---

[41] Sophia Lee, *The Recess; or A Tale of Other Times*, ed. April Alliston (Lexington: University Press of Kentucky, 2000), 18.

[42] Ibid., 19.

memory, will I see again the father of my children; this place shall be my grave, and here, while life remains, I will bless you both, and pray that the sins of your parents may never be visited upon either."[43] Mrs. Colville respects her husband, certainly, but she knows too much to return to England. Once removed from England, her misbehavior ceases to become relevant—her uncles and family are happy to be rid of her, Mr. Colville is happy to have her as his wife, and the knowledge she possesses remains safe, buried under the "sincerity of her conduct" and the distance between Jamaica and the metropole. Her redemption appears complete. However, once her son returns to British soil the image of perfect British matriarch falls apart: her two illegitimate children by Lord Scrope—Mrs. Marlow and young Mr. Colville—meet and marry. Mrs. Colville's revealed knowledge (via deathbed confessional letter) is simultaneously corrupting and preserving. The letter arrives in time to prevent consummation of the marriage, but it is deeply destructive to both the happiness of the son and the future prospects of the daughter. Insulated on the Jamaican island, redemption occurs; once there is a return to the metropole (via her son), the worst happens. Exile is necessary because those women who are banished know "too much"—once the gaze gets returned to England, information sheds light on past wrongs which took place in the metropole. But sometimes, the knowledge that returns to the metropole destroys people who should be destroyed.

Delarivier Manley's "The Physician's Stratagem" is a little-studied novella in her collection *The Power of Love in Seven Novels*. The theme of virtue avenged or rewarded resounds most significantly throughout the collection, and the plots in the novellas consistently punish the unvirtuous and reward the virtuous, though often in paradoxical ways. In "The Physician's Stratagem" (the only text of the collection whose source text has not been identified and which is suspected to be an original work), the exemplary virtuous character, Mariana, is persecuted and cheated out of her own virtue and her opportunity for a happy life, separating her forever from her intended (and much loved) husband Fonteray. The stratagem of Fauxgarde (the titular physician) is only possible through his exploitation of the maid, Caton, whom he then exports to the West Indies. Hoping to marry up, Fauxgarde seduces and impregnates Caton. Jealous of her mistress, Caton agrees to drug Mariana so that Fauxgarde can impregnate her, too, without her consent or knowledge. Fauxgarde then acts the "hero" and marries Mariana, thus saving her reputation, and he removes the only witness to his crime, Caton, by sending her to the West Indies.[44] The pregnant maid gets tricked into being shipped off to the Caribbean:

---

[43]   Ibid., 20.

[44]   The story takes place in France, and the metropole referred to is Paris, which would make the "West Indies" mentioned an island such as St. Kitts. But just as Lee's "Spanish Jamaica" reads more like an eighteenth-century British Jamaica, so do the "French" locales of Manley's story read like London and Jamaica. For the purposes of my argument, the exact locale is not as important as the cultural implication of what "West Indies" means in terms of moral laxity, too much knowledge, and the price of returning to the metropole.

Caton understood no *Geography* but what had been taught her, to her Cost, in the Country of Love, whence *Fauxgarde* might unsuspectingly betray her to his wish. They both Embark'd in a Ship outward-bound to the *West-Indies*, though unknown to her. The Doctor, pretending he had forgot something of Consequence on Shoar … went on board a Boat that followed him for that Purpose. The Ship's Crew knowing his Intent, having taken a good piece of Money of him to carry *Caton* to the Plantations and sell her for a slave, crowded all their Sail, the Wind favouring their Design, whilst the Doctor whish'd her the *bonne Voyage*, made what haste he could to Shoar."[45]

Caton is configured as the erring, immoral, fallen woman, and her punishment is exile to the colonies. But she is not removed just because of her immoral behavior. More important, she is removed because of what she knows—as an accomplice to the crime Fauxgarde commits, she becomes a witness and assistant. Her knowledge of how Mariana becomes pregnant (something even Mariana cannot account for) has the potential to unravel the life that Fauxgarde has created for himself. Like Mrs. Colville's knowledge, it can only be preserved away, out of site of the metropole. Fauxgarde's mistake is in thinking this knowledge is as safe in Europe as it is in the West Indies.

Fauxgarde eventually recalls Caton home, and his own pride causes Mariana to know how she was tricked. Caton and her information become the center of a lawsuit that Mariana files against Fauxgarde—Caton has the power to point out some of the worst aspects of bad patriarchal behavior. In carrying back her knowledge, she carries back with her the chance for Mariana to regain her fortune and previous lover, Fonteray. Unfortunately the scene does not play out—Fonteray kills Fauxgarde in a duel, and both lovers retire to convents to live lives of celibate devotion. Caton's role becomes that of the overly licentious and indulgent woman who gets what she deserves in being tricked into West Indian slavery. The island itself does not redeem her or make her successful; she must depend on Fauxgarde's generosity to her for that, but the information she knows, which has the power to set Mariana's world to rights, implies that a kind of moral reckoning has taken place through the journey itself.

The West Indies in Manley's novella are more a shadow of a threat offstage than a player in the actual drama of Caton's mistakes and reformation. There is no actual description of a creolized space in the text—no recitation of a slave narrative, no story of Caton's island experiences. Rather, the exile looms as a vague menace in the background. And this is what I find most intriguing about it. Manley has, in this novella, used the West Indies as shorthand, a way to code Caton's behavior and character type and Fauxgarde's ruthlessness and determination. Manley expects the eighteenth-century reader to "get" all of this— the horrific conditions, the type of woman who finds herself in such a hellish

---

[45] Delarivier Manley, "The Physician's Stratagem," in *The Power of Love in Seven Novels* (London, 1720). Eighteenth Century Collections Online, http://find.galegroup.com. ezp.lib.unimelb.edu.au/ecco/, 99.

place, the kind of future behavior expected of her, the chance for her to redeem her past and her involvement by coming clean with regard to Fauxgarde's plot. The hybridism of such a space is, for Manley, a given in this particular text. The creole space in Manley's text silently represents a contradictive space with moral laxity, uncanny representations of life back home, and dubious stances on sexual behavior, and the possibility to offer redemption from past crimes. Manley uses Caton's return to explicitly condemn Fauxgarde's sexually exploitative actions. Lee uses Mrs. Colville's knowledge to expose but not condemn Lord Scrope's sexually exploitative actions. In both cases, however, the return of the knowing woman redeemed by performing respectability in Jamaica explodes the illusory stability built by men: rehabilitation is dependent on exile.

Eighteenth-century Jamaica is represented in British texts and art as a space of contrasts, but through the lens of creolization, such contrasts can be better understood to embody several cultural factors. Most important to understanding the role of the fallen woman exiled to Jamaica is reading the way in which creolized space creates an uncanny Britain, a home away from home where such characters can remake their moral pasts much in the same way male characters remake their fortunes. Factors such as climate, absenteeism, and transportation cause Jamaican space to be morally flexible. While many fallen women characters are exiled to Jamaica as punishment, there are also examples of how this exile effects moral change; but rehabilitation is conditional, only possible in the creolized space itself. Because the detritus women of empire know too much about patriarchal irresponsibility, they can refocus the gaze in Jamaica, turning a scrutinizing eye back upon the metropole. Their pasts cannot be completely eradicated, only refocused in Jamaica.

Chapter 3
"Going Native":
Geography, Gender, and Identity in Lady Mary Wortley Montagu's
Turkish Embassy Letters

Ambereen Dadabhoy

In a letter to Lady Mary Wortley Montagu that he sent while she was en route to the Sublime Porte, Alexander Pope suggests that her advance into Ottoman territories will yield a systematic transformation of identity:

> I shall look upon you no longer as a Christian, when you pass from that charitable court to the land of jealousy where the unhappy women converse with none but eunuchs, and where the very cucumbers are brought to them cut. I expect to hear an exact account, how, and at what places, you leave one Article of Faith after another as you approach nearer to Turkey ... Lastly I shall hear how the very first night you lay at Pera, you had a vision of Mahomet's paradise, and happily awaked without a soul. From which blessed instant the beautiful body was left at full liberty to perform all the agreeable functions it was made for.[1]

The letter, dated November 10, 1716, anticipates the Montagu embassy's progress from the Viennese court into Ottoman-controlled Europe, and in its charged eroticism it accesses conventional tropes of the Islamicate societies. The metamorphosis Pope hypothesizes rests on his association of the east with hypersexuality and femininity. As she actively throws off her Christian identity, figured in Pope's letter through the metaphor of dress and undress, Montagu is reborn in Pera (a Christian suburb of Istanbul) as a Muslim woman. Indeed, Pope's Ottoman Montagu is not just any Muslim woman, but an occupant of "Mahomet's paradise," one of its mythical houris, made for heavenly and sensual delights. Pope's epistolary reconstruction of Montagu as a Muslim woman depends upon proximity: he aligns her gradual movement into the Ottoman Empire with her change in identity. Ironically, Pope forecasts the shift in Montagu's subjectivity that occurs during her residence in Ottoman domains, yet this change as narrated in the *Turkish Embassy Letters* is devoid of the fetishized female sexuality that characterizes Pope's fantasy.

---

[1]   Alexander Pope, *The Correspondence of Alexander Pope*, ed. George Sherburn, vol. 1 (London: Oxford University Press, 1956), 368.

I employ Pope at the beginning of my analysis because his letter exposes anxieties about gender, identity, and geography as they intersect with Ottoman-Islamic difference. Moreover, his representation of Montagu offers a stark counterpoint to the way she writes herself. The literary medium of the familiar letter gives her the opportunity to present what she has seen and experienced during her travels across Europe and into the Ottoman Empire, and more significantly, to contemplate her own subjectivity as an Englishwoman and writer through the lens of cultural and spatial difference. The project of self-examination and fashioning observed in the *Letters* not only facilitates extended considerations of gender, geography, sexuality, and national identity, but also allows Montagu to construct herself as woman writer. I argue that while Montagu is authoring other places and people, she is also authoring herself: in other words, through the representation of the foreign she forges her own subjectivity. Like Pope, I find that geographic proximity, with its potential to "go native," plays a crucial role in Montagu's experimentation with identity, so that the further she travels into the Ottoman Empire the more porous and permeable her identity and body become.

Before moving on to a detailed discussion of the *Turkish Embassy Letters*, I would like to excavate an additional element of Pope's letter: its implicit Orientalism. The geography and space he alludes to in his missive reproduces the sex-segregated space of the harem, which was seen as a synecdoche of the Ottoman Empire, so that the east was stereotypically represented as degenerate and sexualized. Indeed, the Orient circulates within his letters to her not as an actual place but as a constructed, discursive site of accumulated knowledge. In another letter he writes, "If you do not now write and speak the finest things imaginable, you must be content to be involved in the same imputation with the rest of the East, and be concluded to have abandoned your self to extreme effeminacy, laziness, and lewdness of life."[2] His knowledge of the east and its mores comes not from his own experience but from secondary sources, yet this same knowledge allows him to write to her from a position of authority (albeit with a patina of irony). His letters operate within the theoretical methodology of what Edward Said has critiqued as Orientalism, that it is "a Western style for dominating, restructuring, and having authority over the Orient."[3] Said claims that the legitimacy of knowledge about the Orient comes from the accumulation of "antecedent authority," which results in "Orientalists treat[ing] each other's work in … a citationary way."[4] He finds that "the Orient is less a place than a *topos*, a set of references, a congeries of characteristics, that seems to have its origin in a quotation, or a fragment of a text, or a citation from someone's work."[5] Thus, the Orient is made into itself through the weight and power of texts that represent it as such.

While Pope's letters do not explicitly cite the work of other writers about the Orient, his representation of the Ottoman Empire does rehearse accumulated

---

[2]   Ibid., 406.

[3]   Edward Said, *Orientalism* (New York: Pantheon, 1978), 3.

[4]   Ibid., 176.

[5]   Ibid., 177.

common knowledge on the topic. Montagu's letters, on the other hand, overtly and aggressively contend with travel writing about the Orient and in this way, it appears that her work participates in the project of Orientalism. She makes use of the writings of those who have traversed—or only written about—the same geographical region, referencing writers such as Sir Paul Rycaut, Richard Knolles, Aaron Hill, Jean Dumont, and Antoine Galland. In addition, through her eyewitness account—"I have now, madam, passed a journey that has not been undertaken by any Christian since the time of the Greek emperors, and I shall not regret all the fatigues I have suffered in it if it gives me an opportunity of amusing … by an account of places utterly unknown amongst us"[6]—and her repeated claims of authenticity—"I will try to awaken your gratitude by giving you a full and true relation of the novelties of this place"[7]—Montagu constructs a narrative of the Ottoman Empire in the Orientalist style: through her "real and true" letters she speaks for and represents the other.[8] Recent scholarship on Montagu's *Turkish Embassy Letters* has either demonized her perceived Orientalism or valorized her cultural relativism and identification with Ottoman women.[9] Current postcolonial studies of the *Letters* have interrogated the binary of Orientalism, finding that the Western dominance of the East through representation, power, and knowledge obfuscates other forms of power relations such as those grounded in gender, class, and race. Such work argues for a reading of the *Letters* and Montagu's treatment of the Ottoman Empire in which she manipulates the Orientalism of her day because of her cultural openness and interest in women.[10] Why such mixed reaction to a

---

[6]   Lady Mary Wortley Montagu, *Turkish Embassy Letters*, ed. Anita Desai (Athens: University of Georgia Press, 1993), 55.

[7]   Ibid., 69.

[8]   Said, *Orientalism*, 6.

[9]   See Srinivas Aravamudan, "Lady Mary Wortley Montagu in the Hammam: Masquerade, Womanliness, and Levantinization," *ELH* 62 (1995): 69–104; Meyda Yeğenoğlu, *Colonial Fantasies: Towards a Feminist Reading of Orientalism* (New York: Cambridge University Press, 1998); Lisa Lowe, *Critical Terrains: French and British Orientalisms* (Ithaca: Cornell University Press, 1991); Reina Lewis, *Rethinking Orientalism: Women, Travel, and the Ottoman Harem* (New Brunswick, NJ: Rutgers University Press, 2004); Joseph W. Lew, "Lady Mary's Portable Seraglio," *Eighteenth-Century Studies* 24 (1991): 432–50; and Billie Melman, *Women's Orients: English Women and the Middle East, 1718–1918* (Ann Arbor: University of Michigan Press, 1995).

[10]   See Arthur J. Weitzman, "Voyeurism and Aesthetics in the Turkish Bath: Lady Mary's School of Female Beauty," *Comparative Literature Studies* 39 (2002): 347–59; Teresa Heffernan, "Feminism against the East/West Divide," *Eighteenth-Century Studies* 33 (2000): 201–15; Patricia Plummer, "'The free treatment of topics usually taboo'd': Glimpses of the Harem in Eighteenth- and Nineteenth-Century Literature and the Fine Arts," in *Word and Image in Colonial and Post Colonial Literatures and Cultures*, ed. Michael Meyer (New York: Rodopi, 2009): 47–68; Nicolle Jordan, "Eastern Pastoral: 'Female Fears' and 'Savage Foes' in Montagu's 'Constantinople'," *Modern Philology* 107 (2010): 400–420; Ahmed K. Al-Rawi, "The Portrayal of the East vs. the West in Lady Mary Montagu's *Letters* and Emily Ruete's *Memoirs*," *Arab Studies Quarterly* 30 (2008): 15–30.

seemingly straightforward travelogue? The answer, I claim, lies in the complicated position of the Ottoman Empire within European colonial (or in this specific case, proto-colonial) discourse and the importance of Montagu's gendered subjectivity.

During the eighteenth century the Ottoman Empire lost many of its eastern European domains and was forced to cede parts of its Black Sea territories to Russia. At the time of the Montagu embassy, the Ottomans were at war with the Austrians, losing a significant portion of Serbia and the fortress at Belgrade.[11] Even after these humiliating defeats, however, total collapse of the empire was not yet imminent. While the balance of power was shifting in favor of Europe and the empire had lost much of its vaunted military strength, it was still beyond Europe's colonizing grasp. Thus the other being constructed within the dyad of Orientalist discourse was not a colonial subject or subaltern but an "unsubjugated subject" with agency.[12] Furthermore, Montagu's writing on the Ottoman Empire is complicated by her gender because her gaze, unlike that of her Orientalist predecessors, is not a masculine one. Indeed, as a woman, she is already Other to masculine/normative, British/European subjectivity; therefore, her letters function as an intervention within a characteristically masculine discursive mode and create a space through which she can critique patriarchal relations of power in Britain and the Ottoman Empire and articulate her own agency and that of Ottoman women.[13] Montagu employs Orientalist methodology in the *Turkish Embassy Letters* through her claims of mimetic representation in order to buttress her own authority; at the same time she challenges that discourse through her concentration on and representation of gender, offering alternative narratives of subversion and power. The result is a self-fashioning achieved through the reflection of and, more important, an identification with a desirable and even possible other identity. Montagu's letters are crafted to offer oblique appropriations of Ottoman subjectivity and moments where she occupies a hybrid position and "goes native."

Geographic movement and the obvious gendering of geography occasion the shift in Montagu's identity signaled satirically in Pope's letter: "I shall look upon you no longer as a Christian, when you pass from that charitable court to the land of jealousy."[14] As "the land of jealousy" the geography of the Ottoman Empire is constructed in gendered terms: it is a locale of masculine jealousy based upon the fear of female sexuality. Such a representation depends on a skewed understanding of the Ottoman-Islamicate practice of sex segregation. Segregated spaces and veiling are facets of the Qur'an-mandated practice of seclusion, resulting in limited access

---

[11]   Suraiya Faroqhi, *The Ottoman Empire and the World Around It* (New York: I. B. Tauris, 2004), 31.

[12]   Lewis, *Rethinking Orientalism*, 6.

[13]   Reina Lewis, Cynthia Lowenthal, Billie Melman, Jill Campbell, Joseph Lew, Felicity Nussbaum, Elizabeth Bohls, Arthur J. Weitzman, Teresa Heffernan, Nicolle Jordan, and Ahmed K. Al-Rawi all focus on how gender creates a position through which Montagu can alter the discourse of Orientalism.

[14]   Pope, *Correspondence*, 368.

to society for women and embodied in the ideology of *mahram and na'mahram*.[15] The chapter "The Light" in the Qur'an delineates specific actions for men and women regarding sexual temptation. While men are instructed to "turn their eyes away from temptation and to restrain their carnal desires," women are commanded to "draw their veils over their bosoms and not to display their finery except to their husbands, their fathers, their husbands' fathers, their sons, their step-sons, their brothers, their brothers' sons, their sisters' sons, their women-servants, and their slave-girls; male attendants lacking in natural vigor, and children who have no carnal knowledge of women."[16] The Qur'anic safeguarding of women's bodies and limitation on mobility is transformed in the Ottoman Empire and other Islamicate cultures into institutions and architectural spaces designed for the surveillance and control of Muslim women. In Pope's imperialist view the strict patrol of Ottoman women points to their dangerous sexuality. Such a formulation requires the site of women's experiences—the all-female domestic space of the harem—to be one of confinement, imprisonment, and degeneracy.[17] The geography and spaces of the Ottoman Empire are, then, discursively constructed around ideological and imperial biases: constituted as simply a "sexual space," the empire can be transformed into a "space to be colonized."[18]

The stereotypical Orientalist construction of sex-segregated spaces rests in their impenetrability to the male gaze. Montagu's narrative reconstitutes Ottoman women's spaces, rescuing them from the realm of European male fantasy, because of her access to Ottoman women and her experiences within the sex-segregated private, domestic realm.[19] Both her gender and her class facilitate her entry into elite Ottoman female society, and so she constructs her own discursive geography of the Ottoman Empire where the "politics of location" and gender obtain.[20] Her

---

[15]   According to Islamic law, *mahram* is one with whom sexual relations are taboo—close unmarriageable relatives—and *na'mahram* is the opposite.

[16]   *The Koran*, trans. N. J. Dawood (New York: Penguin, 1999), 248.

[17]   Sara Mills notes that confinement is the dominant trope of spatial relations in a colonial context, yet she argues that more contingent and space/geography-specific analysis can open up analysis of women's spaces in colonial contexts. Sara Mills, "Gender and Colonial Space," *Gender, Place and Culture: A Journal of Feminist Geography* 3 (1996): 125.

[18]   Alison Blunt and Gillian Rose, *Writing, Women and Space: Colonial and Postcolonial Geographies* (New York: The Guilford Press, 1994), 9.

[19]   Linda McDowell notes that the project of feminist geography must include analysis of the ways in which men and women "experience spaces and places differently and to show how these differences themselves are part of the social constitution of gender as well as that of place." Linda McDowell, *Gender, Identity and Place: Understanding Feminist Geographies* (Minneapolis: University of Minnesota Press, 1999), 12.

[20]   As Blunt and Rose point out, Adrienne Rich's terminology "politics of location" indicates the need to be attentive to "the specificity of a particular woman." Blunt and Rose, *Writing, Women and Space*, 7. In this case, Ottoman women and their agency within sex-segregated spaces and institutions should not be taken as exemplary of all Muslim women's experiences.

experience with the material conditions of Ottoman women's lives invests her and, spectrally, Ottoman women with agency. For Montagu, mobility and liberty are generated by the adoption of Ottoman clothing: her Ottoman costume (of which there are numerous portraits) displays her status and receptivity to a new culture, and the veil—which creates around it a mobile space of seclusion and security— facilitates her easy movement into public and forbidden arenas. The politics of Ottoman dress in the *Letters* point to the confinement and liberation of Ottoman women: the costume itself is fitted and yet provides free and easy movement, just as the women are fettered and still able to finds subversive means of mobility. Thus, once she is suitably clothed, Montagu can and does "enter zones forbidden to men, such as harems, and interrogate the ways in which women occupy, manage, and control contested spaces."[21] While Ottoman practice restricted women to the domestic, it also institutionalized certain public areas where women could gather, such as the *hamam* (*bagnio*). These sites were strictly regulated by social convention and religious laws pertaining to access, yet from Montagu's letters we see how Ottoman women, even Montagu, are able to craft agency, manipulate the "meanings and representations associated with certain places," and "transform" spaces within the bounds of their physical confinement.[22]

To understand the formation and function of Montagu's self-fashioning we must consider the geography wherein her identity is reconfigured, specifically the sex-segregated women's spaces within the Ottoman Empire. The institution of the harem has long held special significance in the European imagination: for early modern (and even to an extent modern) writers it functioned as a sign *par excellence* of Ottoman tyranny, Islamic degeneracy, and sexual licentiousness. As Billie Melman points out, "for a long stretch of time … the odalisk, the domestic despot, and the harem had been the most repeated, most enduring *topoi* of the Muslim Mediterranean."[23] The word "harem" has two seemingly contradictory meanings: to be sacred and to be forbidden. As a space within an Islamic household, the harem is a sacred or protected area, where general access is forbidden.[24] Within its Ottoman context the word "harem" is a "term of respect, redolent of religious purity and honor and evocative of the requisite obeisance."[25] All harems, and especially the sultan's, were segregated spaces signifying the domestic, private realm, utterly separate from the public spaces within the home or the palace. Indeed, the home was bifurcated into two distinct areas: the *selamlık*, a public

---

[21]   Diane Long Hoeveler and Jeffrey Cass, introduction to Hoeveler and Cass, eds., *Interrogating Orientalism* (Columbus: Ohio State University Press, 2006), 5.

[22]   Ghazi-Walid Falah and Caroline Nagel, introduction to Falah and Nagel, eds., *Geographies of Muslim Women: Gender, Religion, and Space* (New York: The Guilford Press, 2005), 4.

[23]   Melman, *Women's Orients*, 60.

[24]   Leslie P. Peirce, *The Imperial Harem: Women and Sovereignty in the Ottoman Empire* (New York: Oxford University Press, 1993), 4.

[25]   Ibid., 5.

receiving area, and the *haremlik*, a private family domain. The harem, then, was a gendered space, governed by its own hierarchies to be sure, but a woman's world nevertheless. Because it was a space inaccessible to European travel writers, it became a fetishized site of male fantasy and unbridled female sexuality. In the letter that began this chapter, Pope writes that "the unhappy women converse with none but Eunuchs, and where the very cucumbers are brought to them cut," rehearsing the trope of the harem's sex-starved inmates, who cannot be trusted with phallic vegetables lest they deploy them as dildoes. Pope's innuendoes are not original: in the seventeenth century Robert Burton in *The Anatomy of Melancholy* commented that Turkish wives "are so penned up they may not confer with any living man, or converse with younger women, have a cucumber or carrot sent into them for their diet, but sliced, for fear, &c."[26] The cultural capital that accrued to the degeneracy of Islamicate sex-segregated spaces within the European imagination furthered the Orientalist agenda that emptied the east of all but the erotic and exotic. Writing within this tradition but separated from it because of her gender, Montagu sets herself the task of debunking the hypersexuality of European male fantasy and, in its place, offering an image of the private world of Ottoman women as a site of culture, civility, and agency.

Montagu's first intimate dealings with Ottoman women occur not in the domestic and drawing room–like arena of the harem but in the *hamam*, which, like the harem, circulated in the European imagination as a site of sexual deviance. By structuring her narrative from public *hamam* to private harem, Montagu showcases her ability to traverse and be accepted in a variety of elite Ottoman women's spaces. In the *Letters* she recounts two important visits to the *hamam*: one in Sofia and the other in Istanbul. Much has been made of her account of the *hamam*, specifically that it is Orientalizing and voyeuristic. (Indeed, this letter is the basis of Ingres' famous nineteenth-century painting *Le Bain Turc*). However, I read the letters detailing her visits to the *hamam* as framing her experience with Ottoman women and providing a geographic, linguistic, and representational space in which she experiments with her subjectivity. In fact, as she travels deeper into the empire her identity becomes increasingly fluid: from her first tentative steps into Ottoman women's space to her adoption of Ottoman costume, the veil, and the inoculation of her son, her narrative demonstrates how geographic progress and continued exposure to the foreign is transformative. The first epistle mentioning the *hamam* is addressed to an unknown lady, written in Edirne or Adrianople (the first Ottoman capital in Europe), but about a *hamam* in Sofia, Belgrade. The specific locations are important because they illustrate the geographic progress being made by Montagu into Ottoman territory: her movements mimetically reproduce her openness to Ottoman culture and identity. Montagu begins this letter by telling her anonymous friend, "I am now got into a new world, where

---

[26] Robert Burton, "The Anatomy of Melancholy," rpt. in *Race in Early Modern England: A Documentary Companion*, ed. Ania Loomba and Jonathan Burton (New York: Palgrave Macmillan, 2007), 204.

everything I see appears to me a change of scene."[27] The relation that follows is one in which multiple layers of identity are presented as palimpsest. Identity and difference become difficult to differentiate until the abrupt interjection of proper English patriarchy at the close seems to appropriately reposition the participants.

Beginning her story with the specific details of how she arrived at the *hamam*, Montagu writes:

> Designing to go incognito I hired a Turkish coach. ... In one of these covered wagons, I went to the bagnio about ten o'clock. It was already full of women. ... the portress stood at the door. Ladies of quality generally give this woman the value of a crown or ten shillings and I did not forget the ceremony. ... I was in my traveling habit, which is a riding dress, and certainly appeared very extraordinary to them.[28]

Montagu's use of "design" and "incognito" suggests that her visit contains a hint of impropriety, which is why she must conceal her identity as the English ambassador's wife. Contradictory elements of titillation and protocol, then, frame the entirety of her *hamam* visit. While there remains an element of the illicit at this early stage, she is still compelled to point out that like Ottoman "ladies of quality," she, too, compensated the "portress" for her hard work. Very much aware of the hypersexual coding of the *hamam* in European writing, Montagu manipulates convention: her narrative also entices and skirts the salacious, but in order to effect a shift in her audience's expectations.

In setting the stage for her excursion, Montagu deliberately points out that while she may travel in the Ottoman fashion, she still dresses in English clothing—an important point, since clothing functions as a symbolic sign of identity, marking rank and nationality. However, clothing is also problematic and unstable, since it can be easily adopted or divested. Her seemingly ordinary British riding habit is an "extraordinary" curiosity for the Ottoman women in its difference to their own clothing, and also, as Montagu goes on to explain, because clothing is extraneous in the *hamam*. In her description, she notes almost as an aside that the women are naked: "The first sofas were covered with cushions and rich carpets, on which sat the ladies, and on the second their slaves behind them, but without any distinction of rank by their dress, all being in the state of nature, that is, in plain English, stark naked, without any beauty or defect concealed."[29] The luxurious furnishings provide a fitting background to the bare, natural beauty of the women. Montagu points out that the geography of the *hamam* is one that appears to erase rank distinction and social hierarchies: a space where women are free from all forms of social constrictions and regulations. Montagu's elision of the realities of rank, present in her cognizance of the arrangement of slaves and mistresses,

---

[27]   Montagu, *Letters*, 57.

[28]   Ibid., 58.

[29]   Ibid., 59.

is conspicuous. Hierarchies thus remain, but only between free women and their slaves, not between women of rank.[30]

By mentioning the Ottoman women's dishabille, Montagu evokes the discursive strategies of European male writing about Muslim women's sexuality, hinting that her own account may tread the same ground. For other travel writers, in whose tradition Montagu situates her letters, the world of both the *hamam* and the harem excited prurient interest and fostered false and fantastic accounts of aberrant female sexuality. Nicholas de Nicolay, in his *Navigations*, writes that women in the *hamam*

> Do familiarly wash one another, whereby it cometh to pass … sometimes [they] become so fervently in love the one of the other as if it were with men, in such sort that perceiving some maiden, or woman of excellent beauty, they will not cease until they have found means to bathe with them, and to handle and grope them everywhere at their pleasures, so full are they of luxuriousness and feminine wantonness.[31]

The erotic tableau of the Turkish bath becomes a recurring and fetishized image of Muslim women's sexual desire, not only for Nicolay but for other early modern travelers as well. George Sandys, in *Relation of a Journey* (1615), writes, "Much unnatural and filthy lust is said to be committed daily in the remote closets of the darksome bannias: yea, women with women."[32] The space of the *hamam*, sex-segregated and free from patriarchal surveillance, becomes a site of promiscuity and aggressive female sexuality. To shift her reader's perspective away from the stereotype of the *hamam* and toward a representation that rehabilitates the scene to one of beauty and sociability, Montagu offers the decisive disclaimer, "there was not the least wanton smile or immodest gesture amongst them."[33]

Nonetheless, critics have accused Montagu's own description of the *hamam* of reproducing the sexual anxiety characteristic of male writers, perhaps because her presentation of these women seems to reproduce the Orientalizing and eroticizing masculine gaze.[34] Her *hamam* ekphrasis depicts women reclining and lounging at ease, self-conscious neither of one another nor of the stranger within their midst. In fact, Montagu's tableau quite pointedly removes her person from the representational frame. This moment presents the first instance of her unstable subjectivity: as an observer and outsider not just in the Ottoman Empire, but also

---

[30] Peirce argues that the women's societies of the sultan's harem developed rigid hierarchies based on age and favorite status. Peirce, *The Imperial Harem*, 7.

[31] Nicholas de Nicolay, *The Navigations, Peregrinations and Voyages, Made into Turkie*, rpt. in Loomba and Burton, *Race in Early Modern England*, 117.

[32] George Sandys, "Relation of a Journey," rpt. in Loomba and Burton, *Race in Early Modern England*, 195.

[33] Montagu, *Letters*, 59.

[34] See Aravamudan, "Lady Mary Wortley Montagu in the Hammam"; Yeğenoğlu, *Colonial Fantasies*.

in the *hamam*, Montagu utilizes multiple mechanisms—like clothing and aesthetic framing—to reinforce her difference, which in its confrontation with the basic, shared identity of "woman" appears endangered. At this stage in her travels, she has only recently set foot in the empire: while this letter is written from Edirne, it recounts events in Sofia, on the frontiers of the empire. She is, then, new to this world just as this is "a new world" to her. As she penetrates deeper into the empire, she more readily and easily embraces Ottoman identity. In this visit to the *hamam*, Montagu appropriates the artistic, masculine gaze in order to accurately represent Ottoman women. In fact, she even expresses a proscribed desire to have the artist Jarvis present: "To tell you the truth, I had wickedness enough to wish secretly that Mr. Gervase could have been there invisible."[35] Introducing a man into this gynaeceum is both forbidden and titillating, but unlike her male counterparts, Montagu's improper desire is motivated by the demands of her narrative for mimetic representation, not erotic fantasy:

> I fancy it would have very much improved his art to see so many fine women naked, in different postures, some in conversation, some working, others drinking coffee or sherbet, and many negligently lying on their cushions while their slaves (generally pretty girls of seventeen or eighteen) were employed in braiding their hair in several pretty manners. In short, 'tis the women's coffee house, where all the news of town is told, scandal invented etc.[36]

Montagu accomplishes through ekphrasis what, according to her judgment, Jarvis cannot do with his paintbrush: gracefully depict women in their natural state.[37] More important, she turns prosaic what for other writers is a sexually chargedtableau. Indeed, the comparison of the *hamam* to the coffeehouse, where matters of news and gossip circulate, attempts to sterilize the scene. The correlation emphasizes the social space of the *hamam* and illustrates the advantages of Ottoman sex-segregated society over British society, for the coffeehouse as a public institution in England was the province of men and there was no comparable public space for women.[38] Ottoman women, then, have access to public spaces, even if they are kept separate based on gender, in a way that British women do not.

Montagu elaborates on the oblique social commentary contained in her comparison by contrasting her study of the Ottoman women with their study of her. This move turns the critical gaze that appears to objectify the other toward the self, and cedes agency to the other gazing subjects, thereby destabilizing her position within the hierarchy of subject-object, voyeur-object relations. Montagu reminds her reader that just as these women are objects of curiosity for her, just

---

[35]   Montagu, *Letters*, 59.

[36]   Ibid.

[37]   Weitzman argues that Montagu's participation in the developing genre of literary picturesque style problematizes the Orientalist critique. Weitzman, "Voyeurism and Aesthetics," 352.

[38]   Lew, "Portable Seraglio," 441.

as her gaze is directed at them, so, too, is she an object of curiosity for them and their gazes are focused on her. By welcoming her into their world, which requires that she divest herself of her habit, the material object that signifies her cultural identity and join them simply as a woman, they, too, erase the distinction between subject and object. At this point, however, at a *hamam* in Sofia, on the border of the European and Ottoman contact zone, Montagu's English mores prohibit her from joining them. She does partially satisfy the exigencies of the *hamam* by opening her shirt:

> The lady that seemed the most considerable amongst them entreated me to sit by her and would fain have undressed me for the bath. I excused myself with some difficulty, they being however all so earnest in persuading me, I was at last forced to open my shirt, and show them my stays, which satisfied them very well, for I saw they believed I was so locked up in that machine, that it was not in my own power to open it, which contrivance they attributed to my husband.[39]

By disrobing, Montagu reveals that the cultural markers of her identity are impossible to undo, as they appear grafted onto her body. The Ottoman women interpret her stays as bondage to patriarchal order. While they are confined to their homes, their physical bodies are free from the restraint that British women must endure. Perhaps Montagu wants to be free, but it is not in her power. She attributes this transgressive thought to the Ottoman women, yet we see not just from the rest of her epistles but also from her biography that the stays are metaphorical as well as literal. Confronted by women whom she will later refer to as "freer than any ladies in the universe," here Montagu finds humor in their misreading of her corset.[40] Although there may be a misunderstanding of her undergarments, the Ottoman women do ironically point out the semblance between their subjectivities: both groups experience spatial and bodily confinement. Just as the stays are presented as a symbol of masculine power, Montagu's *hamam* visit ends with the intrusion of her husband into the narrative. The disruption effectively dissolves the *hamam* society, pulling the focus back from the intimacy of the female world to the greater duties required by the embassy. Montagu notes that she would "have been very glad to pass more time with them, but Mr. Wortley [was] resolving to pursue his journey the next morning early."[41] The stays and Wortley serve as reminders that while she may enter the secret world of Ottoman women, she is not one of them and so must be recalled to her proper identity.

Residence in Edirne presents Montagu the opportunity not just to recount her fabulous visit to the *hamam*, but also to adopt Ottoman fashions and customs. Her letters from Edirne to various correspondents, both male and female, illustrate her easy acceptance of Ottoman culture. In a letter to her sister, Lady Mar, that follows swiftly on the heels of the *hamam* narrative, Montagu writes that she is "now in

---

[39] Montagu, *Letters*, 59–60.
[40] Ibid., 134.
[41] Ibid., 60.

[her] Turkish habit" and that "'tis admirably becoming."[42] Her English clothes have been shed for new ones in the Ottoman style. The long description that follows mimics in prose the portrait Montagu intends to send and is characteristically rich, sensual, and sensational, focusing on brocade, silk, gauze, diamonds, and pearls.[43] We might imagine, because of the meticulous detail, that Montagu is wearing her "Turkish habit" as she writes the letter, so delighted is she in having acquired it. Unlike the Viennese habit she was forced to wear for her audience with the empress, in which she "was squeezed up in a gown, and adorned with a gorget and the other implements thereunto belonging; a dress very inconvenient," Ottoman clothing elicits not a word of complaint.[44] It is both easy and delightful for her to wear. Within the course of this same letter, the beauty of her "Turkish habit" gives way to the convenience and "liberty" of the veil:

> 'Tis very easy to see they have more liberty than we have, no woman, of what rank so ever being permitted to go in the streets without two muslins, one that covers her face all but her eyes and another that hides the whole dress of her head, and hangs half way down her back and their shapes are so wholly concealed by a thing they call *ferace* which no woman of any sort appears without. ... You may guess how effectually this disguises them, that there is no distinguishing the great lady from her slave and 'tis impossible for the most jealous husband to know his wife when he meets her, and no man dare either touch or follow a woman in the street. This perpetual masquerade gives them entire liberty of following their inclinations without danger of discovery.[45]

Montagu sees the Islamic practice of veiling—an extension of sex-segregated spaces—as offering perfect freedom to women. Her positive view of the practice obscures the ideological function of the veil as "an embodied spatial practice through which women are inserted into relations of power in society."[46] For Montagu, the power of the veil is in the literal space it creates for elite Ottoman women (and those who want to appropriate such an identity and pass as such) in the public realm. They can walk the streets without fear of harassment; moreover, the anonymity and protection of the veil decreases the danger associated with the public street. Furthermore, as Joseph Lew points out, "Turkish women ... convert enforced anonymity ... into a tool subversive of the established order it is meant to protect."[47] Ottoman women access public spaces by manipulating the patriarchal structures and modes of bodily control that work to confine and police their activity. Montagu takes full advantage of the protection and agency of the veil when she

---

[42]   Ibid., 69.

[43]   Ibid.

[44]   Ibid., 17.

[45]   Ibid., 71.

[46]   Anna Secor, "Islamism, Democracy, and the Political Production of the Headscarf Issue in Turkey," in Falah and Nagel, *Geographies of Muslim Women*, 204.

[47]   Lew, "Portable Seraglio," 449.

uses it to visit mosques and markets in both Edirne and Istanbul. The veil opens up public spaces for her, so she can occupy those spaces without fear.[48] Unlike male writers who object to the veil because it obstructs Islamic femininity from their gaze, Montagu's insider perspective, one cultivated by repeated use of the veil, argues that it is a mechanism for Ottoman women's liberation. Male writers read the veil as another sexualized eastern, Islamicate practice, but Montagu divests it of this hypersexual coding and presents its advantages for women.[49] The veil becomes a moveable space of anonymity, protection, and, most important, access. She knows how free these women are because she has enjoyed the veil's freedom: "The yaşmak, or Turkish veil, is become not only very easy but agreeable to me."[50] Ottoman identity, which the veil confers, allows her to move about the city without restriction; furthermore, it erases her European identity and signifies only woman, thereby assimilating her into the community she encounters and transforming her into an ersatz Ottoman subject.

The freedom of movement facilitated by the veil allows women even greater liberties, as Montagu indicates. The "disguise," anonymity, and "perpetual masquerade" function in the service of sexual freedom, since even "the most jealous husband" would not know his own wife. By employing the veil to carry out clandestine affairs, Ottoman women subvert its symbolic and political meanings, contesting and negotiating the segregated space it constructs. The liberty Montagu represents somewhat enviously, then, is the sexual liberty of Ottoman women.[51] However, her remarks about such freedoms are quickly followed by the observation that Ottoman women are free in another, more important way:

> Neither have they much to apprehend from the resentment of their husbands those ladies that are rich *having all their money in their own hands*, which they take with them upon a divorce with an addition which he is obliged to give them. Upon the whole, I look upon the Turkish women as the only free people in the empire. The very Divan pays respect to them and the Grand Signor himself, when a pasha is executed, never violates the privileges of the harem (or women's apartment) which remains unsearched entire to the widow. They are queens of their slaves, which the husband has no permission so much as to look upon except it be an old woman or two that his lady chooses.[52]

---

48   Gillian Rose notes that public spaces have occupied a contentious position in feminist discourse because of the fear and unease they generate. Women have lacked security in public spaces, the right to occupy them. Gillian Rose, *Feminism and Geography: the Limits of Geographical Knowledge* (Minneapolis: University of Minnesota Press, 1993), 34

49   Since her account offers a counterpoint to travel writing by men, Montagu takes pains to point out that male travel writers have no access to women's spaces (public or private) and so cannot adequately speak to their situations. See Montagu, *Letters*, 85, 134.

50   Ibid., 127.

51   Felicity A. Nussbaum, *Torrid Zones: Maternity, Sexuality, and Empire in Eighteenth-century English Narratives* (Baltimore: The Johns Hopkins University Press, 1995), 91

52   Montagu, *Letters*, 71–72, added emphasis.

Islamic law guarantees women's inheritance as well as their right to keep their own property, even after marriage. Such freedom as practiced by the elite Ottoman classes gave the women with whom Montagu interacted much power. The freedoms that Ottoman women enjoy come about because they are able to retain their property after marriage, a practice allowed British women only in the nineteenth century with the Married Women's Property Act (1870). Additionally, her list of Ottoman women's advantages indicates that unlike the situation in Britain, women's spaces in Edirne and Istanbul were exempt from male penetration, for even the sultan, she notes, "never violates the privileges of the harem."[53] When Montagu takes up the veil and ventriloquizes Ottoman identity, she attempts to access the liberty of Ottoman women, to "create an imaginative resistance to the domestic confinement at home."[54]

In the structure of her narrative it is significant that with her entrée into the harem she crosses a crucial threshold, since it is, as noted previously, a space both sacred and forbidden. In Edirne she visits the harems of the Grand Vezier's lady and the kabya's (second in command) lady, while in Istanbul she obtains access to the harem of the sultan's widow, Sultana Hafise. Passing into increasingly elevated circles of Ottoman society, Montagu takes special care to make her readers aware that her experiences are uncommon: "It must be under a very particular character, or on some extraordinary occasion when a Christian is admitted into the house of a man of quality, and their harems are always forbidden ground."[55] Penetrating the inner recesses of Ottoman society reflects Montagu's own elevated status.[56] Access to authority in the Ottoman Empire was structured along the lines of interior movement; one got closer to power by moving into private spaces.[57] Her audiences with successively important Ottoman women show her traveling up the social ladder and becoming intimate with some of the most important women in the empire. The visits also allow her to fashion an account of the harem that plays with stereotype while simultaneously revealing it as a fiction designed by those who never gained any familiarity with Ottoman women. By offering correctives and positioning herself with Ottoman women, Montagu strengthens her identification with them.

Her visit to the harem of Fatma, the kabya's lady, is important for its allusions to the *hamam*, since both instances of access into Ottoman women's spaces figure as fantastic spectacles of beauty. Indeed, it is Fatma herself whose beauty exceeds Montagu expectations: "her beauty effaced everything I have seen all that has been called lovely either in England or Germany and must own that I never saw

---

[53]   Lew, "Portable Seraglio"; Montagu, *Letters*, 446.

[54]   Nicole Pohl, *Women, Space, and Utopia 1600–1800* (Burlington, VT: Ashgate, 2006), 138.

[55]   Montagu, *Letters*, 85.

[56]   Peirce, *The Imperial Harem*, 12.

[57]   Ibid., 8.

anything so gloriously beautiful."[58] The private world of the Ottoman harem lives up to the stereotype of the exotic and erotic east, where the women are as beautiful and seductive as their surroundings. They play and dance with beauty, grace, and sensuality:

> This dance was very different from what I had seen before. Nothing could be more artful or more proper to raise certain ideas; the tunes so soft, the motions so languishing, accompanied with pauses and dying eyes, half falling back and then recovering themselves in so artful a manner that I am very positive the coldest and most rigid prude upon earth could not have looked upon them without thinking of something not to be spoke of.[59]

About such scenes in Montagu's narrative, Felicity Nussbaum argues that "utopian sites, forbidden to men's view evoke heightened libidinal desire with homoerotic undertones in the Western women who describe them."[60] Montagu's unwillingness to name the sensations aroused by the dance certainly suggests an element of illicit desire; moreover, her closing remarks regarding Fatma's harem point to the same: "I retired through the same ceremonies as before, and could not help fancying I had been some time in Mohammed's paradise, so much was I charmed with what I had seen."[61] Fatma's beauty is supernatural and hypersexual and so Montagu can only compare her to the mythical houris that populate the Muslim paradise. Yet, ironically, to have been in "Mohammed's paradise," Montagu would have to be a Muslim. Her analogy points both to her eroticized gaze and her shifting subjectivity.

The Sultana Hafise's harem, unlike Fatma's, is a more solemn and elevated site where beauty is still present, but not eroticism. Through conversation with the sultana, Montagu is intent on "learning all that I possibly could of the seraglio, which is so entirely unknown amongst us."[62] The sultana's account of the inner workings of the imperial harem present an authentic narrative of a space closed to outsiders:

> She assured me that the story of the Sultan's throwing a handkerchief is altogether fabulous and the manner upon that occasion no other but that he send the Kuslir Aga to signify to the lady the honor he intends her. She is immediately complimented upon it by the others and led to the bath where she is perfumed and dressed in the most magnificent and becoming manner. The Emperor precedes his visit by a royal present and then comes into her apartment. Neither is there any such thing as her creeping in at the bed's feet. She said that the first he makes choice of was always after the first in rank and not the mother of the eldest son, as other writers would make us believe. Sometimes the Sultan diverts

[58] Ibid., 89.

[59] Ibid., 91.

[60] Nussbaum, *Torrid Zones,* 137.

[61] Montagu, *Letters*, 91.

[62] Ibid., 116.

himself in the company of all his ladies, who stand in a circle round him, and she confessed that they were ready to die with jealousy and envy of the happy she that he distinguished by any appearance of preference. But this seemed to me neither better nor worse than the circles in most courts where the glance of the monarch is watched and every smile waited for with impatience and envied by those that cannot obtain it.[63]

The sultana explains the hierarchy of the harem, the civil arrangement of the sultan's erotic liaisons with the women, and their very natural emotions of elation and jealousy. Montagu's equation of the harem with the European court further desexualizes the scene and sets the experience of the harem women on a par with what she herself has experienced as a member of court. The harem narrative, then, is a spectacle that realizes European fantasy at the same time that it strives for an accurate, intimate, and private portrayal of the world of women, "pivotal to Ottoman culture and society."[64]

Just as Montagu's letter detailing her visit to Sultana Hafise in Istanbul offers a definitive and accurate account of the realities of the imperial harem, so, too, is it in Istanbul that Montagu most fully occupies Ottoman identity. She has advanced in her "oriental learning," which prompts Alexander Pope to respond, "I long for nothing so much as your Oriental self" and insinuate that familiarity with and extended exposure to a foreign culture can displace identity.[65] Montagu has "gone native" in another way as well: writing to Anne Thistlethwayte from Pera (Istanbul) in January, she remarks that she is pregnant, immediately following with a long explanation of how female virtue in Ottoman culture is observed in fecundity: "in this country it is more despicable to be married and not fruitful than it is with us to be fruitful before marriage … The French Ambassadress is forced to comply with this fashion as well as myself."[66] Montagu ironically points to her compliance with the Ottoman fashion of pregnancy, yet her jest indicates her ease in seeming to adopt Ottoman practices. In fact, we see this willingness when she inoculates her son against smallpox, again in the "Turkish" fashion.[67] Writing about Montagu's pregnancy and lying-in, Mohja Kahf also notes Montagu's Ottoman-influenced sensibilities, claiming "she has allowed the Turkish practice to transform her sense of her body and liberated herself from the English custom."[68]

Freed from conventional British mores, Montagu visits another *hamam*, thereby enclosing her experience with Ottoman women within the frame of

---

[63]   Ibid., 116–17.

[64]   See Elizabeth Bohls, *Women Travel Writers and the Language of Aesthetics: 1716–1818* (New York: Cambridge University Press, 1995), 40, for the harem as spectacle and Melman, *Women's Orients*, 84, for its importance in Ottoman culture.

[65]   Pope, *Correspondence*, 494.

[66]   Montagu, *Letters*, 107.

[67]   Ibid., 81.

[68]   Mohja Kahf, *Western Representations of the Muslim Woman: From Termagant to Odalisque* (Austin: University of Texas Press, 1999), 120.

women's spaces. The letter detailing this visit contains the stories of four other women, and is emblematic of Ottoman women's experiences. At the *hamam* in Istanbul Montagu once again sees something unique: the preparation of a bride on her wedding day. Like the narrative of the *hamam* in Sofia, the scene in Istanbul is also one of naked female beauty; however, this time Montagu omits giving an account of her own reception at the *hamam* and whether she wore her British habit, or her "Turkish" one, or whether she followed the example of the Ottoman women and "threw off [her] clothing" as well.[69] Does she assume that her readers trust her to retain her native modesty within this space as she did during her first visit? Or are we to assume, based on her eager Ottoman self-fashioning, that she has disrobed and fulfilled the politic demands of the *hamam*?

The answer, I believe, lies in the narratives that follow—in the anonymity of the Ottoman woman found dead because she had taken advantage of the "liberty" of the veil and pursued her "evil inclinations" by committing adultery and the "romance" of the admiral's wife. The story of the dead woman, following quickly upon the happy relation of a bridal celebration, illustrates the dark side of Ottoman women's freedom and seclusion. Because women are kept separate and it is forbidden for non-family members to look upon them, they have no public identity. Their subversion of the veil can and does become threatening; thus, their agency becomes their undoing. The account of the admiral's lady that follows contains a similar element of danger but also the possibility of inclusion, creating an avenue that opens up the possibility of Ottoman identity. Introducing the topic by saying, "I am well acquainted with a Christian woman of quality who made it her choice to live with a Turkish husband, and is a very agreeable sensible lady," Montagu broaches the controversial subject of exogamous marriage. The story that follows contains the standard tropes of medieval and early modern romance, concerning a virtuous Christian woman, an evil, lecherous Muslim man, and a perilous journey. Once more Montagu manipulates convention and transforms a story of rape into one of possibility and agency, seeing within the lady's narrative the appropriation of power. The Spanish woman, never identified by name, is captured at sea with her brothers by a Turkish admiral. Montagu does not mention the rape she endures and simply alludes to it: "The same accident happened to her that happened to the fair Lucretia."[70] Her beauty captivates the admiral and he releases her and the ransom he received for her, but knowing the fate she would endure at home—seclusion in a convent—the woman tells him to make restitution through marriage: "her infidel lover was very handsome, very tender, fond of her and lavished at her feet all the Turkish magnificence. She answered him resolutely that her liberty was not so precious to her as her honor, and that he could no way restore that but by marrying her."[71] The "veil of romance" that covers Montagu's relation disguises the violence of Ottoman society and the dangers facing women

---

[69] Montagu, *Letters*, 134.

[70] Ibid., 136.

[71] Ibid.

when they leave or are not a part of the "sacred" and "protected" space of the harem.[72] While male violence and aggression are realities of women's lives, Ottoman or otherwise, Montagu employs this story to highlight a different aspect of Ottoman culture: assimilation. The admiral's lady becomes an Ottoman woman through marriage and her national origin and race—a topic not mentioned in the parts of the narrative that take place in the Ottoman Empire—are subsumed in this new identity. Thus when her husband dies, she attains the privileges of Ottoman inheritance laws, becomes "one of the richest widows in Constantinople," and, according to Ottoman custom, remarries.[73] The admiral's lady's story illustrates the possibility of a new subjectivity, of an exalted social standing without the prerequisite of birth. In this way, the Ottoman Empire truly is, for Montagu, "a new world."

Montagu cannot, however, remain in the Ottoman Empire forever. Because she is the wife of a British ambassador her stay is always temporary, and since Wortley (conspicuously absent for much of the narrative) is not particularly successful, the Montagu embassy ends sooner than anticipated.[74] Her journey out of the empire takes her through the geography of the classical past, over the paths of Achilles and Alexander, and symbolically repositions her in a European tradition. Montagu's need to situate herself back within acceptable European culture and discursive modes points to her changed subjectivity. The strength of the Ottoman influence must be banished by traversing the ground of Homer and Virgil, and while Montagu leaves the Ottoman Empire, she takes with her its practices and concerns. In England she advocated smallpox inoculation, entering the public and masculine realm of medicine with the strength and evidence of her Ottoman experience. Her exile in Europe, struggle for erotic and economic freedom, in addition to her commitment to revising and rewriting the letters from her Ottoman journey point to her attachment to Ottoman culture. Through the *Turkish Embassy Letters* Montagu was able to lift the veil and uncover the faces and places of Ottoman women and through them construct a space for herself.

---

[72]   Cynthia Lowenthal, *Lady Mary and the Eighteenth-Century Familiar Letter* (Athens: University of Georgia Press, 1993), 93.

[73]   Montagu, *Letters*, 137.

[74]   The former ambassadors to Turkey had held 10- and 15-year posts, respectively. Wortley's perceived Turcophilic attitude prompted his swift recall. See Isobel Grundy, *Lady Mary Wortley Montagu* (New York: Oxford University Press, 1999), 156–60.

Chapter 4

Margaret Bryan and Jane Marcet: Making Space for "Space" in British Women's Science Writing

Kristine Larsen

For millennia, from the lunar goddesses of ancient cultures to Urania, the classical muse of astronomy, the feminine form has symbolized the heavens, and thus outer space. However, since the time of the ancient Greeks the human practice of astronomy as a science has been an overwhelmingly male discipline. Men held sway over all aspects of astronomy, from observing and teaching through cataloging celestial objects and publishing professional treatises and research papers. Similarly, from the dawn of classical physics with Isaac Newton in the mid 1600s, this new science has also existed as a largely male space, and women found limited roles open to them. With the birth of the popular science movement in Britain in the late 1700s, women and children were at last considered at the very least an appropriate audience for basic-level introductions to science, and a new space opened within the scientific culture, namely that of popular, expository scientific literature. While men initially dominated this field, as they had others in science, women found a way to make their own space for "space" by excelling in a new style of science writing called the familiar format. This essay will review the limitations placed on women in astronomy and physics in this time period, and use the examples of two British female authors of astronomy and physics texts—Margaret Bryan and Jane Marcet—to illustrate this process of creating a female voice in science writing.

With the invention of the telescope in the early 1600s, women found a limited role in family observatories, where they acted as recorders and assistants to a brother, father, or husband. When they tried to strike out on their own, they quickly found that their skills were not appreciated. An often-touted example is Maria Margaretha Winkelmann (1670–1720), the daughter of a minister. She was taught astronomy by Christoph Arnold, a well-known amateur, who introduced her to Gottfried Kirch, Germany's leading astronomer. After becoming Kirch's second wife in 1692, she assisted her husband in their family observatory and made contributions to astronomy in her own right, including calculations for calendars, observations of aurora, and the discovery of a comet in 1702.[1] As Schiebinger notes, Winkelmann was only allowed (limited) entrance into the male space of

---

[1]   Edgar C. Smith, "Some Notable Women of Science," *Nature* 127 (1931): 976.

professional astronomy in a domestic observatory and in the clearly subservient role of an assistant to her much older husband.[2]

When Kirch became the official astronomer of the Berlin Observatory his observations moved from the attic of the family home to a public institution, which signaled the predictable decline of Winkelmann's astronomical career. As Schiebinger demonstrates, such a shift of the observatory from domestic space to public space essentially eliminated women from the astronomical observatory.[3] As a result, when Gottfried died in 1710, Maria was heartily rebuked by the Council of the Berlin Academy of Science when she dared apply for the position of assistant calendar maker, a position for which she was eminently qualified in skill, but deemed unsuitable because of her gender. When her son Christfried was named joint head observer of the Berlin Observatory in 1716, his mother tried to assume the role of his assistant, but she was soon reprimanded by the Academy for "talking too much to visitors" and "meddling too much" in the Observatory. The Academy sternly suggested that her role was to find a house near the observatory "so that Herr Kirch could continue to eat at her table."[4] Thus Maria Winkelmann Kirch was forced back into the domestic space, as were the vast majority of women who expressed an interest in outer space rather than desiring to be limited to the "inner space" of home and hearth.

Winkelmann's cardinal sin was in trying to enter the space of "professional" astronomer, a field in which the normally assigned tasks (before the twentieth century) were the computation of data for municipalities, merchants, and the military (all clearly male-dominated spaces as well). However, Britain's most famous woman astronomer of the eighteenth and nineteenth centuries, Caroline Lucretia Herschel (1750–1848), gained acceptance, both because her work was clearly rooted in the "amateur tradition" of observing celestial bodies for their own sake and she only made accidental discoveries in the process, and because she clearly limited her role to that of assistant to her brother with their garden telescopes.[5] Herschel was born in Hanover, Germany, and had followed her older brother William to England in order to pursue a career as a singer, but instead became William's assistant in telescope making and observing.

After discovering the planet Uranus in 1781, William became an international sensation and gave up his own musical career to focus on astronomy, aided with a royal pension. Caroline assisted him at the telescope, at first by recording his observations and doing simple arithmetic calculations, and later by observing the heavens, searching for new star clusters and nebulae as well as comets. She made

---

[2]   Londa Schiebinger, "Maria Winkelmann at the Berlin Academy," *Isis* 78 (1987): 179.

[3]   Ibid., 199–200.

[4]   Ibid., 192.

[5]   Johan H. Knapen, "Scientific Collaborations in Astronomy Between Amateurs and Professionals," in *Stellar Winds in Interaction*, ed. Thomas Eversberg and Johan H. Knapen, 2010, 77, http://www.stsci.de/pdf/arrabida.pdf.

eight independent discoveries of comets, and in five cases was the first person to see the comet in question. After her first cometary discovery she became "the pet of the astronomical community" and was granted the title "Assistant Astronomer" and a small pension by King George III.[6] The wording of this description of Herschel is no accident; she herself claimed that she had done nothing "but what a well-trained puppy-dog would have done" for her brother, and referred to herself as "a mere tool which my brother had the trouble of sharpening."[7] So while on the surface Herschel might seem a singular case in terms of her unusual acceptance by the monarchy and astronomical community, she was actually occupying the limited accepted feminine space of earlier years of astronomy. By assisting her brother on his property, she did not violate the rules of propriety, and in acting as her brother's assistant, she was fulfilling the acceptable subservient role. She was not breaking new ground, but rather following in the earlier tradition of only allowing women entrance into the space of the observational astronomy in a domestic setting and in the role of dutiful assistant.

Caroline was awarded a Gold Medal in 1828 by the Royal Astronomical Society, and in 1835 she and Mary Somerville became the first female honorary members of that society. In bestowing the Gold Medal on the then elderly Herschel (in absentia), the Society pronounced that "as an original observer she demands ... our unfeigned thanks," but then undercut the originality, that is, masculinity of her work in the succeeding lines, where it was said that "A sweeper [telescope] planted on the lawn became her object of amusement; but her amusements were of the higher order," leading to the discovery of several comets. It is also noted that "during these hours of enjoyment" she discovered a number of nebulae afterwards included in her brother's catalogue, and "we scarcely know whether most to admire the intellectual power of the brother, or the inconquerable industry of the sister."[8]

The Royal Astronomical Society's pronouncements clearly delineate the differences in the roles of William and Caroline, and paint her as a dutiful assistant—the acceptable feminine role. To this day, historians of science debate the value of Caroline's work, leading to yet another limiting of the "space" for women in the mainstream recounting of the history of science. For example, historian Michael Hoskin argues that Caroline's cometary discoveries, "though of widespread popular and professional interest, had little impact on the history of astronomy."[9] However, he does admit that in proving that star clusters and nebulae could be discovered with even a modest telescope (giving her brother the idea

---

[6]   Marilyn Bailey Ogilvie, "Caroline Herschel's Contributions to Astronomy," *Annals of Science* 32 (1975): 155.

[7]   Agnes M. Clerke, *The Herschels and Modern Astronomy* (London: Cassell and Co., 1895), 140; Edward S. Holden, "The Three Herschels," *The Century Magazine* 39, no. 2 (1885): 182.

[8]   James South, "Gold Medal to Miss Herschel," *Monthly Notices of the Royal Astronomical Society* 1 (1828): 63.

[9]   Michael Hoskin, "Caroline Herschel as an Observer," *Status* (June 2006): 5.

for a systematic search for and cataloging of such objects), the "consequence of Caroline's modest discoveries was immense."[10] Hoskin's sentiment is echoed in the ongoing tension in the astronomical community as to the relative value of original research, education, and popularization. As this paper demonstrates, this mindset had important consequences in the eighteenth century as women created new roles for themselves in science through literature.

In the seventeenth century, the Newtonian revolution in physics made a rigorous discipline out of the study of forces in nature such as gravity, electricity, and magnetism. In this regard, physics' relationship to astronomy is crucial to both fields, because, like astronomy, the construction of this new discipline affected and was profoundly affected by gender norms. In particular, physics, especially Newtonian physics, differs from astronomy in its dependence on increasingly complex mathematics, a dependence that distanced it from the world of women, who were generally less well educated in mathematics. The exceptions were women who studied at the side of a male family member or husband, such as Gabrielle Émilie Le Tonnelier de Breteuil, Marquise du Châtelet (1706–1749). The long-time paramour of Voltaire, she wrote the physics textbook *Institutions de Physique* (*Lessons in Physics*) in 1740 for her son, and a posthumously published translation of Isaac Newton's *Principia Mathematica* from Latin into French, with commentary and new mathematical derivations.[11]

If astronomical observation and experimentation in physics were largely closed to British women from the very beginning, in the seventeenth century, what space was open to them? In the late 1700s and early 1800s there was a growth of popular-level science in Britain, most notably manifested in public lectures sponsored by universities and professional institutions. These lectures were opened up to interested women, who attended in large numbers.[12] However, since these same women were still largely denied access to formal university courses in the sciences, there was a need for published background material which would explain the lectures and experiments to the attendees. Hence, British authors began producing popularized science books aimed at a non-technical audience, especially children and women. Written in an easily accessible language (in sharp contrast to the treatises found in professional science journals), their aim was to both amuse and inform.

One of the most popular early examples of this trend in publishing was Tom Telescope's *The Newtonian System of Philosophy, Adapted to the Capacities of Young Gentlemen and Ladies* (1761). "Tom Telescope" is considered a pseudonym

---

[10]   Hoskin, "Caroline Herschel as Observer," *Journal for the History of Astronomy* 36 (2005): 396.

[11]   Judith P. Zinsser, "Translating Newton's 'Principia': The Marquise du Châtelet's Revisions and Additions for Audience," *Notes and Records of the Royal Society of London* 55, no. 2 (2001): 235.

[12]   Barbara T. Gates, *Kindred Science* (Chicago: University of Chicago Press, 1998), 36.

for the book's publisher, John Newbery (1713–1767), who is often credited with the development of children's books as a separate genre.[13] In this work, a series of schoolboys gathers over the holidays to play games at the home of Lady and Lord Twilight, but Tom Telescope admonishes them that playing at the study of astronomy and physics would instead "not only divert the mind, but improve the understanding."[14] The remainder of the work is indeed a series of conversations between Tom Telescope, his friends, and a number of interested adults, in which they perform simple experiments and discuss the laws of nature.

The use of conversation, written in a common vernacular, as a literary device and the location of the action in a home setting formed the core of what is now known as the "familiar format" for science writing.[15] Between 1780 and 1830, this format was adopted by a number of writers of science works for children and women, and afforded an opportunity for women to find a space within science writing that was considered gender-appropriate. The reappearance of science in a domestic setting, although limited primarily to informal, amateur experimentation and popular books, paralleled the progressive educational philosophy of feminist writer Mary Wollstonecraft (1759–1797), who suggested that education should "be grounded in everyday individual experience."[16] Thus the transmission of scientific knowledge became a part of the expectations of "good mothering"[17] and afforded these teacher-mothers additional opportunities to reinforce moral lessons and an appreciation for scriptural teachings.[18] As A. Fyfe notes in her survey of children's science literature, the volume of children's science books published in the early nineteenth century demonstrates that learning science had become "a standard part of childhood."[19] In addition, this new role for women writers depended on giving these women the opportunity to learn science in the first place, so that they could properly transmit it to their audience. Again, because women were largely denied formal advanced education in the sciences during this time, many of these science writers gained their knowledge through tutoring by the men in their lives, or by attending those public science lectures and reading such scientific literature as their backgrounds permitted. In translating professional scientific works into the common vernacular and everyday examples, these women played an important

[13]   A. Fyfe, *Science for Children*, vol. 1 (Bristol: Thoemmes Press, 2003), xii.

[14]   Tom Telescope, *The Newtonian System of Philosophy, A New and Improved Edition* (Philadelphia: Jacob Johnson, 1803), 2.

[15]   Ann B. Shteir, *Cultivating Women, Cultivating Science* (Baltimore: The Johns Hopkins University Press, 1996), 81.

[16]   Ibid., 82–83.

[17]   Barbara T. Gates and Ann B. Shteir, eds., *Natural Eloquence: Women Reinscribe Science* (Madison: University of Wisconsin Press, 1997), 9.

[18]   Ann B. Shteir, "Elegant Recreations? Configuring Science Writing for Women," in *Victorian Science in Context*, ed. Bernard Lightman (Chicago: University of Chicago Press, 1997), 247.

[19]   Fyfe, *Science for Children*, xiii.

role in transmitting scientific knowledge not only to children, but also to other women and members of the lower socioeconomic classes, who appreciated the generally low cost of these works and their readability.[20]

Women science writers used the familiar format to transition from the paradigm of the male scientist as sole repository of scientific knowledge (a patriarchal model of the transmission of knowledge) to a new model, where the mother, or the female tutor or teacher who acted as a surrogate mother, has the responsibility of teaching science to children. The acquisition of a basic scientific understanding, and the transmission of this knowledge to children, therefore became an expected part of good mothering. Science itself also became more than merely a portion of rote schoolwork, but became considered "a part of daily life and the general education of young people."[21] Simple experiments could be done at home rather than the laboratory, using modest equipment such as household chemicals and tools. Because appreciation for science could teach morals and theology as well as its own basic principles, such study was therefore rooted in a culture of self-improvement rather than an esoteric search for greater knowledge, which was not "a defensible female pursuit."[22]

This seemingly revolutionary effect of "domestic science" was quickly countered, however, by devaluing the women's role. Women science writers found themselves pigeonholed into this increasingly gendered role and, as with other stereotypical "women's work," the familiar science book became devalued and even openly derided by some male authors by the middle of the nineteenth century. A clear distinction was drawn by both the women themselves and scientists between the female authors of popular-level works, who merely transmitted the knowledge without endeavoring to make hypotheses of their own, and the scientists who did the original research about which the women wrote. Thus these women, segregated within the space of scientific literature, were clearly seen as inhabiting a second tier (or even a third tier, beneath the male authors of textbooks for leading universities such as Cambridge). To some extent these same prejudices remain today; even male astronomers who concentrate on the popularization of science are looked at with suspicion at best and derision at worst by their colleagues, the most famous example being the late Cornell University astronomy professor Carl Sagan. But as Ann Shteir notes, the skills possessed by a successful popular science writer are different, not inferior, to those of a successful researcher. In her words, "The creation of knowledge and the dissemination of knowledge are equally important to science culture."[23] Theoretically, there is sufficient space for researchers, educators, and authors in science; however, that space has not been divided or valued equally between the genders, especially in the physical sciences—astronomy, physics, and chemistry.

---

[20]   Ibid., xii.

[21]   Gates and Shteir, *Natural Eloquence,* 8–9.

[22]   Shteir, *Cultivating Women,* 62.

[23]   Ibid., 101.

Another type of gendered segregation existed within the popular-level scientific literature of the 1700s and 1800s, namely that of the specific science being discussed. Certain sciences and subspecialties were considered appropriate for women, while others were deemed the province of men. Perhaps the premier example of a female-friendly science was botany. During the decades following the development of the Linnaean system of taxonomy (1760–1830), women found a place in British scientific circles as collectors of botanical specimens, botanical illustrators, and authors of descriptive catalogs, botanical poetry, and books for children and other women.[24] Most of the last of these were written in the familiar format, such as Priscilla Wakefield's *An Introduction to Botany, a Series of Familiar Letters* (1796) and Sarah Fitton's *Conversations on Botany* (1817). Women were so successful as authors of botany books for general readers that there was an eventual backlash by the scientific community, as male scientists sought to professionalize, that is, masculinize botany in the mid-nineteenth century. The physical sciences were seen as a male bastion, and there were far fewer women writers in these fields. Even other women writers recognized that these sciences fell outside the established gender roles. For example, Lady Charlotte Murray wrote in her work *The British Garden* (1799), "The expensive apparatus of the observatory, and the labours of chemistry, confine the science of Astronomy, and the study of Minerals to a few. ... But the study of Botany ... is open to almost every curious mind ... ."[25]

Despite these obstacles, two female science writers of the late eighteenth and early nineteenth centuries pushed the envelope of both the familiar format and the conventional wisdom that astronomy, physics, and chemistry were appropriate for male writers alone: Margaret Bryan (fl. 1797–1816) and Jane Marcet (1769–1858). These women played pivotal roles in the progression of female science writers in Britain from being authors of descriptive botanical catalogs to having the opportunity to become writers of influential works in astronomy and physics in the late nineteenth century, thus paving the way for the illustrious careers of later British women science writers such as Mary Somerville and Agnes Clerke.

Bryan and Marcet inherited a form with a number of male-oriented conventions. For example, in the *Natural System of Philosophy,* despite the fact that the subtitle claims that the work is appropriate for child readers of both genders, the active characters in the books are young boys, including the narrator, Tom Telescope, and several adult males. Several adult women (the wives of the male characters) do take part in the conversation, but are relegated to largely passive roles. The six-volume work *Scientific Dialogues* (1800–1805), written by Reverend Jeremiah Joyce, the former tutor of the Earl of Stanhope's sons, was advertised as a "complete compendium of natural and experimental philosophy" designed to instruct both

---

[24]   For a detailed discussion on the role of women in botany in the eighteenth and nineteenth centuries, see Shteir, *Cultivating Women.*

[25]   Ibid., 59.

"young people" and adults attending public science lectures.[26] Although written as a series of conversations, the teacher figures are both male (a male tutor and a father), and the students include two boys, Charles and James (named for the Earl of Stanhope's sons), and a girl, Emma. Joyce's work was extremely popular, enjoying several editions through 1892. One of its most famous readers was John Stuart Mill.[27]

The works of Margaret Bryan stand in stark contrast. Very little biographical information is known about Mrs. Bryan, so it is hard to know where her knowledge or independent approach to science writing might have originated. Mary T. Brück cites the *The Dictionary of National Biography*, identifying Bryan as a "beautiful and talented schoolmistress" married to an equally mysterious Mr. Bryan.[28] Gates and Shteir offer that she taught science at girls' schools in London and Margate and based her writings on these experiences.[29] She penned at least three physics and astronomy books for young readers: *A Compendious System of Astronomy* (1797), *Lectures in Natural Philosophy* (1806), and *An Astronomical and Geographical Class Book for Schools* (1816). An engraving of Bryan and her two daughters appeared in the frontispiece of her first work and pictures her with her left hand resting on the base of a celestial globe, her writing quill in her right hand.[30] Other scientific instruments are included in the picture, including a telescope. The illustration paints her as more than a passive transmitter of knowledge, and indeed Bryan's writings demonstrate that she had skill in the use of astronomical instruments. For example, an 1811 letter to William Herschel discusses her attempts to observe a comet that year.[31]

Bryan's works were well received by the scientific community, and *A Compendious System* included a letter from Charles Hutton, professor of mathematics at the Royal Military Academy, who had reviewed the manuscript and rejoiced that "the learned and more difficult sciences are thus beginning to be successfully cultivated by the extraordinary and elegant talents of the female writers of the present day."[32] The second (1799) edition of *A Compendious System* boasted a list of 400 subscribers that included the Archbishop of Canterbury and the Secretary at War, as well as Reverend William Lax, professor of astronomy at Trinity College, Cambridge, and Reverend Dr. Nevil Maskelyne, the Astronomer Royal.

---

[26]   Reverend Jeremiah Joyce, *Scientific Dialogues* (London: Knight and Son, 1852), i.

[27]   John R. Issitt, "Jeremiah Joyce: Science Educationist," *Endeavour* 26, no. 3 (2002): 98.

[28]   Mary T. Brück, *Women in Early British and Irish Astronomy* (Dordrecht: Springer, 2009), 15.

[29]   Gates and Shteir, *Natural Eloquence*, 8.

[30]   A portrait based on the engraving is held by the National Portrait Gallery, London, and can be found at http://www.npg.org.uk/collections/search/portrait/mw42469/Margaret-Bryan-with-her-daughters?s.

[31]   Brück, *Women*, 17–18.

[32]   Margaret Bryan, *A Compendious System of Astronomy, in a Course of Familiar Lectures* (London: Leigh and Sotheby, 1797), xi.

These properties of her works already set her apart from the archetypical female "familiar format" science writer, but there are both glimpses of the classic format and other, more important distinctions, as well. She was certainly both a mother and a mother surrogate for her students; indeed, in her preface to *Lectures in Natural Philosophy* she writes, "I rejoice in the titles of Parent and Preceptress," thus openly embracing traditional feminine roles.[33] The same work opens and closes with addresses to her (female) students, a traditional audience for women science writers. She defends her straightforward language, what she calls "a familiar manner" of writing, by explaining in the preface to *A Compendious System* that more elegant language would make her books "less intelligible to my pupils."[34] In fact, she further notes in the same preface that the book was "written for my pupils and not originally designed for public inspection."[35]

Her works contain numerous moral lessons and religious references, also in keeping with the traditions of familiar format works. For example, the concluding address to *Lectures in Natural Philosophy* contains an overview of the moral duties of a female life, including the expected behaviors of a woman as a sister, friend, and wife.[36] In her preface to *Lectures in Natural Philosophy*, she explains that the purpose of the work was not only to instruct her students in the laws of physics, but "to impress them with a just sense of the attributes of the Deity; and thus, by unequivocal deductions, to strengthen and confirm their moral and religious principles."[37] Bryan acknowledges that the book was heavily influenced by Anglican theologian William Paley's *Natural Theology* (1802) and, like Paley's work, sought to provide evidence of the "divine wisdom and omnipotence of our great Creator" through the laws of nature.[38] Bryan further explains in *A Compendious System* that "no subjects tend more to invite us to the exercises of all religious and social duties than those of Astronomy and Natural Philosophy," a philosophy that she strictly adheres to in both of her most famous books.[39] For example, in the introductory address to her students in *Lectures in Natural Philosophy*, she explains that in providing to her students evidence of the divine in the laws of physics, she was also providing them with a "defense against the vain sophistry of the world … which will secure you from all pernicious doctrines and guard your religious and moral principles against all innovations."[40] The obvious assumption here is that any new ideas in either theology or morality are to be avoided at all costs.

---

33 Ibid., vi–vii.
34 Ibid., 141.
35 Ibid., vii–viii.
36 Ibid., 290.
37 Ibid., viii–ix.
38 Ibid., xi–xii.
39 Ibid., 164.
40 Ibid., iv–v.

While Bryan's works reflect the morals and religious values central to the traditional space for women, she occasionally subverts the traditional role of woman science writer, that of a mere reporter of the works of male scientists without consideration of the author's own knowledge or opinions. Bryan humbly describes herself as merely "a reflector of the intrinsic light of superior genius and erudition" of "many learned men," but in this same preface to *Lectures in Natural Philosophy* she provides her own credentials as "eight years' study of the facts ... aided by seven years' practical experience."[41] In the laudatory letter to her most loyal supporter, Dr. Charles Hutton, which graces the beginning of *Lectures in Natural Philosophy*, Bryan notes that she could not "boldly assert my opinions and exhibit my inherent capacity independently" of his support, but assert them she does within the pages of her books.[42] She does this with some hesitation, explaining in the preface to *A Compendious System* that she is relying on the indulgence of those who rise "superior to the false and vulgar prejudices of many, who supposed these subjects too sublime for female introspection."[43]

One such foray into personal hypothesizing is found in *A Compendious System*, when Bryan appeals to theology for her personal explanation for the existence of the moons and rings of Saturn. "As nothing is created in vain," she explains, the sunlight reflected from these objects is "essential to the comfort of the inhabitants of the planet," because due to the extreme distance of Saturn from the sun, the direct rays from our star would be insufficient to warm the planet.[44] In the same work she "reasons from analogy" that the light emitted by comet tails is caused by a discharge of excess heat similar to the discharge of excess electric charge through a visible spark. She makes the bold assertion concerning her hypothesis that if "any arguments can be produced to invalidate it, I am open to conviction; but till then I shall retain it and think myself excusable in advancing my ideas on the subject... ."[45] Clearly Bryan was no mere "reflector of the intrinsic light of superior genius and erudition," but rather openly modeled the scientific method for her students by posing testable hypotheses based on current observations and known facts.

Bryan's works also cross over from the realm of the feminine/passive format to a more masculine/active structure in their layout. Indeed, the label "familiar format" seems a bit of a stretch for Bryan's works when considered in their totality. While her intended audience is undoubtedly her female students, she is speaking directly to them in a lecture format. The sections of her books are termed lectures, not conversations, and while she does include everyday examples to illustrate the scientific concepts (such as condensation on the interior of windows in a warm house, the effects of drafts on the flame of a candle, and the use of steam engines

---

[41]   Ibid., ix–x.

[42]   Ibid., iii.

[43]   Ibid., viii–ix.

[44]   Ibid., 89–90.

[45]   Ibid., 92–93.

to provide drinking water), she spends a great deal of time explaining the use of scientific equipment, such as a mercury thermometer, a quadrant, a mechanical planetarium/orrery, and most especially, celestial and terrestrial globes. *Lectures in Natural Philosophy* concludes with 111 solved astronomical and geographical problems using these globes, followed by 20 pages of additional questions. Similarly, she explains in *A Compendious System* that a study of plane and spherical trigonometry, while central to a deep understanding of astronomy, is beyond the "sphere of knowledge I wish to conduct my pupils in, being unnecessary to their peculiar province in life,"[46] yet includes in that same volume an appendix on the basics of trigonometry, an appendix explaining the mathematical tables found in a popular astronomical ephemeris, and set of trigonometric problems using the quadrant and compass. Perhaps Reverend Jeremiah Joyce was correct in the assertion of his *Scientific Dialogues* (published three years after *A Compendious System* and six years prior to *Lectures in Natural Philosophy*) that "no introduction to natural and experimental philosophy has been attempted in a method so familiar and easy as that which he now offers to the public."[47] Bryan was clearly setting the bar a bit higher for her own readership, and her books were not only read by a general audience, but were used as textbooks in both girls' and boys' schools.

In contrast with the mysterious Mrs. Bryan, the life of Jane Haldimand Marcet is known in some detail. Born in 1769 to a wealthy London merchant and his Swiss wife, she married Alexander Marcet, a physician in London who conducted research in chemistry, lectured at Guy's Hospital, and became a Fellow of the Royal Society. In addition to raising three children, Jane increased her own scientific knowledge through attending lectures at the Royal Institution in London, including Thomas Young's lectures in physics and Humphrey Davy's in chemistry. Her social circles included the scientists Davy and William Hyde Wollaston, as well as women who were noted authors in their own right, such as the science writer Mary Somerville, novelist and children's author Maria Edgeworth, and noted social theorist Harriet Martineau.[48]

Marcet openly embraced the familiar format in many of her writings; her first (and most famous) work, entitled *Conversations on Chemistry* (1806), included the subtitles *In Which The Elements of That Science are Familiarly Explained and Illustrated by Experiments* and *Intended More Especially for the Female Sex*. This work was followed by a number of similar works: *Conversations on Political Economy* (1816), *Conversations on Natural Philosophy* (1819), *Conversations on Evidences of Christianity* (1826), *Conversations on Vegetable Physiology* (1829), and *Conversations for Children on Land and Sea* (1838). These works followed the format of a female figure discussing the topic at hand with several children, with the interesting exception of the conversation on Christianity, in which an adult male leads the discussion. In the remaining works (excepting the last), the

---

[46] Ibid., 103.

[47] Joyce, *Scientific Dialogues*, i.

[48] Brück, *Women*, 62.

discussion takes place between a female teacher/mentor named Mrs. B. and two sisters, Emily and Caroline. In the final book, which was apparently written for a younger audience than the previous works, Mrs. B. is the mother of the children she instructs: Edward, William, Sophy, and Caroline. The name of the main character— Mrs. B.—is nowhere explained or expanded, leading some contemporaries of Marcet to suggest that these works (originally published anonymously) were in fact the works of Margaret Bryan. For example, in his preface to the 8th American Edition of *Conversations on Natural Philosophy*, Rev. J. L. Blake refers to the author of the work as "Mrs. Bryan."[49] While it is certainly possible that Marcet named her main character in tribute to Bryan, no one who has carefully read both women's works could possibly confuse their writing styles.

In her preface to *Conversations on Chemistry*, Marcet explains that the work was precipitated by her own experiences. She found that when she originally began attending public experimental lectures, she had not gained much knowledge from them, but when she afterwards began discussing the science with others and conducting a variety of simple experiments (both of which we may assume involved her chemist husband in some way), her understanding of the subject grew to an extent that when she attended Davy's public lectures at the Royal Institution she could follow them far better than others in the audience. Based on her experiences, she wrote the book in order to instruct beginners and most especially women in the basics of chemistry by mimicking the form of her own instruction: conversation and experimentation. Marcet noted that as a woman "venturing to offer to the public, and more particularly to the female sex, an Introduction to Chemistry," she needed to explain to her audience (and those male reviewers who might look askance at such a bold work) her own background in the subject.[50] Despite the fact that she admitted some apprehension in proposing a work which might be considered by some "unsuited to the ordinary pursuits of her sex," she "felt encouraged by the establishment of those public institutions, open to both sexes, for the dissemination of philosophical knowledge, which clearly prove that the general opinion no longer excludes women from an acquaintance with the elements of science."[51] However, it must be noted that there is a significant difference between allowing women to attend public lectures in the physical sciences and accepting them as authors of works in these historically male sciences, especially a work which was originally published anonymously.

What we might call Marcet's leap of faith in her society turned out to be well founded, at least in terms of the acceptance of her own works. *Conversations on Chemistry* was widely acclaimed and enjoyed numerous editions. In the United States, the book became the most popular chemistry textbook of its time, with

---

[49]   Reverend J. L. Blake, Preface to Jane Marcet, *Conversations on Natural Philosophy*, 8th American ed. (Boston: Lincoln and Edmonds, 1826), iii.

[50]   Jane Marcet, *Conversations on Chemistry*, vol. 1, 5th ed. (London: Longman, Hurst, Rees, Orme, and Brown, 1817), 5.

[51]   Ibid., 6.

its 23 editions used in both girls' and boys' schools. Susan M. Lindee notes that there is "also evidence that young men attending mechanics' institutes used Marcet's text, and medical apprentices favored it in beginning their study of chemistry."[52] The work's most famous reader was scientist Michael Faraday, who received his first introduction to electrochemistry through its pages while he was a young bookbinder. In his later years he fondly referred to Marcet as his "first instructress."[53]

While *Conversations on Chemistry* was the first of her works to be published, it was not the first to be written, as the former's readers could have guessed from its opening sentence: "As you have now acquired some elementary notions of NATURAL PHILOSOPHY, I am going to propose to you another branch of science ... ."[54] *Conversations on Natural Philosophy* was based on her experiences attending Thomas Young's public lectures at the Royal Institution in 1801–1803, and, like the volume on chemistry which ultimately preceded it in publication, the work was written in the form of a conversation between Mrs. B. and the two sisters, heavily punctuated by simple experiments. While this volume is not as famous as its chemical cousin, it, too, was well accepted and was utilized as a textbook, especially in the United States.

The delay in publication of this work is certainly interesting. In her preface to *Conversations on Natural Philosophy* Marcet notes that

> The encouraging reception which the Conversations on Chemistry, and Political Economy, have met with, has induced her to venture on publishing a short course on Natural Philosophy; but not without the greatest apprehension for its success. Her ignorance of mathematics, and the imperfect knowledge of natural philosophy which that disadvantage necessarily implies, renders her fully sensible of her incompetency to treat the subject in any other way than in the form of a familiar explanation of the first elements, for the use of very young pupils.[55]

Was it simply her own self-consciousness over her lack of mathematical expertise which stayed her hand in offering the work to the public, or was it also the imposing nature of physics and astronomy, considered the province of men more than others sciences? Certainly Margaret Bryan's earlier works had proven that a woman could successfully publish general interest books on these subjects, and that such books did not require the inclusion of mathematics (if one ignores the optional appendices of Bryan's works). And if Marcet was initially so hesitant about publishing her introductory work on physics and astronomy, what event served

---

[52] M. Susan Lindee, "The American Career of Jane Marcet's *Conversations on Chemistry*, 1806–1853," *Isis* 82, no. 1 (1991): 9.

[53] Brück, *Women*, 63.

[54] Marcet, *Conversations on Chemistry*, 5.

[55] Jane Marcet, *Conversations on Natural Philosophy*, 4th ed. (London: Longman, Hurst, Rees, Orme, Brown, and Green, 1824), iii–iv.

as the impetus for her to overcome her fears? Brück suggests that the catalyst for Marcet's change of heart was her first extended meeting with Mary Somerville in Geneva in 1818, a meeting which was the foundation of a lifelong friendship. Although in 1818 Somerville was nearly a decade away from beginning work on own her first science book, she had already acquired a reputation for being skilled in mathematics and astronomical theory.[56] She may well have inspired Marcet to throw her hat into the physics and astronomy publishing ring.

Regardless of the ultimate reason for her publishing *Conversations on Natural Philosophy* when she did, this work and *Conversations on Chemistry* are masterful examples of popular-level science books which, on the surface, are more faithful to the classic familiar format than Bryan's earlier works but, like Bryan's works, allowed Marcet occasionally to push the boundaries of the role of the demure popularizer of others' original works. Central to Marcet's works, like most popular-level science books of her time, is the concept of using science to bolster one's faith in the divine. For example, in *Conversations on Natural Philosophy* Marcet explains to her pupils that "Every step that you advance in the pursuit of natural science, will fill your mind with admiration and gratitude towards its Divine Author … no study can then tend more to purify the heart, and raise it to a religious contemplation of the Divine Perfections."[57] Marcet uses the conversation format to put into the mouths of the young students a number of common misconceptions, which she can thereby redress. For example, in *Conversations on Natural Philosophy* Emily voices a misconception about the cause of the seasons, which national polls continue to demonstrate are widespread to this day, namely the belief that the earth is closer to the sun in summer and more distant in winter.

Marcet masterfully weaves together conversation in the common vernacular and everyday examples to illustrate the scientific concepts, aided by descriptions of experiments using both common household items and scientific instrumentation. Mrs. B. and the sisters experiment with a pyrometer, a vacuum pump, and a mercury barometer, and demonstrate that a candle is extinguished in a closed container when the oxygen is depleted. The concepts of heat conduction and insulation are illustrated by the wooden handle of a teapot and a flannel nightgown, and the chemistry behind soap, cheese making, clothing dyes, perfumes, and oil paints is described. Emily and Caroline correctly apply abstract physical principles to the concrete examples of a windmill, a garden water pump, and a drawing-room mirror, all under the careful eye of Mrs. B.

Harriet Martineau noted that Marcet "always protested against being ranked with authors of originality, whether discoverers in science or thinkers in literature. She simply desired to be useful."[58] However, like Bryan before her, Marcet did not shy away from giving her own informed scientific opinion on areas with multiple hypotheses or incomplete knowledge. For example, through the words

---

[56] Brück, *Women*, 64.

[57] Marcet, *Conversations on Natural Philosophy*, 20.

[58] Shteir, *Cultivating Women*, 101.

of Mrs. B., Marcet explains her opinion that the other planets and our moon are inhabited, and that the stars are merely suns which also have their own retinues of inhabited planets (which current technology was insufficient to view). As was the case with Bryan, Marcet bases this opinion on a theological argument, stating that "we should find it more consistent with our ideas of the Divine Wisdom and beneficence to suppose that these celestial bodies should be created for the inhabitation of beings, who are, like us, blessed by His Providence."[59] In another conversation Mrs. B. describes the ongoing discussion in the scientific community as to whether meteorites fall from the moon or another planet, or are formed in the earth's atmosphere. Caroline notes that it makes no sense for iron meteorites to be formed from an atmosphere composed of oxygen and nitrogen, and Mrs. B. concurs, stating her opinion that a lunar origin is much more likely.[60]

After her husband's death in 1822 Marcet turned the bulk of her attention to works for young children, including *Bertha's Visit to Her Uncle in England* (1830), *The Seasons: Stories for Very Young Children* (1832), and two grammar books, one for girls published in 1838 and a parallel volume for boys published in 1845. While some of her later books included a smattering of science—mainly observations of the natural world, such as the flora and fauna of various locations— none of these works rivaled the pure science value of her earlier chemistry and physics/astronomy books.

Perhaps the breadth of Marcet's influence on science writing is best seen in the short-lived expansion of the familiar format which her works sparked. Even famed geologist Charles Lyell began writing a work to be entitled *Conversations in Geology* in 1827. However, after reflecting that Marcet's style might not translate well to the topic and tone he was considering, Lyell instead wrote his classic (and traditional lecture-style) text *Elements in Geology* (1838).[61] The decade after *Conversations on Natural Philosophy* saw an increasing backlash against women science writers, especially in botany, where they had been most successful—so successful, in fact, that the science had become feminized and thus of a lesser stature than the more masculine sciences such as physics, chemistry, and astronomy. Shteir describes the efforts of the professional botanical scientific community to take back the science from the hands of women, in many ways paralleling the shift in Victorian literary circles away from women novelists to a masculinization, and hence perceived higher social class, of the field.[62] For example, in his book *The First Lines of Botany* (1827), John S. Forsythe painted women writers in botany as "pedantic spinsters," a term which clearly did not fit either Margaret Bryan or Jane Marcet.[63] No such disparaging remarks were directed towards these women, perhaps because they were deemed examples too singular and isolated to cast

---

[59] Marcet, *Conversations on Natural Philosophy*, 85.

[60] Marcet, *Conversations on Chemistry*, Vol. 1, 186–87.

[61] Gates, *Kindred Science*, 42.

[62] Shteir, *Cultivating Women*, 165–66.

[63] Ibid., 165.

doubt on the male authority of the physical sciences. Indeed, in these sciences British women continued to play a minor role in popular science writing well into the Victorian period. But Bryan and Marcet were powerful role models for several singular British women science writers, most notably Mary Somerville (1780–1872), Marcet's long-time friend.[64]

In his 1886 review of Agnes Clerke's *A Popular History of Astronomy*, William W. Payne reflected that "the years are few since the time that a woman either could or would have written a book on astronomy for popular reading in Europe or America, because the *savants* would have thought such an undertaking strangely unorthodox according to any scientific creed."[65] Those few years can be traced along a line from Bryan and Marcet, considered so singular and groundbreaking in their time, to a new generation of British women science writers. In this way, we see that Bryan and Marcet were able, through example, to create a culturally acceptable literary and cultural space for British women to write about outer space and its underlying physical and chemical principles for a wide range of audiences.

---

[64]   For more information on Mary Somerville, see Kathryn A. Neeley, *Mary Somerville: Science, Illumination, and the Female Mind* (Cambridge: Cambridge University Press, 2001), 78.

[65]   William W. Payne, "Book Notes: A Popular History of Astronomy During the Nineteenth Century," *The Sidereal Messenger* 5 (1886): 158–59.

PART II
Borderlands

Chapter 5
The Space of British Exile in Frances Burney's *The Wanderer* and Germaine de Staël's *Corinne*

Pamela Cheek

What is the difference between cosmopolitanism and exile? While the first involves a deliberate refusal to belong to a single nation, a self-styling as a "citizen of the world," and the second the loss of or expulsion from a nation, both, in their unmarked universalism, have been persistently figured as male. To imagine an exile one must first imagine a citizen, and this may account for why the idea of women in exile is so formless in fiction prior to the twentieth century. Cosmopolitanism and exile equally depend on nationality and citizenship; these are statuses that western women have held only contingently, through their relationships with their fathers and husbands. Unable to possess nationality or citizenship in their own right, women could not lay claim to cosmopolitanism or bear the status of exile. Nonetheless, without a nationality or citizenship, women were, in a sense, necessarily cosmopolitans or, ultimately, exiles *avant la lettre*.

Corinne ou l'Italie, published in 1807 by Germaine de Staël, and *The Wanderer; or, Female Difficulties*, published in 1814 by Frances Burney, analyze the contingency of women's nationality on fathers and husbands. Critical studies to date have highlighted the cultural hybridity of the heroines of these novels, while discussions of Staël have noted her central preoccupation with exile. Both novels reflect a transformation in discourse about woman's cultural identity by situating cosmopolitanism in the past and redefining women's non-nationality as a melancholic exile. Mourning the loss of an eighteenth-century cosmopolitanism that had been supported by the institutions of Enlightenment sociability and hypothesized in sentimental writing on either side of the Channel, both writers reworked the existing spatial codes of the novel to invent the fleeting figure of the woman exile. Katie Trumpener has written that, "To explore the ways in which the romantic novel takes up and reworks the nationalist debates of the late eighteenth century is to watch a process through which ideology takes on generic flesh."[1] To explore how Staël and Burney sound the national meanings that different forms ascribe to space is to watch an attempt to resist nineteenth-century nationalist ideology and, most particularly, the role it assigned to women.

---

[1] Katie Trumpener, *Bardic Nationalism: The Romantic Novel and the British Empire* (Princeton: Princeton University Press, 1997), xv.

For Staël's protagonist, Corinne, and for Burney's wanderer, Britain is the primary site of exile to which the heroine returns as a stranger in her own land. Such a displacement of the site of exile defied both recent history and the current of writing on either side of the Channel. From the beginning of the French Revolution, France loomed large as a homeland unwillingly left behind by unfortunate *émigrés*. Over the course of the 1790s, 100,000 people emigrated from France to England, with perhaps as many as 25,000 fleeing at the height of the Terror.[2] Among officially classified French *émigrés*, only 15 percent were women, although the actual numbers may have been higher.[3] The French clergy emigrated to England in such large numbers that they became a particular object of charity. Burney herself wrote a plea to the women of England on behalf of "these destitute wanderers," pitching her claims in unusually antinationalist terms by calling on her readers to recognize that we are "all the creatures of one Creator."[4] After Britain declared war on France in 1793, the British were displaced as well, but it was chiefly men who traveled when they were marshaled to fight in large numbers; perhaps a fifth of the male population was involved in the war by 1803.[5] Napoleonic campaigns also made migrants of Central European men, women, and children.[6] It was more likely to be exceptional British women, like the writers Frances Burney, Maria Williams, and, possibly, Charlotte Smith, rather than representative ones, who found themselves away from home in the periods when *The Wanderer* and *Corinne* take place or, indeed, when these two novels were being written.

In the *émigré* fiction of the 1790s, the focus fell more generally on men who had been forced to flee their homeland and men in flight from France. The emphasis on exile from France allowed authors to capitalize on the extraordinary material, as author Sénac de Meilhan described it in his novel *L'Émigré* (1797), offered by the Revolution and the Terror:

> All presents the semblance of truth and all is *romanesque* in the revolution of France ... The most extraordinary encounters, the most surprising circumstances, the most deplorable situations become common events and surpass even what the authors of novels can imagine.[7]

---

[2]   Stuart Curran, "Romanticism displaced and placeless," *European Romantic Review* 20, no. 5 (December 2009): 642.

[3]   Donald Greer, *The Incidence of Emigration During the French Revolution* (Cambridge: Harvard University Press, 1951), 91.

[4]   Adriana Craciun, *British Women Writers and the French Revolution: Citizens of the World* (New York: Palgrave MacMillan, 2005), 150; Frances Burney, "Brief Reflexions Relative to the Emigrant French Clergy" (1793), Project Gutenberg (Ebook #29125), http://www.gutenberg.org/cache/epub/29125/pg29125.txt.

[5]   Curran, "Romanticism displaced," 641.

[6]   To the classes of "displaced persons" in the 1790s, Curran adds the convicts forced to emigrate to Botany Bay in Australia, of whom only 20 percent were women. Curran, "Romanticism displaced," 642.

[7]   Sénac de Meilhan, *L'Émigré* (1797), quoted in Stéphanie Genand, *Romans de l'émigration, 1797–1803* (Paris: Honoré Champion, 2008), 13.

As Adriana Craciun points out, "While conservatives in the tradition of Burke used the *émigré* theme to idealize Britain as a refuge from French atheism and anarchy, the true home of liberty and justice, progressive writers used the *émigrés* to critique everything from homegrown British xenophobia, to Britain's injustices against its own subjects, to Britain's role in fomenting war and thus contributing to the Terror."[8]

In *Corinne* and *The Wanderer*, the protagonists are not young men who have come to Britain fleeing France, but young women, exiled from England at birth, who later return *incognita*, only to suffer an exile from within. Their internal exile fits between two bookends in literary history. Their perspective of "estrangement from one's own culture,"[9] one that enables the progressive criticism of home outlined by Craciun, had been inaugurated in women's writing by Françoise de Graffigny in her 1747 sentimental novel *Lettres d'une péruvienne*, which both Burney and Staël had read and referred to in their work.[10] The heroines' position as victims of their families' disavowal of them—made manifest in a succession of scenes in which the heroine peers into interiors she would rightfully inhabit, were she not an outcast—anticipates nothing so much as the exile of Frankenstein's monster and the concealment of a somehow monstrous parentage in Mary Shelley's Romantic and Gothic novel of 1818.[11] Staël's and Burney's "*emigré*" novels, about women exiled from Britain rather than men exiled from France, cycle through the novelistic forms and related spatial codes that were available between 1747 and 1818. Staël's work was received by male critics, as Madelyn Gutwirth has shown, as evidence that she was poorly inserted into her gender.[12] With the publication of *The Wanderer*, Burney was criticized for being a traitor to the sentimental form, which she had previously been hailed as having mastered, and for being too antiquated in her style to address the realities of a post-Revolutionary age.[13] Yet the novelists' meditations on woman's non-nationality, which proceed through a reworking of existing novelistic spatial codes, reveal not a betrayal of form or of gender but a prescient sense that the two have become linked. Staël and Burney

---

[8]   Craciun, *British Women Writers*, 141.

[9]   Paul Gilroy, *Postcolonial Melancholia* (New York: Columbia University Press, 2005), 67.

[10]   Margaret Anne Doody, "Missing Les Muses: Madame de Staël and Frances Burney," *Colloquium Helveticum: Cahiers suisses de littérature générale et comparée* 25 (1997): 101, 103.

[11]   Dierdre Shauna Lynch, "The (Dis)locations of Romantic Nationalism: Shelley, Staël and the Home-Schooling of Monsters," in *The Literary Channel: The Inter-National Invention of the Novel*, ed. Margaret Cohen and Carolyn Dever (Princeton and Oxford: Princeton University Press, 2002), 205.

[12]   Madelyn Gutwirth, *Madame de Staël, Novelist* (Urbana: University of Illinois Press, 1978), 26.

[13]   George Justice, "Burney and the Literary Marketplace," in *The Cambridge Companion to Frances Burney*, ed. Peter Sabor (Cambridge: Cambridge University Press, 2007), 160–161.

blend the spatial conventions of the sentimental novel, the historical novel, and the Gothic novel, choosing formal hybridity in a melancholic reaction to the nationalist implications of the gendering of form in the nineteenth century.

Pre-Revolutionary sentimental fiction juxtaposed national characters, presenting them as intriguing features of the present age. In contrast, *Corinne* and *The Wanderer* yoke the viability of national types to moments in history through chronotopes for the three possible national romantic choices available to the male protagonist. The nationality of the two heroines remains a mystery for much of each novel. Staël withholds an account of the family and national origins of her heroine until the fourteenth book of a 20-book novel, while Burney virtuosically reveals nothing directly until the ninth book of ten. To shield innocent people, the heroines of *Corinne* and *The Wanderer* must hide their true identities. Thus, the reader, along with the other characters, especially the male lovers, can only judge the heroines on the basis of their behavior and in comparison with other female characters. Each novel sets up a nationally marked triad of women: more mature women who possess qualities associated with French femininity, adolescent incarnations of British identity, and the *incognita* heroines—Staël's Corinne and Burney's wanderer, whom the reader comes to know by her accidental alias, Ellis, and later her first name, Juliet.

The stories of the female characters who personify the French national type, Madame d'Arbigny and Elinor Joddrel, are narrated more or less retrospectively. Staël's Madame d'Arbigny mixes "calculation with passion" and displays "that art of forging the truth that is so frequently encountered in countries where the desire to produce an effect by one's sentiments is more powerful than the sentiments themselves."[14] Burney's Elinor Joddrel, an Englishwoman who travels to France seduced by the Revolutionary chimera of liberty for women and humanity, is equally given to a feminine "Machiavellian policy" and serves as a vehicle for collecting a variety of stereotypes about the stridency of women in public.[15] Like Madame d'Arbigny, who feigns illness, pregnancy, and Revolutionary attacks on her fortune, Elinor parades her emotions, using illness, histrionic scenes, and a public suicide attempt in an unsuccessful scheme to keep the hero of the novel in her thrall (Burney's portrayal of Elinor's loquacious and overly dramatic espousal of suicide doubtless satirizes Staël's espousal of suicide in *Reflections on Suicide* and in the novel *Delphine*). These women who perform French femininity are potential love objects only in France during the early years of the French Revolution (prior to 1793) and during a period that precedes the time of the story. While Burney creates a milder and more authentically French version of French femininity in the character of Gabrielle, the friend with whom Ellis (Juliet) has been raised in France, Gabrielle shares with Elinor and Madame d'Arbigny the central quality of

---

[14]   Germaine de Staël, *Corinne ou l'Italie*, ed. Simone Balayé (Paris: Gallimard, 1985), 322. This and all subsequent translations from the work of Germaine de Staël are mine.

[15]   Frances Burney, *The Wanderer; or, Female Difficulties*, ed. Margaret Anne Doody, et al. (Oxford: Oxford University Press, 2001), 161.

having no imaginable future. In Gabrielle's case, the aristocratic despotism of her French husband and his inability to recognize that he can no longer rely on *ancien régime* privilege lock her in the past, an imprisonment conjured forcefully in the novel by Gabrielle's perpetual mourning for her young son (a noble French heir), who has died prematurely.

Commentators throughout the eighteenth century, including Germaine de Staël in *De la littérature*, often pointed to the active participation of privileged women in public cultural life when they sought to explain the politeness, sociability, wit, and cultural radiance of France. Exaggerating the sentimental novel's conventions for tracing national character, both Staël and Burney obviate the eighteenth-century model of "French" femininity and locate the possibility of successful romance and positive sexual attraction to a woman with wholly French qualities in the historical and narrative past.

Staël's and Burney's heroines each have younger half-sisters, daughters of their father's second marriages to British women from aristocratic families, who fully incarnate British femininity and serve as potential erotic rivals for the male protagonists' affections. Staël's Lucile Edgermond has been raised by her strict and retiring mother near the border with Scotland in Northumberland. When Corinne sees Lucile, she compares herself with the young girl who is utterly artless, in both senses of the word:

> [Corinne] found herself so inferior, she exaggerated to herself so deeply, if it were possible to exaggerate it, the charm of this youth, this whiteness, this blonde hair, this innocent picture of the spring of life, that she felt it almost humiliating to do battle with her talent and intelligence, with gifts that she had acquired, or at least perfected, against graces provided by nature itself.[16]

Like Staël's Lucile, Burney's Lady Aurora Granville is hemmed in by a prejudiced older female relative and incarnates innocence and inexperience:

> Lady Aurora, who had just reached her sixteenth year, was now budding into life, with equal loveliness of mind and person. She was fair, but pale, with elegant features, a face perfectly oval, and soft expressive blue eyes, of which the "liquid lustre" spoke a heart that was the seat of sensibility ... of compassionate feeling for woes which she did not suffer.[17]

Based in the discourse of British and French national contestation, the women embodying the polar erotic choices in the novels have self-evident identities with clear geographic and temporal coding. Whether *ancien régime* or Jacobin in their politics, Madame d'Arbigny and Elinor Joddrel share the French vice of manufacturing passions for public effect. The time for their space is over, as the heroes' ultimate erotic choices, the time of the story, and their own comparatively

---

[16]   Staël, *Corinne*, 481.

[17]   Burney, *The Wanderer*, 117.

advanced ages make clear. The profoundly British and extremely young Lucile Edgermond and Aurora Granville are the daughters by a second marriage of English peers; aristocratic and English on the maternal and paternal sides, they have been raised by severe and powerful older women to operate only in private, domestic circles. While they are frequently rendered powerless by their sensibility, they exert little genuine attraction because they are without art. In *De la littérature*, Germaine de Staël sketched the English social model into which she would insert Lucile in the novel *Corinne*: "The English live retired in their families or gathered in public assemblies for national discussions. The intermediary that is called society hardly exists among them; and [yet] it is in this frivolous space of life that wit and taste are nonetheless formed."[18] For all that the English model entails giving up "society," the perfect incarnations of British femininity, Lucile and Aurora Granville, represent a confined and artless women's future, as their youth and the incomplete narration of their stories imply.

The heroines that Staël and Burney devise are possessed of an extraordinary sensibility which, in sentimental novels, "can be passed on by birth," as April Alliston has suggested, "as if it were a racial characteristic, but when it is so inherited, it tends to mark a hybridization of national character."[19] National hybridity allows an eighteenth-century sentimental heroine like the eponymous protagonist of Sophie von La Roche's *The History of Lady Sophia Sternheim* (1771) to enjoy marriage with a British nobleman and to use her exceptional talents to foster an ideal cosmopolitan community at a remove from corrupting society. In contrast, over the course of *Corinne* and *The Wanderer*, the hybridity of the heroine veers from its cosmopolitan signification toward abjection.

Both *Corinne* and *The Wanderer* rely on pre-histories revolving around the fathers' erotic choices in a first marriage—choices that jeopardize the aristocratic and Protestant lineages of their families and overdetermine the heroines' fates. This was a formula for sentimental fiction that Burney had, in fact, helped to establish with her first novel, *Evelina*, almost 30 years before. The first marriage of Corinne's Scottish father, Lord Edgermond, is to an Italian Catholic woman, and Corinne is raised at first in Italy, where she acquires the talents that allow her to become a gifted improvisational performer who accompanies herself on the lyre. Nonetheless, in Staël's schema of national character, Corinne is not Italian by nature, despite the identification of the heroine with the country in the title *Corinne or Italy*, since she refuses to feminize men, recognizes the importance of subordinating individual talent to the larger good of civic virtue, and has a cosmopolitan appreciation of the varied cultural contributions of European nations. As an adolescent, she goes to England to live with her father and her

---

[18]   Germaine de Staël, "De la littérature considérée dans ses rapports avec les institutions sociales," in *Oeuvres complètes de Mme. De Staël*, vol. 13 (Brussels: Auguste Wahlen et cie, 1820), 234–35.

[19]   April Alliston, "Transnational Sympathies, Imaginary Communities," in *The Literary Channel: The Inter-National Invention of the Novel*, ed. Margaret Cohen and Carolyn Dever (Princeton: Princeton University Press, 2002), 137.

rigid stepmother, but after her father's death she flees the restrictive gender role imposed on her in Northumberland and returns to Italy, promising her stepmother to pass for dead and not to reveal her family name so as not to dishonor her younger half-sister, Lucile. When she performs, she is described not as acting but as communicating something that emanates from her natural sensibility. Lord Oswald Nelvil, Corinne's lover, describes her to her rigid British stepmother as having "those talents that come from the soul, and cannot exist without the most elevated character, without the most feeling heart, those talents that are tied to the most touching goodness to the most generous heart."[20] Corinne follows Lord Nelvil back to England in disguise so as not to violate her vow to her stepmother, where she finds that his guilt over his father's death has drawn him to Lucile, his father's choice for him.

In the pre-history of *The Wanderer*, Ellis/Juliet's father, Lord Granville, marries a commoner and hides this from his father by sending his young family to France, where his daughter is placed in a French convent and benefits from the guardianship of an aristocratic French bishop and his sister. In France, Ellis/Juliet acquires the talents that are surprised out of her once she returns, *incognita*, to England. She plays the harp and sings beautifully, and like Corinne too, she draws. Juliet/Ellis's remarkable performances, like Corinne's, are represented as deriving from nature. When she spontaneously fills leading roles in some private theatricals, for example, the spectators speculate about the source of her exceptional performance: "Whether this excellence were the result of practice and instruction, or a sudden emanation of general genius, accidentally directed to a particular point, was disputed by the critics among the audience ... . This, however, was nature, which would not be repressed; not art, that strove to be displayed."[21]

The heroines' performances emanate naturally; Corinne and Ellis/Juliet produce art without being artful. For Burney, the natural performance marks anxiety about the impropriety of a woman's appearance in public.[22] For Staël, it registers modest feminine subscription to the cult of sensibility. For both writers, it reconciles femininity with genius. Female genius derives from the heroines' cultural hybridity, evident in their capacity to speak both English and French perfectly. Corinne's French is accented with English in a reminder of her British origin and as an indication of how her incarnation of the female artist is distinct from the French artfulness of a Madame D'Arbigny, while her delivery of Italian is entirely unaccented.[23] Juliet/Ellis's English is accented with French as a reminder of her childhood exile from her homeland, of her distinctive taste and talent, and as an indication that she cannot be fully assimilated to English society

---

[20]   Staël, *Corinne*, 458.

[21]   Burney, *The Wanderer,* 95.

[22]   Sara Salih, "*Camilla* and *The Wanderer*," in *The Cambridge Companion to Frances Burney*, ed. Peter Sabor (Cambridge: Cambridge University Press, 2007), 48.

[23]   Batsaki, Yota, "Exile as the Inaudible Accent in Germaine de Staël's *Corinne, ou l'Italie*," *Comparative Literature* 61, no. 1 (Winter 2009): 35.

as an adult. The hybrid heroines straddle cultures in a way that should represent an ideal cosmopolitanism.

Yet when they cross into England, they return home to a place where they are not acknowledged as rightful daughters and heirs. For their border crossings into England, Corinne and Ellis/Juliet each adopt costumes of mourning for a self that fails to fit acceptable categories, choosing not to disappear into the crowd with their disguises but to stand out as culturally exotic, wounded ghosts or apparitions. Their blackness and evident suffering contrast with the appearances of their half-sisters: Lucile's "whiteness" or "fairness" (*blancheur*) and Lady Aurora Granville's "fair" and "pale" complexion, as well as her "feeling for woes which she did not suffer." Aware of her own "black hair, her complexion somewhat darkened by the sun of Italy and her pronounced features," and languishing with an unnamed illness, Corinne decides to wear a "black dress in the Venetian style" and covers "her face and her waist with the mantua worn in that country."[24] For her Channel crossing, Ellis/Juliet deliberately paints her "hands and arms of so dark a colour, that they might rather be styled black than brown." She gives her "muffled up face" an "equally dusky hue," while "a large black patch" covers half of her left cheek and a "broad black ribbon" binds a "bandage of cloth over the right side of her forehead."[25] Sara Salih has read Ellis/Juliet's disguise as indicative of how, in *The Wanderer*, "Burney problematically and opportunistically equates slavery with the oppression of white middle-class women."[26] This is an apt criticism, equally applicable to Staël's fiction, particularly her exoticist stories "Pauline" and "Zulma." The choice made by both heroines to don blackness, the blackness of Catholicism and the blackness of the slave, on their return to the land from which they have been exiled also points to acknowledgment of their own exoticism and abjection.

Reading *Corinne* and *The Wanderer* first as sentimental novels—examining how they map gender roles onto national space by relying on conventional eighteenth-century sentimental codes—brings the two novels' attempts at cosmopolitanism into focus. In *The Literary Channel: the Inter-National Invention of the Novel*, Margaret Cohen has argued that the sentimental novel "served as a privileged site for the exchange of literary codes and observations concerning national character and difference, along with reflection on the process of exchange and translation itself."[27] Both *Corinne* and *The Wanderer* certainly fill this brief, but they do so through negation. They construct French space as a no longer viable option. They make British space exilic. And they turn the "process of exchange and translation itself," of crossing the Channel, into an experience of hybrid abjection. In a sense, then, these are antisentimental novels in that they mourn the end of the age of the

---

[24]   Staël, *Corinne*, 488.

[25]   Burney, *The Wanderer*, 20.

[26]   Salih, "*Camilla*," 50.

[27]   Margaret Cohen, "Sentimental Communities," in Cohen and Dever, *The Literary Channel*, 107.

cosmopolitan hybrid heroine. The use of chronotopes to distribute national models of femininity along a timeline involves the overlay of a new "historical" strategy onto an older "sentimental" strategy.

When *Corinne* and *The Wanderer* are examined in relation to the spatial coordinates of the historical novel, their ambivalence toward a national model of femininity becomes readily apparent. In *Atlas of the European Novel,* Franco Moretti has suggested that external borders between states offer sites of adventure. They "easily generate narrative—but in an elementary way: they take two opposite fields, and make them collide." In contrast, internal borders "work differently, and focus on a theme which is far less flamboyant than adventure, but much more disturbing: *treason.*"[28] The "veritable phenomenology of the border" offered by adventurous collision and treason arose in the era of Napoleon, when, Perry Anderson has written, "The sense of national community, systematically orchestrated by the State … may well have been a greater reality … than at any time in the previous century."[29] Read according to this schema, *Corinne* and *The Wanderer* offer narratives of external borders in their double layers of pre-history. The fathers' decisions to marry outside of the Protestant British nobility and then to hide their daughters abroad generates conflict and action, just as do Lord Nelvil's and Elinor Joddrel's prolonged stays in France and their attraction to the ways of French women. In contrast, the experience of the daughters/heroines in England occurs chiefly in outlying areas along internal borders. Corinne wanders along a northern border region between Northumberland and Scotland,[30] while Ellis/ Juliet wanders along a southern triangle of coastline and an interior of forests, cathedrals, and ruins between Brighton, Salisbury, and Torquay. Wandering along internal borders corresponds to the heroines' treason against the British gender model of retiring domesticity that their half-sisters embody. In the fateful letter that becomes a postmortem paternal injunction to Lord Oswald Nelvil not to marry the woman he loves, Nelvil's father asks his friend Lord Edgermond to marry Lucile Edgermond to his son. Corinne (Lucile's older half-sister) is the wrong match because, as the one father explains to the other:

> Our life in the countryside, our domestic habits would, of necessity, thwart all her tastes. A man born in our happy country must be English before everything else. He must fulfill his duties as a citizen since he has the happiness to be one. And in the countries where political institutions give men honorable opportunities to act and to prove themselves, women must remain in the shadow. How can you expect someone as distinguished as your daughter to content herself with such a fate?[31]

---

[28] Franco Moretti, *Atlas of the European Novel, 1800–1900* (London: Verso, 1998), 37.

[29] Perry Anderson, *Arguments within British Marxism* (London: Verso, 1980), 37–38, quoted in Moretti, *Atlas,* 29.

[30] Cf. Alliston, "Transnational Sympathies," 137.

[31] Staël, *Corinne,* 467.

By presenting two heroines whose treasonous behavior consists in being too talented to remain in the shadows, Staël and Burney reluctantly concede that an emerging model of male national citizenship traced in the father's letter requires women to efface themselves in domestic space. Staël and Burney offer a phenomenology of the border, registering the death of the cosmopolitan appreciation for and discrimination among different cultural gender models that had been hallmark of sentimental novels like Graffigny's *Lettres d'une péruvienne*. Their historical novels argue that the nation is founded on the sacrifice of the heroine's hybridity.

Sentimental novels, historical novels ... *Corinne* and *The Wanderer* also deploy the spatial codes of the Gothic novel—a form, as Jerrold Hogle writes, that "rehearses the death of an old order" and expresses anxiety "on the birth of a new order."[32] In exile, the heroines are drawn into "gothic machinery"[33]—the tomb of the father, a drawn carriage, a roadside ditch, and the castle of the father in *Corinne;* a seaside grave, a tomb, Salisbury Cathedral, Stonehenge, and the bloody attic of a poacher's cottage in *The Wanderer.* Yet these spaces are nothing compared to the representative Gothic and British spaces of the novels, the domestic interior ruled by ill, prejudiced, and sadistic older women. These older women, or "furies," as they are called in *The Wanderer*, torture the heroines because they cannot submit to the living death of the tea room that their half-sisters inhabit. The Gothic *Corinne* and *The Wanderer* paradoxically express both a longing for the return of *ancien régime* authority through the characters' absorption in seeking to fulfill the wishes of the dead fathers and a longing for a new order of Protestant and bourgeois civic virtue and national identity through their privileging of the complementary gender roles that should underwrite this order. The impossibility of embracing either the old or the new order is registered by the way that the heroines always exceed the space of the tea room, bursting out to become exiles once again.

The Gothic *Corinne* and *The Wanderer* indict the fathers for not having displayed the courage to challenge the old order and to honor openly their attraction to other cultures and other social classes. Because the fathers consign romantic choices of foreign women to the level of covert and transitory personal liaisons rather than elevating them to substantive, visible social ties, Corinne must pass for dead in England and Juliet/Ellis must pass for never having been born. In other words, the hybrid, neither/nor status of both heroines is a function of their fathers' inability to legitimate the positive value of alterity or to argue for the recognition of alterity as a civil responsibility incumbent on the individual living in the world. Because of the fathers' failure to sanction the potential of their own cross-class and cross-cultural relationships, the hybridity of the heroines amounts to a condition of non-nationality. Their non-nationality registers as a repressed cosmopolitanism, evident in their extraordinary social talents, and as an expressed abjection in exile. Harriet Guest explains that in Gothic novels, revelation of the

---

[32]   Jerrold E. Hogle, "Introduction," in *The Cambridge Companion to Gothic Fiction*, ed. Jerrold E. Hogle (Cambridge: Cambridge University Press, 2002), 2.

[33]   Margaret Anne Doody, "Burney and Politics," in Sabor, *Cambridge Companion*, 96.

secret of the past liberates the heroine from her martyrdom and allows her to be redeemed as an exemplary figure of chaste British femininity.[34] As such, *Corinne* and *The Wanderer* are Gothic novels but in reverse, for the secret of the heroines' births—the very cultural hybridity that has yielded their excellence—has made them monstrously unfit to inhabit the space of perfected British femininity. The Gothic culmination of each novel, the revelation of the heroine's secret hybrid national identity, expresses longing for the hybrid identity of the eighteenth-century heroine and surrender to the narrow national gender models ushered in by the Napoleonic era.

The impoverished reaction of Staël and Burney to the triumph of the national model is to displace exile onto Britain. They make the country that was discursively privileged in Enlightenment thought for its model of civic virtue and political liberty into the only available space for a woman of virtue. Yet Britain is also a space where exceptional women are condemned to wander or to sacrifice their hybridity, since they cannot pretend to citizenship. The two authors retreat into a melancholic mourning for the international community of sentiment supported by the sentimental novel prior to 1789 rather than proposing a gendered cosmopolitanism or a fully politicized stance of exile for a new age. On the one hand, the reversal of sentimental, historical, and Gothic spatial codes in *Corinne* and *The Wanderer*, as well as the novels' formal hybridity, betray what Paul Gilroy, in a discussion of the limits of contemporary planetary thinking, has called "a failure of political imagination."[35] On the other hand, the transformation of spatial codes involves resistance to the gendering of form in the nineteenth-century novel.

Franco Moretti argues in *Atlas of the European Novel* that different novelistic forms effectively construct the space of the nation in the nineteenth century:

> Think of Austen's world: everything within a circle centering on London (a day, a day-and-a-half away). Well, historical novels show the opposite pattern: a weak centripetal pull, with the story running immediately away from the national capital. ... And that [Walter] Scott's world should end exactly where Austen's begins ... such a perfect fit, of course, is only a (beautiful) coincidence. But behind the coincidence lies a solid reality: namely, that different forms inhabit different spaces.[36]

And, as Moretti indirectly acknowledges through his choice of authors, in the nineteenth century different genders inhabit different forms in different spaces. While the sentimental novel was not a purely female or male form in the eighteenth century, it would, as Margaret Cohen has argued in *The Sentimental Education of the Novel*, become lastingly associated with women writers and readers in the

---

[34]   Harriet Guest, "The Wanton Muse: Politics and Gender in Gothic Theory after 1760," in *Beyond Romanticism: New Approaches to Texts and Contexts, 1780–1832*, ed. Stephen Copley (London: Routledge, 1992), 128.

[35]   Gilroy, *Postcolonial Melancholia*, 5.

[36]   Moretti, *Atlas*, 34.

nineteenth. A truly nineteenth-century genre, the historical novel was written and peopled by men. Moretti confirms this in the list of novels he chooses to illustrate his argument.[37] Published at the cusp of the transition from sentimental to historical fiction and at the tail end of a period in which women and men wrote sentimental historical fiction about French Revolutionary *émigrés*, *Corinne* and *The Wanderer* anticipate and resist the gendering and nationalization of form in fiction. Staël and Burney reworked the spatial codes of available novelistic forms to claim the melancholic transnational space of exile—not for all women, but for exceptional women like themselves. When *Corinne or Italy* and *The Wanderer or Female Difficulties* hover over the "or" in their titles, when a single form cannot describe the heroine's experience and a single space cannot encompass her, when home is equivalent to exile, this reflects an intuition of gendered deterritorialization. Deleuze and Guattari remind us that a minor literature is "that which a minority constructs within a major language" and that it is generated by "the impossibility of not writing because national consciousness, uncertain or oppressed, necessarily exists by means of literature."[38] The 600 pages of *Corinne* and the 900 pages of *The Wanderer*, urgent with the impossibility of not writing, cannot even constitute a minor literature, since consciousness of a woman's citizenship in the nation could only be scripted through the negation of existing forms for imagining national identity.

Coda

The similarity in Burney's and Stael's novelistic designs can be partly understood as the outcome of their interest in each other's work as well as of their own transnational personal histories. In 1793, long before their extended exiles and the publication of their *émigré* novels, Burney and Staël had met in England and formed a short-lived friendship characterized by mutual admiration. Germaine de Staël had narrowly escaped French Revolutionary violence and had taken up residence with a party of fellow constitutionalists in Surrey, near the home of two of Burney's friends. Through these intermediaries Burney met her future husband, Alexandre d'Arblay, as well as the 28-year-old Germaine de Staël. Known since adolescence for her striking conversation in her mother's Parisian salon, Staël had circulated some critical works, published a novella, and was working on her first major piece of criticism, *De l'influence des passions* (*On the Influence of the Passions*). At the time of their meeting, Burney enjoyed an international reputation. Her first novel, *Evelina*, had appeared in 1778 when she was Staël's age; her second novel, *Cecilia* (1782), and her third, *Camilla* (1796), were both well received. All three of Burney's early novels were quickly translated and

---

[37]   Ibid.

[38]   Gilles Deleuze and Félix Guattari, "From *Kafka: Toward a Minor Literature*," in *The Norton Anthology of Theory and Criticism*, ed. Vincent B. Leitch, et al. (New York: Norton, 2001), 1598.

received internationally as models of sentimental fiction. Despite the two women's affinities, Burney followed her father's cue to break off the friendship with Staël, whose extramarital relationship was as notorious in England as her politics.

In 1802, the year that her first novel, *Delphine*, was published, Germaine de Staël was forced out of France for a second time, this time by Napoleon's hostility to her political influence. She took up residence along with her children in her father's Swiss home in Coppet and, unable to return to Paris until 1814, traveled throughout Europe and Russia, using Coppet as a base. The novel *Corinne* partially reproduces Staël's peregrinations skirting outside the borders of France and traveling into Italy.

The same year that Staël went into exile, Frances Burney hurriedly crossed the Channel with her young son to join her French husband, Alexandre d'Arblay, who had renewed his pre-Revolutionary military commission to become a general under Napoleon. The family became trapped in France by both the Napoleonic blockade and the need to show loyalty until 1812, when Burney and her son were finally able to return to England. Burney had to display careful diplomacy on the voyage home, negotiating in English with a British captain who refused to transport her son because he appeared to be French. She also negotiated in French for permission to emigrate with the hefty English manuscript of her final novel, *The Wanderer*, which she had probably begun writing in 1798.[39]

In addition to their experiences of exile, two other biographical similarities contributed to the parallel concerns evinced in the authors' later fiction. First, Burney and Staël had strong relationships with their fathers, both well-known public figures, and devoted considerable energy to commemorating their fathers' lives in print and to negotiating a precarious balance between filial devotion and intellectual and personal independence.[40] Second, neither writer could have considered herself as having a single, clear nationality by the time she wrote her final novel. Burney, who was born and raised in England, married the French *ancien régime* count and Napoleonic general Alexandre d'Arblay. Frances Burney d'Arblay's nationality seems not to have been at issue during her stay in France, but only because she was careful not to draw any attention to herself.[41] Moreover, Burney's maternal grandparents were French immigrants and Roman Catholics (she had learned French from her grandmother), while her father's family was originally Scottish. On both sides, her social position was decidedly common,

---

[39] Frances Burney, *Journals and Letters*, ed. Peter Sabor and Lars E. Troide (London: Penguin Books, 2001), 460–461.

[40] On their relationships with their fathers, see Margaret Anne Doody's *Frances Burney: The Life in the Works* (New Brunswick, NJ: Rutgers University Press, 1988), 10–11, 18–21; and Gutwirth, *Madame de* Staël, 35–45. After her father's death in 1804, Germaine de Staël published *Manuscrits de M. Necker*, preceded by her own preface, "Du caractère de M. Necker, et de sa vie privée." Frances Burney published the three-volume *Memoirs of Doctor Burney* in 1832.

[41] Burney, *Journals and Letters*, 484–85.

although her own fame and her father's carefully crafted cultural prominence as a professional musicologist had helped her secure a position as Second Keeper of the Robes to Queen Charlotte. On her side, Germaine Necker de Staël was Swedish, according to a ruling of Napoleonic jurisprudence, since she had been united in an arranged marriage with Eric-Magnus, Baron de Staël-Holstein, the Swedish ambassador to France.[42] Staël's father was a Swiss Protestant from Geneva; her mother, Suzanne Curchod Necker, was the daughter of a pastor in Lausanne from a Provençal family. Necker's service as finance minister to the king elevated him to a position of nobility, and his wife's salon guaranteed the family impressive social and intellectual credentials. As Margaret Doody puts it, Burney and Staël were on the "cusp of national and class identities" and religious identities as well.[43] So, too, were their exiled heroines.

After Burney submitted to paternal injunction and guiltily abandoned the friendship with Staël, the two writers kept track of each other's subsequent published work and produced clearly intersecting reflections on women's exile in their final novels. In her journals and letters, Burney records anxiety about her relationship with Staël but also her impressions of Staël's works, including *On Germany*, *Reflections on suicide*, and *On the Influence of the Passions upon the Happiness of Individuals and of Nations*.[44] Staël gave her father a copy of Burney's *Cecilia* to provide him with solace after he lost power in the fall of the French monarchy, and she probed the possibility of a renewed acquaintance after Burney arrived in France.[45] Burney's publisher later sent Staël an advance copy of *The Wanderer*. As I have suggested here, *The Wanderer* is in some sense an English translation of *Corinne*, one that retains the heroine's French accent. Long after the pre-Revolutionary and early Revolutionary promotion of international sociability had faded, and despite the material impediment of the Napoleonic blockade, the two writers' continuing engagement with each other's ideas kept to the practice of gendered cosmopolitanism that they mourned in their novels.

One can see Burney, still trapped in France, reaching for a fuller vision of post-Revolutionary cosmopolitanism, based in the sentimental convention of an international marriage, in a letter sent to her father in 1810. Hoping for an end to the war after Napoleon's marriage to the Archduchess of Austria and an end to enforced separation from her English family and friends, Burney wrote:

> Could you but send me a little food for the Hope now in private circulation that the new alliance of the Emperor may perhaps extend to a general alliance of all Europe—ah Heaven! How would that brighten my faculties of enjoyment! I should run about to see all I have hitherto omitted to seek with the ardent curiosity of a traveler newly arrived and I should hasten to re-view and consider all I have

---

[42]   Carla Hesse, *The Other Enlightenment: How French Women Became Modern* (Princeton: Princeton University Press, 2003), 65.

[43]   Doody, "Missing," 84.

[44]   Burney, *Journals and Letters,* 357, 468.

[45]   Ibid., 358, n. 7, 416–17.

already beheld with an alertness of vivacity that would draw information from every object I have as yet looked at with undiscerning tameness. —Oh such a gleam of light would new-model—or re-model me, and I should make you present to all my sights, and partake of all the wonders that surround me.[46]

In her conditional cadence Burney echoes, perhaps, the wanderer of Wordsworth's *Tintern Abbey*, who seeks to see the world again through "the shooting lights" of his innocent younger sister's eyes. Or perhaps she reprises the cry of Shakespeare's Miranda—"Oh brave new world"—at the possibility that the regime of island exile magically enforced by her father may be coming to a close. The idea that "a general alliance of all Europe" would allow her to "re-view" her world as a "newly arrived" traveler appears in the letter as an improbable dream of cosmopolitanism, penned from France in British exile.

---

[46]   Ibid., 430.

Chapter 6

"Ever restless waters":
Female Identity and Coastal Space in
Charlotte Smith's *The Young Philosopher*

Zoë Kinsley

It is often said that Charlotte Smith's final novel, *The Young Philosopher* (1798), is concerned with marginal or liminal locations and states of being, an aspect of the work which has been seen to actively facilitate its critique of the values and power structures of mainstream British society. Elizabeth Kraft, for example, observes that

> the significant exploration of borders—liminal places and psychic spaces—within the narrative proffers a critique of the hegemonic values that underwrite the colonizing impulse as it tries to come to terms with the disorientation of new ways of thinking, new centers, new truths.[1]

This employment of the periphery as a physical and conceptual space from which to appraise and criticize the center characterizes what Eleanor Ty has termed the "ex-centric" nature of the novel, which explores "the out of the ordinary as well as the de-centerd or marginalized."[2] However, whilst the novel's concern with marginality has been noted, it has yet to receive sustained critical attention in terms of the use of geography and space in the novel, something which is perhaps surprising, given the significance of coastal settings in the story of Laura Glenmorris. This essay demonstrates that in *The Young Philosopher*, as in the poetry that preceded it, Smith uses the coastline as a powerfully symbolic space for the exploration of the relationship between female identity and patriarchal authority in its various manifestations. It has been argued that during the course of the eighteenth century the British coastline came to be seen as a clear and "settled" border within which national identity could be forged.[3] Smith, however, represents the fringe of Britain in much more ambiguous terms. Absolutely fundamental to

---

[1]   Elizabeth Kraft, "Encyclopedic Libertinism and 1798: Charlotte Smith's *The Young Philosopher*," *Eighteenth-Century Novel* 2 (2002): 246.

[2]   Eleanor Ty, *Unsex'd Revolutionaries: Five Women Novelists of the 1790s* (Toronto: University of Toronto Press, 1993), 143.

[3]   Linda Colley, *Britons: Forging the Nation 1707–1837* (London: Pimlico, 2003), 17–18.

the narrative direction of the novel, the coastal settings of *The Young Philosopher* are spaces of opportunity, where fortunes change and freedom from oppression becomes a possibility. Yet they are also places of sorrow, frustration, violence, and criminality, where the suffering of women is thrown into sharp relief and the sanctuary offered by nature proves only a temporary refuge from the injustices and oppression which are shown to exist, not only at Britain's borders, but also at its heart.

Charlotte Smith grew up and lived most of her life in the South Downs region of southern England; the landscapes of that area permeate her poetry and her novels, and she has been described as a regional poet.[4] Her childhood home of Bignor Park resonates particularly strongly in her writings,[5] and gave her access to the landscape of the southern English coast, which would become a touchstone in her work. From the 1780s, in her *Elegiac Sonnets*, Smith begins to explore the coastline as a liminal and uncertain space characterized by "moody sadness" and "lamentation," in which she finds an echo and a means of expression for her own sense of marginality and fragmentation.[6] In an early poem—"Sonnet XII. Written on the sea shore October 1784," the speaker inhabits a shoreline location which is "damaged, partial, sundered."[7] From that position she aligns herself with the "shipwreck'd" "mariner": both are "out of reach of society, of community, of help, and figured as becoming voiceless."[8] The sonnet culminates in the death of the mariner—the "exhausted sufferer"—in the rising tide, one of many drownings littering Smith's writings, and one which the logic of the poem insists that we also read as the symbolic death of the female speaker. Smith's depiction of the seashore as a threshold representative of the fragile boundary between life and death anticipates subsequent uses of the coast in her poetry, in which the physical periphery of England's land mass becomes emblematic of various states of liminal or threshold experience. The "giddy brink" of the cliff-top in "Sonnet LXX," for example, is the site where Smith explores the boundary between sanity and madness. The speaker of the poem envies the madness of the lunatic which protects him from the extremes of sorrow she has to endure, and the plate accompanying the poem—one of the four illustrations in the *Elegiac Sonnets* which depict coastal/ seashore scenes—draws a direct correspondence between the female speaker and

---

[4]   Carol L. Fry, *Charlotte Smith* (New York: Twayne, 1996), 19.

[5]   See Florence Hilbish, *Charlotte Smith, Poet and Novelist, 1749–1806* (Philadelphia: University of Pennsylvania, 1941), 28–35.

[6]   Charlotte Smith, "Sonnet LXX. On being cautioned against walking on an headland overlooking the sea, because it was frequented by a lunatic," in *The Poems of Charlotte Smith*, ed. Stuart Curran (New York and Oxford: Oxford University Press, 1993), ll. 9, 7.

[7]   Zoë Kinsley, "'In moody sadness, on the giddy brink': Liminality and Home Tour Travel," in *Mapping Liminalities: Thresholds in Cultural and Literary Texts*, ed. Lucy Kay, et al. (Bern: Peter Lang, 2007), 47.

[8]   Charlotte Smith, "Sonnet XII. Written on the sea shore—October 1784," in Curran, *The Poems of Charlotte Smith*, ll. 9, 10; and Kinsley, "'In moody sadness,'" 47.

the supposed madman she observes on the headland in what has been described as a "powerful statement of identity and alliance."[9]

There is not space here to discuss in full the use and significance of coastal locations within Charlotte Smith's poetry, but it is necessary to emphasize that the sympathetic relationship she establishes between coastal landscapes and the female, marginalized self in *The Young Philosopher* is one she has rehearsed many times before. The themes of drowning and madness found in Sonnets XII and LXX will be significant for Smith's later analysis of female identity in *The Young Philosopher*, and the 1790s, which saw an increased politicization of her fiction writing, gave birth to a number of poems which construct the seashore as a zone of ideological struggle. *The Emigrants* (1793), written in response to the violent developments in France, opens "on the Cliffs" "to the Eastward" of Brighton, and considers the position of French emigrants to Britain during the emerging reign of terror.[10] "Sonnet LXXXIII. The sea view," published in the second volume of the seventh edition of *Elegiac Sonnets* in 1797, develops an explicit antiwar theme, with the "pastoral innocence" of "inland" nature being contrasted with the violence of the battle in the channel,[11] which sees the coastal waters "pollute[d]" with "mangled dead."[12] The cliff-top and shoreline locations in the poems are frequently violent environments, yet as is the case in *The Young Philosopher*, the brutality of the coast is represented ambivalently, offering an opportunity for self-knowledge but also for self-obliteration. In her study of Smith's poetry Jacqueline Labbe draws attention to the significance of the "margin" as a physical, textual, and conceptual space which Smith consciously inhabits: "once she has established herself as *willingly* on the margin, as a woman, as a poet, as a figure on a headland, she fearlessly takes on the authorities she should, by cultural expectation, allow to dominate her voice."[13] In *The Young Philosopher*, I argue, Smith similarly explores the periphery as a place for the potential emancipation and empowerment of women, yet ultimately it is the female suffering which takes place at these marginal locations that is most persistent and most culturally entrenched, and which forces the heroines' hopes toward an alternative coastline.

The Young Philosopher, Charlotte Smith's final novel, was first published in 1798. It has been seen as "the most radical [of her novels] in its claims about the role of women within the British nation," and in fact vociferously challenges the possibility of a positive, coherent national identity for women within the country's boundaries, offering instead "the most developed vision of Smith's cosmopolitan

[9] See Jacqueline M. Labbe's interesting discussion of this plate in *Charlotte Smith: Romanticism, Poetry and the Culture of Gender* (Manchester: Manchester University Press, 2003), 42.

[10] Charlotte Smith, *The Emigrants*, in Curran, *The Poems of Charlotte Smith*, 135.

[11] See Fry's analysis of the poem in *Charlotte Smith*, 27.

[12] Charlotte Smith, "Sonnet LXXXIII. The sea view," in Curran, *The Poems of Charlotte Smith*, ll. 12–13.

[13] Labbe, *Charlotte Smith*, 58, original italics.

feminist alternative to British nationalism."[14] Whilst "her previous tales held out the hope for reform and change," *The Young Philosopher* suggests that the injustices and inequality of British society are insurmountable.[15] The liberal Republican sentiments expressed through the behavior and values of her central characters offer up a scathing critique of the patriarchal structures that govern the nation in which they are all seen to struggle.[16] Though the title of the novel professes the hero to be the "Rousseauesque" George Delmont, this is actually overwhelmingly a novel about female experience, and its principal characters, its heroines, are Laura Glenmorris and her daughter Medora—both of whom are "deracinated bi-nationals," outsiders "whose lack of national identity … is also their best chance for liberty."[17] In "parallel tales of virtue and distress," this mother and daughter pair both suffer violence, exploitation, and oppression, and their stories paint a bleak picture of the vulnerability and powerlessness experienced by women in British society in the late eighteenth century.[18]

The novel opens by directing the reader's thoughts to the British seashore. The Winslows have spent "part of the Autumn at a public place of great resort, about sixty miles from London." This resort is Brighton (then Brighthelmstone), for which Smith had a fondness,[19] but which she nevertheless associates here with female behavior that is trivial and worthy of satirization. Whilst the family travels to the seaside for the treatment of Mrs. Winslow's "nerves," it is implied that the improvement of her condition has little to do with the "marine breezes." Instead, her recovery is attributed to her regular attendance at card parties and to the fact that she has "added five titled friends to her visiting list."[20] Mrs. Winslow is the first of many society women who are depicted within the novel as superficial and self-

---

[14]   Leanne Maunu, "Home is Where the Heart Is: National Identity and Expatriation in Charlotte Smith's *The Young Philosopher*," *European Romantic Review* 15, no. 1 (March 2004): 51; and Adriana Craciun, "Citizens of the World: Émigrés, Romantic Cosmopolitanism, and Charlotte Smith," *Nineteenth-Century Contexts* 29, no. 2–3 (June/September 2007): 176.

[15]   Maunu, "Home is Where the Heart Is," 56.

[16]   For a discussion of the influence of Godwinian, Jacobin politics in *The Young Philosopher*, see A. A. Markley, "Charlotte Smith, the Godwin Circle, and the Proliferation of Speakers in *The Young Philosopher*," in *Charlotte Smith in British Romanticism*, ed. Jacqueline Labbe (London: Pickering and Chatto, 2008), 87–99.

[17]   Elizabeth Kraft, Introduction to Charlotte Smith, *The Young Philosopher*, ed. Elizabeth Kraft (Lexington: University Press of Kentucky, 1999), xxiv; and Craciun, "Citizens of the World," 178.

[18]   Craciun, "Citizens of the World," 178.

[19]   Fry, *Charlotte Smith*, 8.

[20]   Charlotte Smith, *The Young Philosopher*, ed. Elizabeth Kraft, (Lexington: University Press of Kentucky, 1999) 1:7. By the last decade of the eighteenth century, English seaside resorts were serving a dual purpose, catering for "seekers after pleasure, recreation, novelty, as well as votaries of health and rest." John K. Walton, *The English Seaside Resort: A Social History 1750–1914* (Leicester: Leicester University Press, 1983), 156.

serving, whose values and principles are repeatedly criticized and found wanting, providing a stark contrast to the positive maternity and enlightened liberality of Laura Glenmorris. Smith's symbolic use of coastal space alerts us to the difference between these types of women. Mrs. Winslow is attracted to the coast merely because of the society she can mix with there, and we are left with no doubt that her later seaside excursions constitute similar quests for pleasure and social improvement.[21] Laura, on the other hand, is always associated with the coast as a carefully delineated natural environment, the raw energy and turbulence of which echoes her own emotional and psychological state. Through Laura's relationship to the coastal landscape, Smith explores the social and ideological questions concerning women's relationships to patriarchal authority which pervade all of her writings.

The second volume of *The Young Philosopher* is devoted to Laura's story of her youth and the years spent in Britain before her emigration to America with Glenmorris. It traces her movement from the northwest coast of England to the northeast coast of Scotland and details the way in which that journey between shorelines sees one form of violence and oppression being exchanged for another. Sandthwaite, the Lancashire estate to which Laura is removed prior to her elopement with Glenmorris, is the first of her many prisons within the narrative: historically serving as a "fortress," it is a place of confinement and surveillance. Its position on the Lancashire coast is significant in physical and conceptual terms. By removing her to a remote location on the nation's periphery, Laura's parents isolate her from the urban, civilized culture which her newly married sister enjoys, and in doing so underscore her inferior status within the family hierarchy. Her consignment to Sandthwaite, formerly the "principal seat" of her family and now the "repository" for "the rubbish left from generation to generation," associates her with the family's past and its detritus, in contrast to her sister, who embodies their parents' hopes for the family's future social and economic improvement. Significantly, the oppression of Laura within this locale is not presented in straightforward terms as the result of a repressive patriarchal authority; rather, it is the consequence of her mother's "ascendancy" over her increasingly infirm and submissive husband, what Mark K. Fulk has termed "patriarchy cross-dressed."[22] Movement to the nation's margin facilitates female usurpation of male authority, but it is not a role reversal that Smith celebrates: rather, she shows Lady Mary assimilating abhorrent qualities of patriarchy—"violence and arrogance"—that are characteristic of the villains in her fiction.[23] Early on in the novel, removal to the coast enables the questioning of gender roles and upsets the balance of power between men and women, but there is no sense as yet that Smith is working

---

[21] Smith, *The Young Philosopher*, 3:231, 4:267.

[22] Smith, *The Young Philosopher*, 2:91, 2:93; Mark K. Fulk, "Mismanaging Mothers: Matriarchy and Romantic Education in Charlotte Smith's *The Young Philosopher*," *Women's Writing* 16, no. 1 (May 2009): 96.

[23] Smith, *The Young Philosopher*, 2:91–92.

toward a positive vision of transformation here. Instead, the attainment of power by one woman merely leads to the withdrawal of it from another, a maneuver made all the more shocking by the betrayal of maternal instinct that such behavior demonstrates.

The coastal landscape surrounding Sandthwaite is first described as Laura views it through the "gothic windows" of the house, an apt framing device which sets the tenor for the scenes of wildness and suffering that are to follow:

> The country it stood in was wild and gloomy, and from its gothic windows there was a view of the Irish Channel, and an immense extent of sand, covered only at times by the tide, which took off the bold grandeur of a sea view, and left only ideas of sterility, danger, and desolation, in its place.[24]

These initial impressions of the seashore adjacent to Sandthwaite are characterized by distance and separation from the landscape being described. As a mere observer of nature Laura associates it with barrenness and peril. When that separation between subject and object is broken down, however, and distance gives way to increased proximity, these "ideas" about the coastline are replaced by a much more complex, and in many ways more positive, experience of place.

One evening, more than a month into her residence at Sandthwaite, Laura's mother torments her with the "news" that Glenmorris has ruined himself by "gaming." Laura's response is to escape into the garden, in order to "breathe freer, for I felt choked." The narration of her withdrawal from the suffocating atmosphere of the house into the open air invokes a poetic, sensitively detailed account of her coastal surroundings:

> It was a mild evening—the wind blowing from the sea, brought with it the hollow murmur of the waves with the rising tide; they broke shallow and ripling on the broad bed of sand, on which, where it was not dry, and on the surf as it whitened beyond, the trembling lustre of an early moon was reflected.—The very circumstance of being alone, and at liberty for a few moments, was a species of enjoyment, and I soon recovered recollection enough to consider, that what Lady Mary had said was probably unfounded ... .[25]

The murmuring of the waves will come to echo throughout the novel, providing a rhythmic continuity and sense of reassurance for Laura, even at times of deep despair. And the expanse of sand that she had earlier described as sterile now becomes a site of awakening: the "ripling" and "whiten[ing]" of the waves suggest continuity, and a fragile becoming that climaxes in the "trembling lustre of an early moon," which can be seen to symbolize the tentative arousal of Laura's long-oppressed sense of self. That symbolic connection between Laura and the moon—

---

[24] Ibid., 2:91.
[25] Ibid., 2:95–96.

which has a long mythological association with both water and femininity[26]—is continued in the next paragraph, where its light playing upon the wings of sea birds evokes a hopefulness previously absent in Laura's story:

> On reaching its termination towards a sort of salt marsh, I stopped a moment to observe some sea birds, whose white wings catching the moon beams, seemed like transient meteors floating from the sea, which was now covering the sand, where at low water they sought their food. Every thing was so still that I could hear the whispering of their wings, when my attention was suddenly and forcibly arrested by a low yet strong voice, which, issuing from beneath the place where I stood, sang an air … .[27]

The moonlit flight of the birds, which lifts them above the sand where they usually feed, can be read as a metaphor for Laura's desire to transcend her own quotidian existence, a desire which is once again depicted as precious yet frail through its encapsulation in the image of a shooting star.

Much has been said of Smith's interest in nature and of her belief in the healing and restorative potential of engagement with the natural world.[28] Laura's movement into the outside facilitates a heightened sensory engagement with her surroundings, which is depicted in terms of pure and unmediated communion with nature. There is a fleeting moment in the passage where everything surrounding Laura falls away and her existence becomes concentrated in the quiet, mysterious dialogue between herself and the sea birds: "Every thing was so still that I could hear the whispering of their wings." This moment, like the "transient meteors" on which her hopes are carried, is ephemeral, however, and she is wrenched away from that joyous stillness by the sound of Glenmorris singing, her reaction to which, in the context of the preceding narrative, is ambiguous. Whilst Glenmorris's arrival offers the physical fulfilment of Laura's hopes to escape, his appearance also represents the male invasion of female space, and its effect is described in terms of a violent severing of the emotional connection between Laura and her environment.

Glenmorris's appearance instigates another stage in Laura's movement and absorption into the coastal landscape. Whereas when alone, Laura had watched and listened to her natural surroundings from within the confines of the gardens at Sandthwaite, Glenmorris urges her over the threshold of her family estate and

---

[26] See Gilbert Durand, *The Anthropological Structures of the Imaginary*, trans. Margaret Sankey and Judith Hatten (Brisbane: Boombana Publications, 1999), 99.

[27] Smith, *The Young Philosopher*, 2:95–96.

[28] See, for example, Lorraine Fletcher, *Charlotte Smith: A Critical Biography* (Basingstoke: Macmillan, 1998), chap. 5. Laura herself says slightly later in the novel: "Amidst the many sad hours I have passed, I have never failed to feel my spirits soothed by the contemplation of vegetable nature, and I have often thought that, wherever I could gaze on the clouds above, and see the earth below me clothed with grass and flowers, I could find some, though a melancholy, pleasure in existence." Smith, *The Young Philosopher*, 2:128.

onto the sands themselves. The shore becomes Glenmorris's confessional, where he owns up to his dissipations, acknowledges that their estrangement has tempted him to suicide, and proposes that they turn their backs upon the false refinement of modern society and escape to the "Eden" of his native Scotland.[29] Two nights later the sands become the couple's escape route as they flee Sandthwaite with the intention of reaching Glenmorris's family home in Scotland. Whilst the seashore gives the lovers "shelter" for their clandestine meetings, their transition from observers of the seashore to participants on it sees the strand become a place of ambivalent promise, offering the potential of freedom from oppression whilst simultaneously threatening danger and annihilation. The pair almost drowns in the fast approaching waters of the sea tides, but are rescued by a local smuggler when all seems lost. Laura's description of this incident is haunted by images of death, yet by narrating it through the perspective of Glenmorris she emphasizes his terror rather than her own, and foregrounds a form of male inaction that becomes characteristic of the men in the novel.

The "heroes are poor rescuers" in *The Young Philosopher*, a fact that Lorraine Fletcher has argued "undercut[s] received notions of gender and hierarchy."[30] The near-drowning of Laura and Glenmorris is a good example of this. Pursued by the incoming tide approaching more rapidly than he had "calculated," Glenmorris becomes "terrified" and is debilitated by the terrible thoughts which are the product of his "ardent and rapid imagination." He *imagines* Laura's death as she "perish[es] among the rising waves," and *imagines* his own passivity in the instance of her death: "unable to save me he was to stand an helpless spectator." He goes on to murmur that his response to the loss of Laura would be suicide: "I can always, however, escape the misery of surviving her." Overcome by such thoughts, he ceases to move, stopping to watch the water approach "with an eye of despair": imagined inaction has resulted in real inertia.[31] The way in which Smith relates the increasing debilitation of Glenmorris via the narrative voice of Laura means that he lacks agency as the speaker of his own intellectual and emotional responses, just as he is presented as physically inactive in the face of the approaching crisis. He is distinctly feminized within the vocabulary of this passage by being repeatedly characterized as excessively imaginative and emotional, generally perceived to be female traits in this period.

In contrast to Glenmorris, the smuggler who saves the couple is a man of action. He is reluctant to interrupt his journey across the sands, and, unlike Glenmorris, "has no mind to be drowned." Like many of Smith's characters, he is a figure who exists both physically and ideologically at the margins of society, and his inclusion here underscores the northeastern English coastal landscape as a space of uncertain authority. His identity is a dual one which locates him both inside and outside of the moral and political structures of mainstream society, as

---

29   Smith, *The Young Philosopher*, 2:96–98.

30   Fletcher, *Charlotte Smith*, 282–83.

31   Smith, *The Young Philosopher*, 2:102.

he works to both protect and undermine the values of the community he lives on the edge of. "Employed during the day in conducting passengers across these dangerous sands," he works at night "in conveying contraband goods inland from the coast opposite Ireland."[32] Glenmorris is roused into action by the arrival of the anonymous smuggler and attempts to regain control of Laura's safety by asserting authority over the local man, whose compliance is ultimately bought. Whilst Glenmorris's behavior towards the smuggler/guide is based on the presumption of social and economic superiority, the reader is aware that Laura and Glenmorris actually have much in common with their rescuer: like him they have become socially marginal, and have chosen a life that disturbs conventional assumptions regarding the value of the legal, political, and economic hierarchy of supposedly polite and progressive British society.

Despite the Lancashire seashore being used to explore the melancholy, fatalistic character of Glenmorris, the coastline is primarily used as a location through which Smith considers the powerlessness of women in contemporary Britain.[33] The coastline is a place reserved for the detailed exploration of a form of suffering that is marked as peculiarly feminine. Having successfully fled confinement in Lancashire, Laura and Glenmorris travel northwest, getting married en route, to Sutherland in the Highlands of Scotland. The paternal house of Glenmorris, the final destination of their journey, is, like Laura's parents' estate in Lancashire, isolated and prison-like: "it was a stone fortress, built on an almost perpendicular rock, its base beaten by the waves of the German ocean."[34] Whilst offering her temporary sanctuary and glimpses of freedom, the Scottish shore and its caves nevertheless constitute a no man's land where Laura finds herself isolated and alone, the threat of pursuance by male tyranny bearing down on her from one side, destruction by the sea and the elements facing her on the other.

Laura enjoys a brief period of contentment with Glenmorris in their Scottish home as she awaits the birth of their first baby, yet even that felicity is troubled by apprehensions regarding the future: "it seemed as if our happiness was too great to admit of permanence."[35] Those misgivings prove to be well founded when they are attacked by pirates and Glenmorris is abducted, leaving Laura only able to speculate about whether he is dead or alive. Her torment continues when the elderly Lady Kilbrodie, Glenmorris's nearest relation, forcibly removes Laura to the abbey of Kilbrodie, where she becomes the object of the unwelcome and violent advances of the laird. Having lost her baby son at only three days old, and facing the threat of physical and sexual assault by the tyrant Kilbrodie, Laura flees from the abbey and hides in coastal caves, which she perceives as places of death, but which actually prove to be spaces of sanctuary, revival, and salvation.

---

[32] Ibid., 2:103.
[33] See Ty, *Unsex'd Revolutionaries*, 148.
[34] Smith, *The Young Philosopher*, 2:104.
[35] Ibid., 2:105.

As was the case in Lancashire, it is the seashore that offers Laura a means of escape. Her narration suggests that she is somehow subconsciously drawn to that location—"I soon found myself on the borders of the sea"—and in following in the footsteps of the "fishermen and fowlers" who have worn a path through a "chasm" in the cliffs onto the seashore, she is once more aligned with the local community who live and work on the coast. Her initial description of the Scottish beach figures it as "inhospitable" and oppressive, the cliffs towering over and bearing down upon her. The caves "eaten into" the rock by the "ever restless waters" of the sea are perceived as places of "concealment" at this point in the narrative, but they are otherwise figured as spaces for the termination, rather than the sustainment of life. Laura determines to die in one of these coastal caverns, a fate she repeatedly insists is preferable to the violence threatened by Kilbrodie:

> Here I was determined to remain and perish—for such a death, cruel and lingering as it must be, was far preferable in my opinion to being exposed, even for another moment, to the atrocious insults of Kilbrodie.[36]

Her acquiescence to passive suicide by either "hunger" or the "rising waves" echoes the response of Glenmorris to her own (imagined) death on the Lancashire coast, and anticipates the drowning of Elizabeth Lisburne later in the novel. This complex web of imagined, intended, and actual coastal deaths establishes the seashore as a place where lives are lost, yet also emphasizes that death can in itself be a form of escape from worldly suffering, and more specifically patriarchal tyranny. As Lorraine Fletcher has suggested, the recurring motif of drowning within Smith's writing could be seen as "an image of the suffocation of biology, perhaps a frequent dream or escape fantasy."[37]

Thematically, these recurring images of death in *The Young Philosopher* also reach out beyond Smith's own corpus, to the works of other writers. She quotes from Thomas Warton's "The Suicide" (1789) in order to give expression to her heroine's despair,[38] and her novel can in many ways be seen as an alternative, female version of his poem's themes. By ventriloquizing the melancholy persona of Warton's verse through her own characters, Smith forms both Laura and Elizabeth Lisburne in the mold of the archetypal suicidal "wretch" popularized in his poem. Yet she also does more than that, for her reference to "The Suicide" implicitly associates suicidal melancholy with poetic creativity: in Warton's poem the suicide is that of a poet, whose sensibility, his "feeling too refin'd," made him peculiarly susceptible to the "misery" and "horrors" conjured by his "fancy."[39] Smith draws attention to her own fragile emotional and psychological health through this intertextual reference, and alerts us to the suffering that accompanies poetic composition; in

---

[36]   Ibid., 2:119.

[37]   Fletcher, *Charlotte Smith*, 334.

[38]   Smith, *The Young Philosopher*, 2:121–22.

[39]   Thomas Warton, "The Suicide," in *The Poems on Various Subjects, of Thomas Warton* (London, 1791), 69–72.

doing so she uses Warton as a connecting thread which binds her to Laura. This maneuver forms part of a sustained and complex web of associations within the novel, which imprint Smith's identity onto that of Laura by triangulating Smith and Laura with the speaker of the *Sonnets*. It is the coastal setting which enables Smith to establish the relationship between this prose work and her earlier poetry, the shoreline location of Laura's suffering echoing the positioning of the speaker within numerous of Smith's poems and their accompanying illustrations, most explicitly that entitled "On Some Rude Fragment of the Rocky Shore."[40] By replacing the "tumbling flood" of Warton's "brook" with the "ever restless waters" of the "inhospitable coast,"[41] Smith rejects the pastoral in favor of the sublime, depicting the context in which women's suffering takes place as more dangerous and violent than the world of "The Suicide."

Fulk interprets Laura and Glenmorris's flight to the seashore as an encounter with an alternative manifestation of maternal authority after rejection by Laura's mother.[42] That Smith considered the British coastline as a particularly appropriate setting for the exploration of female identity, including her clearly ambiguous feelings regarding the authority of mothers over their children, chimes with modern assumptions about the "incontrovertible femininity of water" and the proposition that, by the latter half of the eighteenth century, "the beach was emerging clearly as the site of extended maternity."[43] Whilst Laura initially articulates the caves on the Sutherland coast as a place to die, her narrative goes on to challenge that bleak representation. Hiding in these recesses of the cliffs, she is sheltered and rejuvenated. Selecting what appeared "the most secure of these caverns," the hiding place she finds is obscure and desolate, yet it provides for her needs: the stones "conceal" her and provide her with a "pillow"; "it happened that the night was unusually mild and still"; and she finds her resting place "perfectly dry." Most important, this environment works to calm her—"the low still sound of the untroubled waves ... murmur[s]" to her once again as it had done in Lancashire—and enables her to grieve for her lost child:

> As my dread of pursuit became fainter, my spirits, subdued by fear and fatigue, lost something of the sullen desperation that I had at first felt—I melted into tears, and tears I had of late been so frequently unable to shed, that I felt my head and heart greatly relieved by them. ... By insensible degrees the wild tumult of my spirits subsided, and I fell into a slumber, confused and broken indeed, but still such as composed and refreshed me, when before day-break the succeeding

---

[40] For discussion of this relationship between *The Young Philosopher* and the *Sonnets*, particularly the way in which Smith "superimpose[s] her own image on the image of the despairing Laura," see Fletcher, *Charlotte Smith*, 281–82.

[41] Warton, "The Suicide," 69–70; Smith, *The Young Philosopher*, 2:119.

[42] Fulk, "Mismanaging Mothers," 101.

[43] Durand, *Anthropological Structures*, 99; also Alain Corbin, *The Lure of the Sea: The Discovery of the Seaside in the Western World 1750–1840*, trans. Jocelyn Phelps (London: Penguin, 1995), 171.

morning I was awakened from it by the cries of gannets, petrels, gulls and sea snipes without, as well as by the gurgling murmurs of the wild pigeons within my cave.[44]

Laura traces her own emotional and psychological cleansing in this passage, and that regeneration is facilitated by the natural environment of the cave which, significantly, is designated her own. In his seminal study of the meaning and representation of the seaside in Western thought, Alain Corbin has suggested that the desire to inhabit the insular spaces of the coastline—spaces which "act as substitutes for the maternal womb"—reflect "the growing quest for privacy within the social body": "the fascination exerted by the creek and the cave corresponds to the longing for a house, a room, a corner of one's own."[45] This is the first space within the novel which Laura has really been able to describe as hers, and her assertion of ownership over it marks a significant point in the narrative. Whilst it may superficially resemble other spaces of confinement in the novel, within her parents' home at Sandthwaite and the abbey of Kilbrodie, it differs from them because whilst those other abodes symbolized the oppressive authority that others wielded over her, the cave enables the discovery of her own agency. The recovery of her strength and her spirits is marked by the dawn of a new day and the recovery of her alertness to the communications of the natural world. As has been said of Smith's description of the hermit's cell in which Laura hides after being rescued by Glenmorris's clansmen: "the point she wants to emphasise is clear: nature alone offers protection to Laura."[46]

Laura's coastal experiences as a young woman are paralleled elsewhere in the novel, forming part of the project of "cross-referencing" which "speaks to a belief in the integration of all things."[47] As has already been mentioned, Laura's contemplations on death and suicide in many ways anticipate the fate of Elizabeth Lisburne, narrated in volume three. Elizabeth, a young woman of uncertain identity, waits at the harbor of Milford Haven in South West Wales for news from her lover. Given sanctuary by a fisherman and his wife, she roams the coastline nightly, but her Hillario never returns and she commits suicide in the coastal waters. Her story serves to remind us that Laura's own fortunes could easily have been very different, and she becomes symbolic of the extreme isolation and suffering experienced by vulnerable women in this highly criticized British society. She is denied interment in the local churchyard, so the fisherman and his wife bury her beneath the cliff-top in a "remote and lonely grave." The inclusion of the story of Elizabeth in some ways appears to be a heavy-handed narrative contrivance through which to emphasize Smith's key concerns about female suffering, and to give Delmont the opportunity to engage with and "philosophize" on the subject.

---

[44]   Smith, *The Young Philosopher*, 2:120.

[45]   Corbin, *Lure of the Sea*, 180. Corbin points to the emerging perception of the "correspondence" "between the cycle of the tides and the menstrual cycle," 169.

[46]   Fletcher, *Charlotte Smith*, 269.

[47]   Kraft, "Encyclopedic Libertinism," 244.

On closer inspection, however, the brief digression on her distress enables Smith to develop "parallel scenes and thematic resonances" which function on a number of different levels. The setting of Elizabeth's story, the nature of her death, and the site of her burial "recall Laura Glenmorris's cavern exile by the sea in Scotland, her despair at the loss of her husband, [and] the surreptitious burial of her dead infant."[48] Furthermore, the description of her plight echoes through the narration of the older Laura's anguished mourning for the loss of Medora on the cliff-tops of Rottendean, near Brighton. Thought by locals to be "disordered in her mind" and likely to "do herself a mischief," the "poor mourner's" position "on an heap of the fallen cliff," "where other fragments beetled fearfully overhead," recalls the grave of Elizabeth, overhung by "beetling rocks, barren, cold, [and] sullen."[49] In addition to these multiple resonances between the distresses of Elizabeth and those of Laura, Elizabeth also becomes metonymic for a number of other suffering women within the work. It is hinted at, but nowhere explicitly stated, that Elizabeth was pregnant by the lover who has forsaken her;[50] she therefore becomes emblematic of the abandoned and fallen women we encounter elsewhere in *The Young Philosopher*, particularly those who are victims of the brutality and abuses of Sir Harry Richmond. And, finally, Elizabeth's status as a poet aligns her with Charlotte Smith herself, who, through her *Sonnets* and their prefaces, frequently figures herself at the margins of society.

The turbulent fortunes and misfortunes of Laura and Elizabeth contrast markedly with Delmont's coastal experience, stranded at Milford Haven in Wales awaiting good weather and passage to Ireland. Frustrated and melancholy, he is himself a character whose values and actions have isolated him from mainstream society, yet the assertion that he is "marginalized like a woman, placed literally and figuratively outside the world of the father" becomes problematic when close attention is given to his status within the narrative.[51] Delmont finds Elizabeth's story suited to his own state of despondency, separated from Medora and compelled to inaction whilst stranded at the Welsh harbor: "I was disposed to indulge the melancholy thoughts this incident had given rise to."[52] However, whilst he pines for Medora and is troubled by the difficult financial circumstances into which he has been thrown by the reckless and selfish behavior of his brother Adolphus, those problems are a far remove from Elizabeth's desperate situation, caused by her unmarried pregnancy, which has driven her to a life of anonymous exile at the brink of society, and from which suicide offers the only form of escape. Despite appearing genuinely moved by the tragedy of Elizabeth, Delmont nevertheless treats her as a curiosity and violates her hard-sought privacy by reading her poetry and gazing upon her grave. By purchasing her books and papers from the

---

[48]   Ibid., 265.

[49]   Smith, *The Young Philosopher*, 4:338, 3:183.

[50]   Fletcher suggests that Elizabeth waits for a month at Milford Haven in order to confirm her pregnancy. Fletcher, *Charlotte Smith*, 334.

[51]   Ty, *Unsex'd Revolutionaries*, 144.

[52]   Smith, *The Young Philosopher*, 3:183.

fisherman he achieves ownership over what little is known of her identity in an act of patriarchal assertion which reminds us how readily women are commodified in this society.[53] Delmont's growing fascination with the tragic fate of Elizabeth offers him a detached, vicarious experience of extreme emotional and psychological suffering upon which he can "philosophise," but from which his gender renders him fundamentally remote.

There is, of course, another facet to the parallels of female experience explored within Smith's final novel. The social injustices and emotional and psychological traumas experienced by Laura are lived again by her daughter Medora in a "twice-told tale" which emphasizes suffering, exploitation, and marginalization as a continuum of female experience which connects one generation to another.[54] Medora is abducted from a hotel in London, where her mother has reluctantly left her "beloved girl" alone whilst she frantically visits one lawyer after another in the hope of securing funds to pay their mounting debts.[55] Her kidnapper is Darnell, the brother of Brownjohn, an attorney with whom Laura is forced to deal, and their intention is to force Medora into marriage with Darnell in order to gain access to the fortune which they know to be rightfully hers. As Ty has pointed out, therefore, "both Medora and her mother are imprisoned, not for themselves as subjects, but for the commodities or objects they will produce: a fortune in Medora's case; an heir in Laura's case."[56] Darnell takes Medora as far north as Yorkshire, and as was the case in Laura's story of her youth, the motif of journeying serves to underscore the extreme nature of the suffering she undergoes. The sense of dislocation and disorientation both women experience is heightened by their enforced travels, which dramatize the physical, emotional, and psychological endurance that are fundamental elements of Smith's depiction of the female self. It is Medora's determined fortitude, along with her intelligent, quick thinking, which enable her to escape her captor. As she tells the story of her abduction to Delmont in the final volume of the novel, she repeatedly emphasizes the fact that it is her mother, who was similarly made a "prisoner" in her youth, who taught her by her own example that enlightened, virtuous stoicism—"that pure morality"—is the only means available to women struggling to survive the tyrannies of a society which continues to repress and marginalize them.[57]

It is Smith's use of topography and space that provides the key to the significance of this repetitive cycle of female oppression. Laura, the mother, experiences persecution and abuse in remote, isolated coastal locations at the periphery of the British Isles. The association with England's violent, feudal past, established through the description of the "fortress" at Sandthwaite, along with the clan traditions of Highland Scotland illustrated through the scenes set in Sutherland, situate Laura's trials within a world of primitivism and barbarity

53   Ibid.
54   Ty, *Unsex'd Revolutionaries*, 143.
55   Smith, *The Young Philosopher*, 3:190.
56   Ty, *Unsex'd Revolutionaries*, 151.
57   Smith, *The Young Philosopher*, 4:306, 4:314.

that could be easily dismissed as characteristic of the nation's Gothic past rather than its enlightened present. However, whilst Laura suffers at the margins of the nation, her daughter, Medora, endures similar hardship at its center, being abducted in London, where she and her mother have repeatedly endured offenses caused by "cold and repulsive" legal men and upper-class women concerned only with self-aggrandizement.[58] This shift in geography and topography illustrates that the barbarity of Britain's margins has equivalence, and is still rife, in the supposedly progressive society of the English metropolis. In fact, by shifting the locus of female pain from the margin to the center, Smith suggests that the oppression of women has become increasingly widespread during the decades that separate the episodes related in *The Young Philosopher*. Laura's experience of physical and sexual violence, because it is enacted in remote locations and enabled by her isolation and solitude, renders it personal and particularized. Medora's story, in contrast, draws attention to the fact that she is not alone in her distress; rather, she is just one of many voiceless women, including Elizabeth Lisburne and the numerous victims of Sir Harry, who fall prey to the abuses perpetrated by those with power.

Charlotte Smith was writing in a period which saw increasing popular interest in the British coastline and the emergence of a dual tradition of practice and representation in relation to it. Whilst British seaside resorts were being quickly developed as social spaces and becoming important centers for both valetudinary and leisure activities, at the same time, within literature and the arts, the seashore was becoming a powerfully symbolic space for a form of Romantic self-discovery that depended on solitude and a positive sense of marginality. Smith's novel rejects the emergent resort culture in favor of the Romantic tradition, which explores the coast as a margin that might offer sanctuary from the centripetal social and political forces which dominate elsewhere in the nation. Indeed, Smith's persistent revisiting of the British coastline in her literary works seems an acknowledgment of the transgressive potential of this as both a topographic and conceptual space which women can inhabit, yet the sustained suffering of the female characters elides any firm suggestion that female transformation and empowerment can be achieved here or elsewhere in the British nation. The matrix of female identity which Smith develops through her use of the strand in *The Young Philosopher*, which connects Laura and Elizabeth Lisburne to the speakers of the earlier *Sonnets*, reinforces her critique of contemporary society by emphasizing the marginalization and oppression of women as universalizing aspects of female experience in Britain at this time, which, lamentably, extend from the center of the country to its very edges. It is in the final pages of *The Young Philosopher* that the British coast holds most promise, as a point of embarkation for a journey—alluded to rather than narrated—to America, where democratic principles, social justice, and a more natural state of life offer hope for the long-suffering female characters who might finally find happiness on that other shore.

---

[58] Whilst Medora's abductor takes her north as far as Yorkshire, it is London where all of her suffering originates.

Chapter 7
Writing from the Road:
Space and the Spectacle of Hortense Mancini, Duchess of Mazarin

Courtney Beggs

Hortense Mancini, Duchess of Mazarin (1646–1699) is acknowledged as the first woman in France to publish a memoir in her lifetime.[1] Born in Italy, educated in France, and a prominent figure in the Restoration court of Charles II, Mancini lived much of her life in transit from one house, convent, city, court, or country to another, usually in an attempt to escape her fanatically religious husband. She was a fascinating figure then and now, and the spectacle she created in print and in life illuminates multiple connections between gender and space in early modern women's lives and writing. This essay will explore the ways in which Mancini used her writing to manipulate physical, cultural, political, and literary spaces to inscribe a "safe" space for herself in the English public's imagination.

While most scholarly work on Mancini is primarily concerned with her memoirs, this essay examines the second half of her life, roughly 1675–1699. Mancini spent this time in England and the life she created there was one that allowed her the pleasure of sociable and esteemed company, modest financial security, a somewhat protected physical separation from her husband, and a prominent place in England's political and cultural imagination. Her escape from her husband in France and the legal battles that followed were well known throughout Europe and England, and the reputation she garnered as a result was infamous. Through privately circulated court lampoons and satires, popular ballads, and published court documents, readers learned of her penchant for cross-dressing and the tricks she and her girlfriend played on nuns in the convents where they sought refuge. The published accounts often read like racy novels, and her husband's writings and confiscated letters from family members, friends, and the occasional rumored lover painted a picture of Mancini as a transgressive woman who was unfaithful to her husband, stubborn with family members who tried to advise her, and unwilling to compromise her freedom. Despite her husband's efforts to prevent her from exercising it, she fervently believed in her right to some sort of pleasurable existence. With the law rarely on her side and few friends or family she could

---

[1]   Margaret of Valois (1553–1615) also recorded a memoir, but hers was not published until after her death.

trust, how then did Hortense Mancini manage to establish one of the most famous intellectual and literary salons of the Restoration?

Using the 1680 poem "The Dutchess of Mazarines Farewel to England," as well as other contemporary writings about Mancini, I will argue that she created a literal and metaphorical space for herself in the Restoration court by constructing a poetic spectacle of the people, places, and events by which she was surrounded. As I will show, the poem may have been key in securing her continued time and support in England. Playing on both her gender and the sense of herself as a victim of a social system that privileges "honor" and thus robs her of freedom and pleasure, she works to ensure a sympathetic response from her English readers. Additionally, she blurs the generic boundaries between poetry and stage by using the last few lines as a goodbye to the theater, where she sees herself being acted "if evil Fortune still pursue[s]." Using her writing as a form of performance, Hortense Mancini was well aware of all the eyes that were upon her. To preserve her freedom of mobility and a space of pleasure for herself in England, she crossed national, legal, and social boundaries. This essay investigates the literary and cultural marks she left while writing from the road.

Born to the Italian aristocrat Lorenzo Mancini and Cardinal Mazarin's sister, Girolama Mazzarini, Mancini was the favorite niece of her wealthy and influential uncle. She received her first marriage proposal when she was just 12 years old. Encouraged by his first cousin, Louis XIV, Charles II proposed to Mancini, but his offer was declined by the cardinal, who would not see his favorite niece married off to an exiled and penniless king. Anticipating the way she would frame her life in later writing, Mancini describes how "Fortune ... started off by pretending to want to make me a queen."[2] Two subsequent marriage arrangements (one with Charles Emmanuel II, Duke of Savoy, and another with the Duke of Lorraine) also failed over negotiations for property.

Unsurprisingly, Mancini had no involvement in any of the marriage discussions, nor did she play a role in the negotiations for her only marriage, which took place in March 1661. The 15-year old Mancini married Armand-Charles de la Porte, who inherited Cardinal Mazarin's fortune and was granted the title of Duc Mazarin. It was a disastrous match from the beginning. Mancini was popular, beautiful, young, and intelligent. Her husband, on the other hand, was known for his religious fanaticism and jealous nature. His deceptive nature and suspicions about anyone who spent time with Mancini prompted him continually to move his wife from place to place throughout Europe. Even the ritual space of childbirth was disrupted for Mancini on account of the duc's obsessive drive to

---

[2]   Hortense Mancini, *Memoirs*, in *Hortense Mancini and Marie Mancini: Memoirs*, ed. Sarah Nelson (Chicago: University of Chicago Press, 2008), 31. Only months later, Charles would be called back to court, and the cardinal quickly recanted his refusal. Though he offered the king a dowry of five million livres, Charles refused.

control all access to and movement of his wife.[3] Eventually separated from her own brothers and sisters as well as the duc's family, at times confined to convents or private quarters in her own home, Mancini carefully records in her *Memoirs* the impossibility of finding any sense of peace or pleasure within the domestic sphere as it is traditionally defined.

Using three primary categories of space—domestic, court, and public—to frame my analysis, I hope to contribute not only to the scholarship that exists on such an important figure in women's literary and material history, but also to current discussions of space in early modern England. The latter is of utmost importance because, as Sara Mendelson and Patricia Crawford explain, "From their own viewpoint, women enacted a mapping of space that was different from the normative strictures decreed by men."[4] This is especially so in the case of Hortense Mancini, who found herself unable to map the domestic space normally afforded to women of her station. Not only did her husband prohibit any form of female authority in the household, but Mancini's class status did not require her to work in ways similar to those women of the middling sort, who often managed to forge female communities that allowed them the pleasures associated with sociability.[5] In escaping her husband's tyrannical control over her physical person and domestic surroundings, the duchess took the calculated risk of becoming a public spectacle, something she would later find a difficult but successful tactic.

As the speaker of "The Dutchess of Mazarines Farewel to England," Mancini invokes the space of the Restoration court, an arena that was inherently under the public gaze and which inevitably made the duchess a political and literary target. During her time as the king's favorite mistress, the court was a space of physical and sexual pleasure for the duchess. However, the space of the court was in no way a refuge from the confinement she faced in her own home with the duc; it merely came with a different set of limitations and expectations for those who wished to be regular members.[6]

---

[3]   She recounts in her *Memoirs* that she was forced to travel even when she was near childbirth (39).

[4]   Sara Mendelson and Patricia Crawford, *Women in Early Modern England, 1550–1720* (Oxford: Clarendon Press, 1998), 205.

[5]   I am using Margaret Hunt's definition of the middling sort as a reference to women who were part of families that were "beneath the gentry but above the level of the laboring classes." Margaret Hunt, *The Middling Sort: Commerce, Gender, and the Family in England, 1680–1780* (Berkeley: University of California Press, 1996), 15. It should be noted, however, that women in the laboring classes would also have the capacity to exercise control of the domestic space, as the survival of the family often depended upon both men and women working to sustain a living.

[6]   In *The Age of Conversation* (New York: New York Review of Books, 2005), Benedetta Craveri cites Louis XIV's understanding of the court as public spectacle when he declared, "We [members of the court] are not as private individuals. We owe ourselves entirely to the public" (246). Such an attitude is certainly on display in the court of his cousin, Charles II, as well.

It may at first seem odd, then, that there is no mention in her "Farewel" of the space that afforded Mancini the most freedom during her time in London: the public space of her salon. Chauncey Tinker similarly concludes that "the one unfailing characteristic of the salon, in all ages and in all countries, is the dominant position which it gives to woman."[7] While not the first to bring French salon culture to London, Mancini makes a unique use of this public space by mapping for herself a safe retreat from the torments of the patriarchal conjugal family that both the court and her husband represented. So why not mention this space in her "Farewel to England"? I would suggest that such an omission is a protective measure. The poem does the work of flattering the king and his court, London and its landmarks, and the English culture, which in turn helps readers to be both more sympathetic to her cause and more understanding of her reputation as one that was fueled largely by rumor and speculation. The result is that Mancini was allowed to remain in England, despite hostile political and religious conditions, and enjoy the private pleasure of a public space and the "psychological emancipation" that it subsequently afforded.[8]

Heretofore, almost no inquiry has been made into the second half of Mancini's life, which was spent in England.[9] In 1675, the duchess claimed to be going to England to visit her cousin, Mary of Modena. From the beginning, however, her motives were a matter of public speculation. Because the publication of her *Memoirs* preceded her arrival in London, and due to the fact that "sightings" of the duchess "on the road were excitedly reported in letters and news accounts," the "Character" of the duchess was already a familiar public persona.[10]

Only five years after arriving, Mancini appeared to have been thinking about returning to France. She was no longer the king's favorite mistress, although they remained friends and he continued to supply her with a generous pension. She had

---

[7]   Chauncey Tinker, *The Salon and English Letters: Chapters on the Interrelations of Literature and Society in the Age of Johnson* (New York: Gordian Press, 1967), 16.

[8]   Jürgen Habermas suggests that this freedom corresponds to a political-economic emancipation as well. *The Structural Transformation of the Public Sphere: An Inquiry into a Category of Bourgeois Society* (Cambridge, MA: MIT Press, 1991), 46.

[9]   Cyril Hartmann's biography, *The Vagabond Duchess*, details Mancini's time in England just as thoroughly as it details her early life. As useful and interesting as it is, however, it remains a biography rather than a critical inquiry or literary study. *The Vagabond Duchess: The Life of Hortense Mancini Duchesse Mazarin* (New York: E. P. Dutton, 1927). In *Publishing Women's Life Stories in France, 1640–1720* (Aldershot: Ashgate, 2001), Elizabeth Goldsmith links Mancini's writing to the history of commercial women's writing in France, and Susan Shifrin makes an equally important contribution by connecting Mancini to the phenomenon of early modern women's border crossings in a recent collection of essays, *"The Wandering Life I Led": Essays on Hortense Mancini, Duchess Mazarin and Early Modern Women's Border Crossings* (Newcastle-upon-Tyne: Cambridge Scholars Publishing, 2009).

[10]   Elizabeth Goldsmith, "Thoroughly Modern Mazarin," in Shifrin, *"The Wandering Life I Led,"* 21.

not, however, given up her efforts to gain the financial support of Louis XIV, as the letters written by her and on her behalf by others in favor of her case against her husband testify. Her other main goal was to protect the Mazarin fortune for her eldest son. It was during this time that she may have penned her only published poem, "The Dutchess of Mazarines Farewel to England" (1680). Just short of two pages in length, the broadsheet is not directly signed by Mancini and thus has heretofore been considered anonymously published; as such, there is no reference to it in either Hartmann's biography or Goldsmith's edition of Mancini's *Memoirs*. Susan Shifrin is the only scholar, to my knowledge, who makes reference to the poem, and she, too, presents the broadsheet as anonymously authored,[11] though she notes that the bookseller for whom it was printed, Langley Curtis, "was fairly well known for his animosity toward the court."[12] While Curtis may have been critical of Charles's court, the broadsheet in question shows no sign of this animosity. In fact quite the opposite is the case, as the poem carries a somewhat sympathetic tone for that class of people whose presence at court would have been seen as necessary for making important family and financial connections. Furthermore, the fact that it was not signed does not support the conclusion that Curtis penned the verse, as almost half of the manuscripts printed for the bookseller between 1668 and 1698 were anonymously authored, and none of these texts constitute attacks—explicit or implicit—on those in the court circle.[13]

A much more logical conclusion is that the duchess herself wrote the poem. The principal reason for suggesting this is that the speaker's tone and the metaphors used sound like Mancini. That is, they are quite similar to the tone, language, and style that we find in her *Memoirs*. The prominent role of fate as the driving agent in her life, the figuring of her travels as forced by the actions of others (rather than her own choosing), and the reflective consideration of her station in life and the consequences that follow both wealth and a famous family name are all strong imprints of the duchess's literary voice.

Another factor supporting this attribution is the marked difference between it and similar "farewell" poems during this period. The most direct comparison is offered by looking at "The Dutchess of Portsmouths and Count Coningsmarks Farwel to England" (1682). Louise de Kéroualle, Duchess of Portsmouth (1649–1734), was the much-hated, long-favored French Roman Catholic mistress of the king, and attacks against her in print were in no small supply.[14] The farewell poem

---

[11] Susan Shifrin, "'Subdued by a Famous Roman Dame': Picturing Foreignness, Notoriety, and Prerogative in the Portraits of Hortense Mancini, Duchess Mazarin," in *Politics, Transgression, and Representation at the Court of Charles II*, ed. Julia Alexander and Catharine MacLeod (New Haven: The Yale Center for British Art, 2007), 149.

[12] Ibid., 170, n. 29.

[13] This statistic is based on the list of titles catalogued and available in EEBO.

[14] See, for example, "Utile Dulce" (1681), "An Essay of Scandal" (1681), and "Julian's Farewell to the Muses" (1685) in John Harold Wilson's *Court Satires of the Restoration* (Columbus: Ohio State University Press, 1976). See also "The Dutchess of Portsmouths and Count Coningsmarks Farwel to England" (London: J. Bayly, 1682).

presented on behalf of Portsmouth and the count has a different printer, form, tone, and purpose than that of Mazarine's "Farewel." It is written in prose rather than poetic form, and the tone is clearly bitter and satiric in nature. It does not reflect fondly on London's pleasures, but instead celebrates the riddance of the title subjects. Portsmouth, for example, is referred to as "the English Plague."

Given the numerous differences between the two "Farewel" pieces and the similarities between Mazarine's "Farewel" and her *Memoirs*, one can say that it is both likely and logical that Mancini authored her own text as a way of currying favor with friends and protectors in England. Although such an attribution cannot be definitive, it does enable a much different reading of the poem, as well as a new understanding of Mancini's literary talent and activity. When juxtaposed with her *Memoirs* and what we know of her salon, attributing authorship to the duchess also provides a useful and provocative analysis of the way she manipulated the public space of the English cultural imagination while she simultaneously protected the private pleasure she cultivated in her borrowed lodgings.

One of the things made clear in her *Memoirs* is her desperate desire to find some sort of pleasure in life. Any relationship or activity that brought her even the slightest bit of pleasure was eliminated as soon as her husband discovered it. The duc saw to it that she was separated not only from her family but from his as well. The company she was not allowed to enjoy in her own home, however, she found in a bustling London circle. Differing slightly from the Parisian salon, Mazarin's apartment was less formal and it gave visitors ample opportunity for gambling, in addition to the sophisticated literary and philosophical conversations and readings they enjoyed. The hostess also differed in that she was less concerned with mingling with her guests than she was with pursuing whatever activity pleased her at the moment.[15] Though no records officially document all the guests who frequented what came to be known as "the little palace," the company included persons such as

> Robert Spence, 2nd Earl of Sunderland, one of the Secretaries of State; Sunderland's political enemy Laurence Hyde, 1st Earl of Rochester ... as well as his wife Henrietta Boyle; Louis de Duras, Earl of Feversham, Chamberlain to Queen Catherine of Braganza and Gentleman of the Bedchamber to Charles II and James II, Ralph Montagu, Frances Villiers, a Teller of the Exchequer; and the oboist and composer [Jacques] Paisible.[16]

The duchess spared no expense in furnishing her apartment with the finest decorations, offered the very best in food and drink and, with the assistance of Saint-Évremond, supplied an extensive library, which served as the main attraction for several visitors. The social makeup of Mancini's salon was a "cosmopolitan and

---

[15]   Denys Potts, "The Duchess Mazarin and Saint-Évremond: The Final Journey," in Shifrin, *"The Wandering Life,"* 170–72.

[16]   Susan Shifrin and Andrew R. Walkling, "'Iddylle En Musique': Performative Hybridity and the Duchess Mazarin as Visual, Textual, and Musical Icon," in Shifrin, *"The Wandering Life,"* 81–82.

wide-ranging crowd of politicians, intellectuals and aristocrats."[17] It is fascinating to consider, then, that it is within this kind of socially diverse and very public crowd that the duchess carved a private space of pleasure for herself.

The poem comes at a time when Mancini seemed to be enjoying all the excess and luxury her life in London could afford. Though she was no longer his favorite mistress, the king had generously restored a £4,000 pension to her, and she easily survived contemporary criticism, which consisted mainly of attacks against her virtue or her Catholic sentiments.[18] Most importantly, the "Farewel" was published when the "pursuit of pleasure was Hortense's only object in life," and her lodging in London had become "a place of reunion for learned and brilliant men as well as for the rank and fashion of the land."[19] These details, as well as a close reading of the poem, suggest that the poem was less about a goodbye to London and the happiness it afforded the duchess and more an effort to articulate the contradictory sort of pleasure she found while living there.

Having the physical freedom to move about London as she pleased, as well as the ability to create a space designed solely for her pleasure, indicates that Mancini did not intend to leave England as long as she could maintain her lifestyle. One of the things the poem makes clear, however, is the contradiction between the speaker's desire for private pleasure and the position of public spectacle: "Happy the Countrey-Swain, who courts the shades, / Whose Privacies no sullen Fate invades."[20] In her *Memoirs*, Mancini frequently cites "Fate" as a determining factor in her life, and this framework is echoed throughout the poem. Because of her unique position—as a woman who had quite publicly fled her husband, who had recorded and published the details of her travels and legal battles, who had temporarily been the king's favorite mistress—Mancini sought happiness and refuge in the only space where it was available to her: the public sphere. While Hartmann may be correct in claiming that Mancini was "devoid of ambition" in the political sense,[21] the duchess had ambition of another kind. Her ambition was for pleasure, which in her case was inherently a public matter.

Her lodging in London was not a private home, which the "separate spheres" theory of space would have us understand as one that afforded protection from outside/public threats or temptations. However, it is also unlikely that Mancini ever knew the kind of empowerment Amanda Flather describes as available to

---

[17]   Potts, "The Duchess Mazarin," 169.

[18]   Comparatively speaking, the English people were much less hostile to Mancini than they were to the "other" Catholic mistress, the Duchess of Portsmouth, who was severely lampooned in contemporary writings.

[19]   Hartmann, *Vagabond*, 231–33.

[20]   "The Dutchess of Mazarine's Farewel to England" (London: Langley Curtis, 1680), 9–10. The original is not lined, so I have provided line numbers for ease of reference. All further references will be to "Mazarine's Farewell."

[21]   Hartmann, *Vagabond*, 27.

many women within the domestic space of the home.[22] Her house in St. James's park did not legally belong to her, but it also did not reflect the patriarchal social organization within which she lived.[23] She used the space as a site of sociability and hospitality, not only for the purpose of accumulating social capital, which I shall discuss later, but also for her own pleasure, something denied to her from the beginning of her marriage. She took advantage of the learned friends who made up her circle and encouraged her "to take an interest in literature and philosophy," and thus gained a "new-found reputation for wit and intelligence."[24]

The poem can be divided roughly in half, with the first half framing the duchess as the speaker who considers herself part of "the Great" crowd, those who have noble births and pedigreed lineage. The speaker uses the first half of the poem to establish herself as one who is being forced by "Fate" to leave all of England's pleasures behind, the first of several rude disappointments that "Dame Fortune" has in store for her. Juxtaposing the relationship between the privileged space that she has been born into and the metaphorical consequences that follow, the speaker considers herself as existing in a sort of in-between space, in which she is a "slave" to "Honor" and cheated of "freedom." On either side of this space, she imagines the happiness and peace of the "Countrey-Swain," "Rural Maid," and "Shepherdess" as well as the exaltation of "a Queen." The latter is "above report" while the "Shepherdess ... innocently cares not for't." The space articulated here is one with which Mancini was all too familiar. On one hand, she was certainly not "above report," but on the other hand she seemed to care about it quite a bit. She knew she could not avoid the public gossip that circulated about her affairs, friendships, and daily habits. In fact, she sometimes contributed to the chatter.[25] She was well aware that her position in London was a precarious one which depended not only on the generosity of the king and other friends but also

---

[22]   In *Gender and Space in Early Modern England* (Woodbridge, UK: Boydell Press, 2007), Flather argues that "Inconsistencies within patriarchal rhetoric that admonished women to be 'neighbourly,' together with the intricate and sometimes contradictory ways in which gender intersected with other social factors such as age, social and marital status, created social maps that were fluid, flexible, and contextually determined" (95). In the home, women's responsibility for domestic hospitality and sociability often led to spatial determinations of power that were more complicated than the "separate spheres" approach has thus far suggested.

[23]   Shirley Ardener, "Ground Rules and Social Maps for Women: An Introduction," in *Women and Space: Ground Rules and Social Maps*, ed. Shirley Ardener (New York: St. Martin's Press, 1981), 12.

[24]   Hartmann, *Vagabond*, 196.

[25]   Mazarin's friend and protector Saint-Réal was not alone in being commissioned by the duchess to write about her. She also commissioned Saint-Évremond to write her funeral oration before her death so that she could see how people might respond to it. Elizabeth Goldsmith, "'Savoir la carte': Travel, Self-Advancement, and Survival in Letters by Women," in *Formes et formations au dix-septième siècle*, ed. Norman Buford (Tübingen: Narr, 2006), 15–34.

on a particular demeanor toward Louis XIV and her husband, who continued to demand her arrest and forced return to France.

She transitions to the second half of the poem by depicting her escape from her husband as something she was "forc'd" to do because he despised both her and her beauty.[26] Wandering "in disguise" as a cavalier, Mancini made the difficult journey to England, thus increasing her reputation as an "intrepid adventuress."[27] This transitional point in the poem usefully lends itself to a consideration of space and spectacle in early modern England. Often commented on by her contemporaries, Mancini's practice of cross-dressing was thought to be just another manifestation of her carefree attitude and resistance to gender norms. Much ado was made of this habit, which is odd, considering that she admits in her *Memoirs* that her efforts were rarely successful; she claims that she was continually recognized as a woman in man's clothes.[28] The spectacle she creates, then, is a transgressive one, but not for the reasons we might normally assume. Not in her self-recognized failure to pull off dressing like a man, but rather in the effort to fashion for herself a space within the cultural imagination as a woman on the run, Mancini transgresses the spatial boundaries assigned to married women of her station. And while I agree with Goldsmith's reading of her travels and correspondence by letter as a method of survival and self-advancement, I think the "Farewel to England" makes it clear that a "stubborn capacity for mobility" is not her primary motivation or goal.[29]

The second half of the poem, which is almost wholly concentrated on England, explicitly reconfigures the national and physical spaces she inhabited. The England to which the speaker bids farewell is the land

... where Peace and Plenty flow,
Where all things to ease wretched Souls do grow;
Where all things fit to make Life sweet abound,
And where I Pleasure, Ease, and Comfort found.[30]

Finally free from those who would confine her, either to a convent, a prison, or her husband's palace, Mancini found herself content with her life in London and saw the opportunity to "settle" there as one worth the sacrifice of the conjugal domestic space in which many women found a sense of authority. While the legal battle with her husband "would become the subject of divorce hearings which were published and debated,"[31] Mancini found "shelter and Relief" in Charles's court.[32] Crediting Charles's "Power" and "bounteous hand," the speaker acknowledges the efforts to

---

[26] "Mazarines Farewel," ll. 30–31.

[27] Hartmann, *Vagabond*, 148.

[28] Nelson, *Hortense*, 61. The duchess writes that "We had been recognized as women almost everywhere."

[29] Goldsmith, "Savoir la carte," 19.

[30] "Mazarines Farewel," 40–43.

[31] Goldsmith, "Savoir la carte," 18.

[32] "Mazarines Farewel," 45.

which the king went to defend her against court orders and written laws that were intended to be enforced, if necessary, with violence. By remaining in England, the duchess transgressed these legal boundaries and created a space in which she existed largely outside of the law.

The king's financial generosity to his mistresses was well known, and Mancini's case was no exception. Securing economic support from him, as well as a few close friends, freed the duchess from the dangers of poverty, which she certainly would have faced, since her husband refused to continue her pension. The physical landmarks of England and its royalty are what signify the space of pleasure for the speaker in the poem: "delightful *Windsor*," the "Silver *Thames*," and "*Whitehal*" offer readers a map of the duchess's most frequented destinations. Mapping her relatively short time in England (just five years at this point), the poem highlights the importance of Mancini's relationship to space. Moreover, it does so in a way that seems to challenge Elizabeth Goldsmith's notion that her unwillingness to stay put or, rather, her "fondness of mobility" became an argument for her extradition to France.[33] While Mancini's flight from her husband is often seen as one motivated by a stubborn desire to move about as she pleased, and although she enjoyed the freedom of mobility while in London, it was the place where the duchess would remain for the second half of her life. At the same time, the speaker's favorable description of these sites appeals rhetorically to English readers, hopefully securing their sympathies for one as fond of their country as the citizens themselves.

If not the sympathy, Mancini certainly had the admiration not only of dozens of English men, but also of several important women. Aphra Behn admired her for being "racy," "witty," and "ambiguous."[34] As someone who had notoriously broken her marital vows, the duchess was then, in some ways, an appropriate choice for dedicatee of Behn's *The History of the Nun*. As Janet Todd notes, the dedication to Mancini was laden with a much more sensual and "homoerotic yearning than Behn usually allowed herself".[35] Though there is no direct mention of it in her dedication to the duchess, surely Behn considered Mancini's marriage the kind to which many women of the period fell victim. It was an ill-suited match, and the theme of change in natural inclinations and human nature in *The History of the Nun* (1688) reinforces the possibility that Behn's readers might somehow be able to identify with the domestic troubles that had plagued the duchess. Thus, the space Mancini occupied in the English public's imagination was constructed from more than her memoirs or the published court documents detailing the accusations she faced from her husband and her attempts to defend herself and negotiate an amenable arrangement of living separately from the duc.[36]

---

[33]   Goldsmith, "Thoroughly Modern Mazarin," 23.

[34]   Janet Todd, *The Secret Life of Aphra Behn* (London: Pandora, 2000), 233.

[35]   Ibid.

[36]   The duchess never sought to divorce her husband, but rather asked the court for the right to live in private quarters. Throughout the entire process, her claims for financial settlements rested on her concern that the duc would eventually waste the remaining Mazarin fortune and thus deprive their eldest son of any financial security he was rightfully due through inheritance.

What space, then, did she occupy in the English public's imagination? Although much evidence suggests that the duchess worked hard to hone her image in the public imagination of the English, members of the French court, and her family, the space she occupied was one over which her control was questionable, to say the least. Visual, textual, political, and legal accounts worked simultaneously to shape a very public space that Mancini would never escape. I would argue, however, that she knew this and accepted it as a consequence of her choice to live separately from her husband and under the protection of the English court. Rather than seeking refuge from the public sphere and the scrutiny and censure of public opinion that accompanied it, the duchess sought "a more open and liberating environment for the formation of the self" in the public eye.[37]

Pierre Bourdieu's work on social space argues that power follows from the ability to mobilize various forms of capital (economic, social, educational, and so forth),[38] and the Duchess Mazarin was quite successful in this regard. Using the house in St. James's Park provided to her by the Duke of York, the duchess established a salon of different social and national groups, men and women, "aristocrats, merchants, artists, and ambassadors."[39] Although Mancini did not own the house, she recognized it as a site where social and cultural capital might be organized and collected. According to Habermas, the salon, by serving society rather than the house or its "intimate circle" of inhabitants, became part of the public sphere at the turn of the century in England.[40] Unable to establish a refuge from this space, one usually formed through the "intimate circle" of the conjugal family, the duchess used the space of her salon to achieve the psychological freedom Habermas and others traditionally associate with the autonomy of property ownership. She transformed the house from a place to a space and mobilized the capital it gained her in order to secure her standing as a cultural icon in English society.

Of course, this did not come without at least some criticism. In "Rochester's Farewell" (1703), we find the most violent attack on Mancini's sexual reputation.[41] Attacks against the king's mistresses (especially Portsmouth) were fairly frequent, especially in court lampoons. The author's virulence in this lampoon, however, is notable in its characterization of Mancini's sexual desire. Despite the fact that she was the king's favorite mistress only for a brief period, Mancini takes the brunt

---

[37] Mary Thomas Crane, "Illicit Privacy and Outdoor Spaces in Early Modern England," *The Journal for Early Modern Cultural Studies* 9, no. 1 (2009): 7. Crane's argument on the relationship between outdoor spaces and the formation of the modern subject is extremely useful, not only in challenging the public/private dichotomy but also in its close study of the overlooked and/or mistaken nature of space outside the home.

[38] Pierre Bourdieu, *Distinction: A Social Critique of the Judgement of Taste* (Cambridge, MA: Harvard University Press, 1987).

[39] Goldsmith, "Thoroughly Modern," 22.

[40] Habermas, *Structural Transformation*, 45–46.

[41] Published in *Poems on Affairs of State: from the time of Oliver Cromwell ....*, 5th ed., vol. 1 (London, 1703), 154.

of the attack rather than the Duchess of Portsmouth or Nell Gwyn. Describing her lust as "well-travel'd," the author blasts the duchess for the expanse of her sexual conquests:

> The great *Pedalion* Youth, whose Conquests run
> O'er all the World, and travel'd with the Sun,
> Made not his Valour in more Nations known,
> Than thou thy Lust, thy matchless Lust have shown.

The dominating image is one of movement. It is the association with unfettered mobility—in this case sexual experience—that helped to shape Mancini's contemporary image. Despite the fact that she had remained fixed in England for at least four years at this point, the author's depiction of the duchess equates her with "The great *Pedalion* Youth, whose Conquests run / O'er all the World." Her promiscuous reputation, which the speaker claims is known by all in Europe, is linked to a perverse, even monstrous sexual desire that spans "All Climes, all Countries." Thus, readers are left with the picture of a highly mobile and sexually insatiable Mazarin, an image of scandal and impropriety that would be further shaped by Mary Astell just a year after the duchess's death.

The Mazarin case was the impetus for Astell's famous *Reflections Upon Marriage* (1700). Although the essay's purpose was to point out the inherent flaws in marriages arranged by self-serving family members and naïve young people, or otherwise based on ill-informed motivations and desires, Astell's comments on the Mazarin case, and the character of the duchess in particular, offer useful insight into contemporary responses to Mancini's behavior. While Astell initially places blame with both parties for the scandal that came to be associated with the Mazarin name and implies that only those who have felt such a "misery" as Mancini's can understand her position, her commentary is focused primarily on the duchess and what she sees as Mancini's "Scandalous Methods" of seeking revenge on her husband by "running away in Disguise with a spruce Cavalier, and rambling to so many Courts and Places … diverting herself with such Childish, Ridiculous or Ill-natur'd Amusements, as the greatest part of the Adventures in her Memoirs are made up of."[42]

Astell goes beyond mere disapproval of Mancini's behavior, eventually condemning the duchess for lacking "Discretion" and "exposing herself to Temptations and Injuries from the Bad, to the contempt, or at the best to the pity of the Good, and the just Censure of all."[43] Making it clear to her readers that Mancini's example should not be followed, Astell then turns to the issues of determining the cause of such "mischief" and how it might be prevented. What she fails to acknowledge in her criticism, however, is that the duchess never spoke out against the institution of marriage. In fact, she claims in her *Memoirs* that

---

[42] Mary Astell, *Some Reflections Upon Marriage, Occasion'd by the Duke & Ductchess of Mazarine's Case; Which is also consider'd* (London, 1700), 5.

[43] Ibid., 6–8.

If Monsieur Mazarin had been content to overwhelm me with sadness and grief, expose my health and my life to his most unreasonable whims, and in short to make me spend my best days in unparalleled servitude, then since heaven had given him to me as master, I would merely have moaned and complained of him to my friends.[44]

Indeed, throughout her accounting of their marriage, the duchess cites countless examples of the small joys she would briefly encounter—company, friendships, or even physical spaces—that would be taken from her the moment her husband discovered the pleasure they brought her.[45] While Astell acknowledges the doomed future of marriages based on an ill choice of partner, she shows little sympathy for those who had no choice in a marriage settlement, which was the case for most women of Mancini's social class. The damage to her image had clearly been done, and the spectacle created by Mancini's escape from her husband and her decision to remain in England cemented her position in the public sphere, within her own lifetime and well after.

Described by Hartmann as the "Vagabond Duchess," Hortense Mancini cannot be so conclusively defined. She may have spent the first half of her life wandering wherever her family or, later, her husband might take her, but her escape from the duc was carefully planned, as was her decision to spend the second half of her life in England. Writing from the road—with her own pen and through the pens of others—she made her mark with the help of those whose economic, social, and intellectual capital empowered the duchess to create a relatively safe physical, intellectual, and emotional space for herself in England.

The mark she left while writing from the road demonstrates that Mancini's travels and the spaces she created for herself were motivated by more than a desire to simply roam nomadically, something she certainly had the opportunity to do, given her connections. Within her apartment at St. James, she positioned herself as the epitome of a Parisian salon hostess and created a "private" space of "Pleasure, Ease, and Comfort" under a very public gaze.

---

[44] Nelson, *Hortense*, 44.

[45] In particular, Mazarin recounts an episode where she was forced to travel only three weeks after giving birth and stay in a house so "miserable" that she was "obliged to stay outside in the meadows all day." Ibid., 42.

PART III
Inside

Chapter 8

New Models for the Literary Garden: Women's Amatory Novels of the 1720s

Mary Crone-Romanovski

Between 1680 and 1730, a period defined roughly by the publication of Aphra Behn's *Love Letters between a Nobleman and his Sister* (1684–1687) and Elizabeth Singer Rowe's *Friendship in Death* (1728), the garden consistently appears as a central space in popular amatory fiction by women.[1] In the same period, new theories of garden design were articulated and illustrated in architectural and gardening books intended for wealthy estate owners wishing to improve their property according to emerging concepts of taste. Bringing this historical interest to bear on amatory novels of the period illuminates the way that women writers both appropriated conventional literary uses of the garden and drew on contemporary theories of garden design to construct new narrative possibilities for dramatizing women's experiences.

This essay uncovers a neglected history of the literary garden: its role as a social and creative space for female characters in woman-authored amatory fiction. Most scholars of eighteenth-century literature have read the gardens of amatory fiction as sexualized spaces, founding their interpretations on the conventional role of gardens in earlier texts, like those by Edmund Spencer and John Milton, as well as travel and exploration narratives that commonly described the landscape in feminized and even eroticized terms.[2] While I recognize that the literary garden

---

[1]   For example, the garden is a significant site in each of the following novels published between 1680 and 1730: Aphra Behn's *Love Letters between a Nobleman and his Sister* (1684–87), *Oroonoko* (1688), and *The History of Agnes de Castro* (1696); Delarivier Manley's *The Secret History of Queen Zarah and the Zarazians* (1705) and *Bath Intrigues* (1725); Jane Barker's *Love Intrigues* (1713); Eliza Haywood's *Love in Excess* (1719), *The British Recluse* (1722), and *Philadore and Placentia* (1727); Penelope Aubin's *The Strange Adventures of Count de Vinevil and his Family* (1721) and *The Life of Madame de Beaumont, A French Lady* (1721); Mary Davys' *The Reform'd Coquet* (1724) and *The Accomplish'd Rake* (1727); and Elizabeth Singer Rowe's *Friendship in Death* (1728).

[2]   See, for example, Karen Harvey, "Spaces of Erotic Delight," in *Georgian Geographies: Essays on Space, Place, and Landscape in the Eighteenth Century*, ed. Miles Ogborn and Charles W. J. Withers (New York: Palgrave, 2004), 131–53; and April London, "Placing the Female: The Metonymic Garden in Amatory and Pious Narrative, 1700–1740," in *Fetter'd or Free? British Women Novelists, 1670–1815*, ed. Mary Anne Schofield and Cecelia Macheski (Athens: Ohio University Press, 1986), 101–23.

often serves as a sexualized space, I am more interested in how women writers drew on specific features of contemporary gardens and garden design theories to revise the traditional meaning of the literary garden and to imagine a new type of novel that featured dynamic female protagonists. In fact, women writers' revision of the literary garden helps define the amatory genre, and their innovation is critical to the development of the novel in the eighteenth century.

My alternative reading of the amatory garden is founded on the assumption that narrative structure corresponds to spatial setting, which is, in turn, informed by gendered experiences of actual space. Space can register in novels in a number of ways, including geographical distance, topographical location, descriptors of movement, and architectural layout. In attending specifically to the garden, I am interested in the architectural details that constitute a character's immediate physical environment. Attending to how space operates as a dynamic source of narrative, rather than mere background setting, opens new avenues of inquiry for the relationships among space, gender, and narrative in literary history. As the central space in amatory fiction, the garden produced new possibilities for female characters, a role that transferred to other types of spaces in later subgenres of the novel—including, for example, the domestic interior in courtship novels. To better understand why women's amatory fiction as a genre coalesced around the space of the garden, I explore intersections between the literary significance of the garden as it appears in women's novels throughout the 1720s and the cultural significance of the garden's changing role in women's lives.

Analyzing the depictions of gardens in Eliza Haywood's *Love in Excess* (1719) and Mary Davys' *The Reform'd Coquet* (1724), I will demonstrate that the gardens in these novels serve as two distinct types of spaces: as a sexualized space reappropriated to serve female desire and as a social space that supports female reason and creativity. First, I show that in *Love in Excess*, Eliza Haywood not only reinforces the conventional literary role of the garden as a sexualized space, but she also uses the garden's potential to support plots of female agency, a move that has been overlooked by most Haywood and amatory fiction scholars.[3] I then show that Mary Davys, one of Haywood's contemporaries, exemplifies a trend in amatory fiction that more fully illuminates an alternative meaning of the garden as a space of female sociability, meditation, and creative expression. I demonstrate that Davys employs the amatory garden as an established literary

---

[3]   Toni Bowers recognizes a similar phenomenon in her discussion of "collusive resistance" in *Love in Excess*. Bowers argues that the novel explores the possibility of female virtue coexisting with female sexual agency. While her goal is to elucidate Haywood's new means of expression for partisan politics, my interest is in how the literary and cultural histories of the garden inform narratives that express a range of female experiences. Toni Bowers, "Collusive Resistance: Sexual Agency and Partisan Politics in *Love in Excess*," in *The Passionate Fictions of Eliza Haywood: Essays on Her Life and Work*, ed. Kirsten T. Saxton and Rebecca P. Bocchicchio (Lexington: University Press of Kentucky, 2000), 48–68.

convention within which the female protagonist can exercise creative power by using the garden's traditional meanings to her advantage.

This theoretical shift—from understanding the garden as an erotic symbol to understanding it as a dynamic source of narrative—demands close attention to the details of garden design, as well as the cultural values associated with both actual and literary gardens in the late seventeenth and early eighteenth centuries. My study, therefore, uncovers some components of garden design and use that were typical before the English landscape garden gained in popularity from the 1730s onward. The recovery of women's literature and life-writing has provided new evidence that women's writing often conceptualized the garden as a space of creativity, as a symbolic site of gendered social relations, and as an important space in women's everyday lives for both housekeeping work and leisure activities.[4]

The significance of specific garden features in women's novels has been obscured by critical attention to the wrong kind of garden design—that of the landscape garden. Rather than incorporating design features of the newly emerging landscape garden, the plots of many of Eliza Haywood's works depend on typical features of older, formal gardens. In *Love in Excess*, the sensory experiences made possible by an ornate, exotic, and enclosed garden design stimulate characters' actions. In the seduction scenes in this novel, the characters feel "intoxicated" by the odors, beauty, textures, and sounds of the gardens, an experience that is distinct from the visual appreciation of landscape gardens.

One of the primary garden scenes in *Love in Excess* links specific features of the garden, reflective of contemporary garden design, to the characters' actions. Each of three characters uses a specific feature of the garden to forward his or her individual scheme: Melantha plans to find and seduce Count D'Elmont, the owner of the property and a friend of her father's; the (married) count seizes the opportunity to attempt to seduce Melliora, his ward; and Melliora uses garden features to avoid seduction and preserve her chastity. The scene begins with the two women deciding to walk through the garden after dark, in an effort to discover the count:

> The ladies walked in the garden for some time, and Melantha searched every bush, before she found the Count, who stood concealed in the porch, which being covered with jessamin and fillaree, was dark enough to hide him from their view, tho' they had passed close to him as they came out. … [H]e watched their turning, and when he saw they were near an alley which had another that led to it, he went round and met them.[5]

The physical elements of the garden bring the characters into contact with each other and provide opportunities for them to act on the desires that they must

---

[4]   Jennifer Munroe, *Gender and the Garden in Early Modern English Literature* (Burlington, VT: Ashgate, 2008), 9.

[5]   Eliza Haywood, *Love in Excess, or, The Fatal Inquiry* (1719), ed. David Oakleaf (Peterborough: Broadview, 2000), 121.

conceal indoors in the presence of others. The garden's conventional function as a sexualized space empowers Melantha to pursue her individual desires, and the spaces of the garden become the means of her (failed) attempts to seduce the count. Likewise, the count uses the garden's "wilderness" and winding paths to attempt to seduce Melliora. Oddly, although the garden conventionally has been a site of seduction, both of these attempts ultimately fail, thwarted by yet additional garden features. Thus, in *Love in Excess*, the garden is not solely a male-dominated space as scholarship often understands the amatory garden; rather, it has the potential to serve competing male and female desires, prolonging the tensions that drive the narrative.

Garden features like winding paths and the wilderness tend to be treated as incidental details when mentioned in the novel, but they were actually central to garden design previous to 1730. From the 1730s through the end of the eighteenth century, many property owners and garden-design enthusiasts renovated older formal gardens to create landscape gardens with sweeping vistas of the lawns, fields, and forests. The wilderness, an artificially constructed and manicured wooded area resembling a labyrinth, actually transcends this shift in garden design and continues to be incorporated into landscape gardens throughout the eighteenth century. Most features of the earlier gardens, however, were redesigned or omitted as the new landscape garden gained popularity. Like the gardens described in Haywood's novel, formal gardens built previous to the popularity of the landscape garden were designed to provide multiple sensory experiences. This ideal is at odds with the landscape garden's focus on wholly visual appreciation of the landscape from a single vantage point. While landscape gardens included open views, natural-looking wildernesses and streams, and hidden boundaries, the older, formal style consisted of intricately designed knots and parterres enclosed by high walls that separated the designed garden from the fields and woods beyond.[6] These earlier gardens sought to please all of the senses by way of paths that wound through the garden, allowing one to experience the garden from within instead of just from a designated viewpoint. This style of garden design privileged the layout of paths and placement of objects to evoke a series of responses: suspense as one wandered through the garden; surprise at finding a statue, grotto, or orange grove hidden behind a curve in the path; and contemplation in response to the new discovery.

Batty Langley's *New Principles of Gardening* (1728) emphasizes the importance of a range of sensory perceptions of the garden, exemplifying garden design before 1730, even while incorporating emerging design features that would become synonymous with the English landscape garden. In his list of rules for garden layout, Langley describes the ideal design for "serpentine meanders" that wind through the garden to reveal pleasing prospects, secluded seats, and

---

[6]   David Streatfield, "Art and Nature in the English Landscape Garden: Design, Theory, and Practice, 1700–1818," in *Landscape Gardens and Literature of Eighteenth-Century England: Papers Read at a Clark Library Seminar, 18 March 1978* (Los Angeles: William Andrews Clark Memorial Library, University of California Press, 1981), 2.

objects for contemplation. Langley declares that clearings should be placed at regular distances along these paths. In each clearing, a new "surprise" should be positioned to delight those that walk along the path. Such surprises could include a fruit garden, a fountain, a statue, or a group of pines.[7] These surprises heightened multiple senses, not just visual, but also aural, olfactory, and even tactile. Langley professed this type of design in order to promote variety as providing the most pleasure in a garden.

The renovated landscape gardens, in contrast, featured designs founded on the concept of visual appreciation. In her study of the relationship between landscape garden theory and theories of vision, Katherine Myers explains that landscape gardens were designed to be viewed from a specific point from which tricks of depth and size created the illusion of two-dimensionality.[8] The ability to "see" a landscape garden correctly, as if it were a painting rather than an actual landscape, became an indication of refined taste. In Haywood's novel, the ability to experience the garden through all of the senses and to experience the emotions of surprise and suspense created by paths, walls, and clearings is central to the structure of the plot and female characters. That is, Haywood's plot depends on the experiences produced by older garden design rather than those of the landscape garden.

While Haywood draws on both older design features and the garden's conventional literary role as sexualized space, she also depicts the sensual experiences of the garden as inspirational to women's creativity and individual agency. In each scene that arises out of the physical features of the garden, a female character attempts to manipulate those features according to her desires. In the scene described previously, after the women have met the count in the garden, Melantha suggests that the three play a game in the wilderness in hopes of being able to secretly join the count while they are separated from Melliora. Later, Melantha prevents Count D'Elmont's seduction of Melliora by coming upon them by surprise, a move enabled by the winding and shaded paths. The count's thwarted seduction encapsulates a dual function of the garden: the garden supports Melantha's illicit behaviors by providing seclusion, and it preserves Melliora's chastity by enabling discovery.

As in this scene, the multiplicity of sensual stimuli in garden spaces inspires storylines of sexual desire and seduction throughout amatory novels before 1720, particularly those by Aphra Behn, Delarivier Manley, and Haywood. These authors use contemporary interest in garden design to adopt and refresh a long literary history of the garden. In ancient myth, religious doctrine, and medieval and early modern literature, the literary garden conventionally operates as a static trope and a symbol of illicit sexual desire, female vanity, and women's vulnerability to

---

[7]   Batty Langley, *New Principles of Gardening* (London: A. Bettesworth and J. Batley, 1728), 198.

[8]   Katherine Myers, "Visual Fields: Theories of Perception and the Landscape Garden," in *Experiencing the Garden in the Eighteenth Century*, ed. Martin Calder (Oxford: Peter Lang, 2006), 24.

temptation. Before 1680, the symbolic importance of the woman in the garden was derived primarily from the Biblical account of the Garden of Eden. Works of early modern literature like Edmund Spenser's *The Faerie Queene* (1590) and John Milton's *Paradise Lost* (1667) reinforce the literary garden as a symbol of sexual desire, temptation, and transgression. In each of these texts, the garden space and the female character become parallel symbols of beauty, desire, and temptation.

Milton's description of Eden in *Paradise Lost* (1667) exemplifies the garden's cultural and literary capital in England before 1680. While most Milton scholarship has focused on the garden's role as a symbolic trope, positioning the text in conversation with early eighteenth-century women's writing illuminates an alternative characteristic of the garden, its function as a lived space.[9] Milton creates a garden with physical details that make it visually and sensually pleasurable, as well as functional, within the everyday life of the first couple. In particular, Milton characterizes the garden as a domestic space, a setting for everyday life and a source for structuring a marriage-like relationship. Milton carefully describes Adam's and Eve's activities in the Garden of Eden as a joint effort at tending to the plant life that provides sustenance, shelter, and pleasure. The couple balances domestic labor and domestic pleasure, working in harmony together to maintain their home and enjoying a companionable relationship in hours of leisure. Of course, Milton's garden is also a representation of the setting of the "first sin" and, as such, clearly encapsulates the garden's already long-standing function as a site of illicit behavior. His adaptation of the creation story, however, emphasizes the garden's role as a functional domestic space for Adam and Eve, and, as a site for the full range of human experiences, including love and happiness, solitude and meditation, temptation and deception, and finally reconciliation. By incorporating this range of human emotions, Milton recognizes the competing possibilities for this space and begins to connect physical details with emotional and social experiences.

English women writers of the 1720s embrace Milton's treatment of the garden as a multifaceted domestic space. In contrast to Milton and his literary predecessors, however, they also characterize the garden as a significant site for dramatizing women's experience in particular, rather than the human condition more generally. By providing particularities of time and space for their gardens, women writers subordinate the garden's symbolic significance to its secular, practical, and narrative functions.[10] Thus, these writers use the garden space to

---

[9]   Shannon Miller's study of *Paradise Lost* offers a revised theory of influence that considers women writers as both influencing and influenced by Milton's work. My claims here depend on a similar approach that uses Milton's poem as a major text that exemplifies a broader literary trend. Shannon Miller, *Engendering the Fall: John Milton and Seventeenth-Century Women Writers* (Philadelphia: University of Pennsylvania Press, 2008), 6.

[10]   Ian Watt describes formal realism as dependent on the inclusion of particularities of time and space in regards to character and setting. Ian Watt, *The Rise of the Novel: Studies in Defoe, Richardson and Fielding* (London: Chatto & Windus, 1957), 24.

create vibrant female characters that adapt to their environments, responding instantaneously to events that the space of the garden enables. As early eighteenth-century women writers adopt and revise the garden, female characters transition from static symbols to dynamic models. As we have seen, Haywood's *Love in Excess* exemplifies this transition by appropriating the garden to serve competing male and female desires.

In a move similar to Haywood's appropriation of the sexualized garden, *The Reform'd Coquet* (1724) by Mary Davys invokes the older meanings of the garden through classical epic and the masculine perspective, but in the end rewrites the garden as a space for female creativity. Early in the novel, the rakish Lord Lofty views a painting on the ceiling of a garden seat while he plans his seduction of Amoranda, the novel's heroine.[11] The painting that he contemplates is of Paris abducting Helen of Troy. The representation of classical myth in the garden nods to the traditional sexualization of the space that derives from its function in myth and religious doctrine. Amoranda, however, manipulates the features of the garden, in effect revealing her awareness of the narrative expectations associated with the garden. Ultimately, Amoranda creates a new story by adapting the conventional treatments of the garden to serve her individual purposes.

The heroine's use of the architectural features of the garden in service of her own agenda depends on the multiple narrative possibilities for the garden. After a decade of appearances in women's amatory novels, the garden no longer enables only narratives of seduction, kidnapping, and other threats; for a savvy heroine, the garden also supports narratives in which she can thwart seduction and kidnapping attempts and further desirable courtship. Davys' employment of the garden resonates with the garden's role in Haywood's *Love in Excess*, where a female character also attempts to use the garden to satisfy her desires. Davys, however, develops this possibility further, allowing her heroine to succeed in revising the garden plot rather than only making the attempt. Davys' novel, thus, marks the conventionality of the literary garden as well as its multiplicity of meanings, two characteristics that continue to shape the garden's appearance in novels throughout the eighteenth century.

The multiplicity of narrative possibilities in the garden coincides with contemporary ideas about women's relationship with gardens and gardening. Debates over the garden encompassed a web of social issues, including emerging constructions of gender, management of property, and ideals of marriage and courtship. Throughout the early eighteenth century, periodical essays, pamphlets, and poetry made clear the significance of the garden to English life generally and to women's experiences in particular. Two essays from *The Spectator*, issued less than a month apart, depict relationships between women and gardens through fictional female characters. Aurelia, described in "*The Spectator* No.

---

[11] Mary Davys, *The Reform'd Coquet* (1724), in *Popular Fiction by Women, 1660–1730: An Anthology*, ed. Paula R. Backscheider and John J. Richetti (New York: Oxford University Press, 1996), 258.

15," exemplifies feminine virtue through her use of the garden, while Leonora, in "*The Spectator* No. 37," challenges the limits of proper femininity as well as proprietorship through her interconnected practices of gardening and reading. The description of Aurelia's retired life and her rural garden contrasts with that of Leonora's elaborate garden of her own design. Aurelia's garden meets expectations for a tasteful appreciation of landscape and for the use of the space for reflection and for conversation with her husband. Leonora's garden, however, is linked to the design of her "Lady's Library," and both are treated with a mixed response from Mr. Spectator, the authorial persona of the essays. First, Mr. Spectator describes the aspects of the "Lady's Library," listing the mix of china ornaments, volumes of romances, and a variety of philosophical and religious texts that line the shelves. Then, he refers to Sir Roger, a more elite and worldly member of the Spectator club, as the source of a lengthy and detailed description of the garden. From Sir Roger's perspective, the description, on its surface, seems appreciative of the garden's beauty and sense of fantasy. According to Sir Roger, Leonora's country seat is

> situated in a kind of Wilderness, about an Hundred Miles distant from London, and looks like a little enchanted Palace. The Rocks about her are shaped into Artificial Grottoes covered with Woodbines and Jessamines. The Woods are cut into shady Walks, twisted into Bowers, and filled with Cages of Turtles. The Springs are made to run among Pebbles, and by that means taught to Murmur very agreeably. They are likewise collected into a Beautiful Lake, that is inhabited by a Couple of Swans, and empties itself by a little Rivulet which runs through a Green Meadow, and is known in the Family by the Name of *The Purling Stream.*[12]

Mr. Spectator's association of the garden design with the type of reading represented in the "Lady's Library," however, complicates the praise of the this passage: "As her Reading has lain very much among Romances, it has given her a very particular Turn of Thinking, and discovers itself even in her House, her Gardens and her Furniture."[13] Although Sir Roger seems enamored of the delightful features of the garden and Mr. Spectator entertained by the description, Mr. Spectator's final evaluation is "a mixture of admiration and pity."[14] At the end of the essay, he laments that a woman so "susceptible to the impression of books" had not turned her attention to something more edifying. Mr. Spectator is clearly disturbed by the potential for romances and female proprietorship to influence the design and decoration of property, which should function as a symbol of male rank and wealth.

---

[12]   Joseph Addison, "*The Spectator* No. 37" (April 12, 1711), in *The Spectator*, ed. Donald F. Bond (Oxford: Oxford University Press, 1965), 158.

[13]   Ibid.

[14]   Ibid.

Comparing *The Spectator*'s description of Leonora's garden with its comments on Aurelia's garden provides insight on the social connotations attached to gardens and garden design. Mr. Spectator describes Leonora as "susceptible to impression" and as having developed a "particular Turn of Thinking" in response to romances.[15] In contrast, he states that Aurelia has "true happiness" and implies that she is wise in her choice of how to spend her time.[16] A major distinction between the two women, aside from their reading practices, is that Aurelia is married to "her bosom friend," and Leonora is widowed and intends never to marry again. The critical difference is that Aurelia enjoys a garden designed and maintained by the male property owner, while Leonora has independently designed her garden. Unlike Leonora's satisfaction, Aurelia's delight in the garden walks is acceptable because she enjoys them with the company, advice, and approval of her husband and for the purposes of spiritual meditation. Aurelia's appreciation of the garden is pointedly different from Leonora's delight in her romance-inspired garden. Leonora satisfies independent, female desire when she creates the luxurious, beautiful, and fantasy-like garden for her personal enjoyment and from sources of inspiration that she has chosen without male direction.

Part of the trouble with Leonora's creation and enjoyment of her garden arises from a shift in the relationship between gender and gardening that occurred with the increasing popularity of landscape gardens. In addition to reducing the range of sensory experiences provided by the garden, the building of landscape gardens resulted in the minimizing of women's involvement in garden design and care overall. Flowers, botany, kitchen gardens, and the design of sociable or intimate garden spaces had traditionally been considered consistent with feminine arts and crafts, hobbies, interests, and housekeeping duties.[17] Thus, the traditional correlation of garden culture with a woman's domain preceded male domination of landscape design. John Dixon Hunt explains that horticulture and agriculture were seen as having central roles in England's recovery from the Civil Wars, and in the late seventeenth century, new theories of gardening and garden design promoted horticulture as a moral and intellectual activity for men.[18] Jennifer Munroe traces a similar shift toward the association of gardening with masculinity. She explains that as gardens became powerful symbols of rank, wealth, and power, and as the profitability of gardening increased, the major work of designing large landscape gardens became conceptualized as primarily a masculine activity. Women continued to use smaller gardens, usually kitchen gardens or small flower gardens,

---

[15]   Ibid.

[16]   Joseph Addison. "*The Spectator* No. 15" (March 17, 1711), in *The Spectator*, ed. Donald F. Bond (Oxford: Oxford University Press, 1965), 68.

[17]   Lisa L. Moore, "Queer Gardens: Mary Delany's Flowers and Friendships," *Eighteenth-Century Studies* 39, no. 1 (Fall 2005): 67.

[18]   John Dixon Hunt, *The Figure in the Landscape: Poetry, Painting, and Gardening during the Eighteenth Century* (Baltimore: The Johns Hopkins University Press, 1976), 25–26.

throughout the eighteenth century, but their involvement in gardening was reduced and circumscribed by the new masculine interest in landscape gardens.[19] As men came to govern decisions and plans for the outdoors, women's involvement in the process of gardening decreased, and the value of the male "view" of the garden replaced the value of women's experience of creating and maintaining the garden.

Participating in this ongoing shift, *The Spectator* privileges female appreciation of a male-built landscape, but criticizes female involvement in garden design and creation. The two essays from *The Spectator* illustrate a web of concepts associated with the garden, including wisdom, economical housewifery, and proper companionship as well as fantasy, sensual experience, and self-indulgence. The conflicting notions of what the garden could or should do and what it could or should indicate about its proprietor multiply the narrative possibilities for fictional gardens. *The Spectator*'s treatment of two distinct types of gardens and their proprietors parallels the conflicting and changing role of the garden in women's novels.

For Davys, the multitude of possibilities in the garden provides her heroine with a means of self-expression that demonstrates wit, creativity, and virtue. Davys positions the garden as an impetus to the turns of the plot throughout the novel, from Lord Lofty's initial contemplation of the classical scene as he plans the seduction of Amoranda, to the scheming of rival suitors to abduct Amoranda from the summerhouse, to the final staging of a marriage in the orange grove. The summerhouse abduction scheme, in particular, consciously mocks the garden as a convention of amatory novels. The features of the summerhouse, and Amoranda's manipulation of them, contribute to a sequence of events that results in a comic scene of cross-dressing, fist-fighting, and general mayhem that occurs with no risk to the heroine. The summerhouse first becomes central to the novel when two of the heroine's suitors, Froth and Callid, meet there and, realizing Amoranda is not seriously considering marriage to either of them, begin to scheme against her. Callid explains the plan:

> I have often heard Amoranda say she passed her whole Evenings in this Summer-house when the Weather is hot; now where would be the difficulty of whipping her out of this low Window into a Coach provided ready and carry her to a House which I have taken care of, keeping her with the utmost privacy, till she resolves to marry one of us, and the other shall share the Estate.[20]

When Froth complains that Amoranda and her maid will surely scream when taken, Callid suggests "a pretty little Gag for a minute or two, till we got them into the coach."[21] The plan thus far closely resembles a conventional amatory plot that depends on the summerhouse: use the warm weather and the opportunity of the woman's routine behavior that leads her to a summerhouse positioned in the

---

19   Munroe, *Gender and the Garden*, 6.

20   Davys, *The Reform'd Coquet*, 263.

21   Ibid.

garden away from the main house, gag her to prevent screaming, place her in a coach, and take her to another house. The potential for danger is clear, and it draws on the convention of amatory novels to figure the garden as a space of surprise. The tone of Davys' work, however, negates the dangerous associations of the summerhouse. Davys presents the schemes of Froth and Callid as ridiculous, as if these two have indeed read many novels in which rakes kidnap heiresses from summerhouses and foolishly assume that it must be as easy as those novels suggest.

In addition to mocking conventional garden plots that use the summerhouse as a pivotal space, Davys revises these plots by drawing on typical physical features of the summerhouse that permit actions, like spying and eavesdropping, which potentially subvert such male scheming. Amoranda's housekeeper is able to inform her of the intended kidnapping because of these features:

> Madam, said she, I went this Afternoon into my little Room over the Summer-house, where you know I dry my Winter-Herbs, and while I was turning them, your Ladyship came in with Mr. Froth, and Callid came to you. You may please to remember, Lord Lofty gave you an opportunity of leaving them, which you had no sooner done, than they began to lay a most dangerous Plot against you.[22]

With the information provided by the eavesdropping housekeeper, Amoranda plans to frustrate the suitors' scheme, thereby revising the types of stories that are generated by the summerhouse and the garden. The scheming and counter-scheming that depend on the summerhouse culminates in a comic scene that transforms the garden from a site for kidnapping or seduction to a site for a female-generated frolic.

The farce of the garden space ridicules the potential danger of the summerhouse by suggesting that such threats can be easily frustrated when a woman recognizes the typical plot pattern associated with a key space. Aware of the possibilities associated with the spaces of the garden and the summerhouse, Amoranda foils her abductors' scheme by instructing her guardian and a servant to dress in ladies' apparel and to sit in the summerhouse in place of herself and her maid. When Callid and Froth run into the summerhouse and attempt to kidnap the women, the men dressed as ladies "began to handle their Cudgels, and laid about them with such dexterity, that the Ravishers were almost knocked on the head, before they could believe they were beaten."[23] By Amoranda's design, the attempted kidnapping turns into a beating of the two foolish suitors and the summerhouse becomes a stage for frolic and farce.

Davys' summerhouse scene bears striking resemblances to previous scenes in amatory fiction, including a scene in Penelope Aubin's *Madame de Beaumont* (1721) in which the villain, Glandore, succeeds in kidnapping the heroine, Belinda, by means of the summerhouse window. Callid and Froth seem to take this very

---

[22]   Ibid., 266.

[23]   Ibid., 274.

scene as a model for their own designs, as if they have just finished reading Aubin's novel. Davys, however, effectually erases the threat of rape that exists in Aubin's novel and that typically dominates such scenes in amatory fiction. For Davys, the garden allows her protagonist to thwart the suitors' plans and display her own creative agency. Instead of succumbing to the sexual threat, Amoranda recognizes an alternative narrative potential of the garden and summerhouse. Amoranda does not allow the surprises lurking in the summerhouse to shape the story, but uses the properties of this space to surprise others and to create her own story.

By the end of the 1720s, women writers were using the garden in a multitude of new ways. Elizabeth Singer Rowe's *Friendship in Death* (1728), in particular, drastically deviates from the older conventions of the literary garden as well as from the more recently established uses. This narrative characterizes the garden as a virtuous, desexualized space that serves sociability, solitude, and spirituality. Letter XVI of Rowe's novel relates the story of a woman appearing after death to warn her brother that he has only a few weeks to live. The woman explains to her brother that she "chose the Opportunity, when [she] found [him] in a clear Moon-light Night, sitting in a pensive Posture, by the Side of a Fountain in [his] Garden."[24] Several of the letters depend on similar moments when characters seek the solitude of the garden to indulge their grief or to contemplate the loss they have experienced. Moreover, Rowe's letters consistently describe a spirit's visit to a loved one as dependent on a moment in which the living are prepared for the meeting by features of the garden that inspire contemplation. Solitary walks in orange groves, moments of contemplation by a fountain, or moonlit wanderings along a garden path are deemed appropriate times for the dead to approach the living with the least amount of shock or surprise. Rowe's using the garden in this way derives from more than a decade of women writers revising the conventional meanings of the literary garden and creating a multitude of narrative possibilities for that space which often depended on women's traditional uses of gardens.

In other words, the ways in which women writers employ the garden to craft original stories suggests that women's fiction actually preserves the pre-landscape garden tradition of women's active participation in gardening. The plots and characters of women's amatory novels depend on the idea of a sense-stimulating garden, the concept of the garden as a space associated with women's housekeeping roles and artistic endeavors, and the use of the garden as a social or meditative space. Amatory fiction develops from the possibility that one could step into these gardens and, while wandering through their pathways, discover a person lurking at the borders, a couple stealing a clandestine interview behind a thick grove, or a young woman reading a private letter in a garden wall recess. Rarely do these novels include landscape descriptions that focus on the "picturesque" nature of a scene, like those in Jane Austen's or Ann Radcliffe's novels written nearly a century later. Instead, amatory fiction presents garden features piecemeal, focusing on a specific spatial aspect that serves the narrative structure. Thus, the "serpentine

---

24   Elizabeth Singer Rowe, *Friendship in Death* (1728) (New York: Garland, 1972), 88.

meanders" and their potential to reveal hidden surprises, like those elaborated by Langley, as well as other specific features of gardens of this era, are central to the plots of women's amatory novels. In amatory fiction, gardens shape plots through the interplay of intoxicating plant life, the potentially disorienting design of paths, and the ever-present possibility of surprise, for instance, that someone else in the garden will turn a corner at just the wrong—or right—moment. More important, however, the heroines of these novels overcome the garden's intoxicating effects and exercise control over the garden space.

Throughout the eighteenth century, the tensions among the potential meanings of the garden, evident in women's amatory fiction, shape the plots of novels concerned with women's circumscribed agency, like Samuel Richardson's *Pamela* (1740) and *Clarissa* (1748), Frances Burney's *Evelina* (1778) and *The Wanderer* (1814), and Jane Austen's *Mansfield Park* (1814). In these novels, the multiple meanings of the literary garden generate a host of narrative possibilities, and the authors continue to adopt new features of garden design, like the ha-ha, to create additional narrative potential. In *Mansfield Park*, for example, Maria Bertram and the rakish Mr. Crawford, claiming only to be desirous of gaining a better view of the house, impatiently pass around the edge of a locked iron gate and brave the depth of a ha-ha to escape the enclosed "wilderness" and the sight and company of the other characters. Before Maria and Mr. Crawford cross over the gate, Fanny Price warns Maria that she may tear her gown on the iron spikes or fall into the ha-ha. Her cautions cannot stop the determined and infatuated Maria:

> Fanny was again left to her solitude, and with no increase of pleasant feelings, for she was sorry for almost all that she had seen and heard, astonished at Miss Bertram, and angry with Mr. Crawford. By taking a circuitous, and as it appeared to her, very unreasonable direction to the knoll, they were soon beyond her eye; and for some minutes longer she remained without sight or sound of any companion. She seemed to have the little wood all to herself.[25]

Maria's actions and Fanny's reflections invoke two conventional and contradictory characterizations of the garden in eighteenth-century novels: a sexualized space that serves as a site for seduction, clandestine meetings, and other illicit activities; and a contemplative space that promotes meditation and sociability in the service of female virtue. The *Mansfield Park* scene is well known and often discussed by scholars of eighteenth- and nineteenth-century literature. The garden scenes of early eighteenth-century novels by women are less familiar, but they are crucial to shaping the significance of Maria's and Fanny's conflicting situations in the garden almost a century later. Maria's actions in the garden recall the older literary tradition that associates the garden with female transgression; Fanny's experience in the garden suggests a newer tradition associating the garden with female reason

---

[25]   Jane Austen, *Mansfield Park* (1814), ed. Claudia L. Johnson (New York: Norton, 1998), 73.

and spirituality. Together, they embody the innovations of the early eighteenth-century women writers that I have been tracing here.

In addition to historical interest in the rise of the landscape garden, the centrality of the domestic interior to later types of novels, like courtship novels, sentimental novels, and Gothic novels, has obscured the innovative use of literary gardens by early eighteenth-century women writers. These writers crafted a new model of the literary garden that shaped the development of the novel over the course of a century, and by doing so they imagined a new type of female protagonist whose wit and creativity found the space of the garden to be a means of agency, even within increasingly restrictive notions of gender.

Chapter 9
Anne Finch's Strategic Retreat into the Country House

Jeong-Oh Kim[1]

When Anne Finch (1661–1720), Countess of Winchilsea, writes, "My hand delights to trace the unusual things, and it deviates from the common and known way,"[2] she retraces the trajectory of her remarkable political retreat into the country house in Eastwell Park. Unlike male and masculine politicians like Lord Bolingbroke, Lord Cobham, and William Pitt, who receded from public life to their estates as a deliberate means of reentering public life in the disguise of disinterested country gentlemen, Finch finds expulsion from the court to be a real disaster and the remodeling of the estate to be an echo of the disaster, not a political manifesto, as it was, for instance, for Cobham at Stowe.[3] She has to invent a way of making retirement tolerable in Eastwell. She turns to her poetry to do so, and this is reflected in how the disasters of the Bloodless Revolution directly commingle with the metaphors of pastoral ease in her verse. Although Finch, as a political failure in the displaced Stuart court, retreats into the country house in Eastwell Park, I argue that her poetic intervention in the high politics of the absent Stuarts makes intervention at a distance feasible. Finch's withdrawal from the court into the country is, for her, a loss of power and influence, but she compensates for it by writing landscape poetry, of which "Upon Lord Winchilsea Converting the Mount into a Terras" is a significant departure from traditional rural idealization. Finch's

---

[1]   I would like to thank Bridget Orr for her helpful comments on earlier versions of this essay, Jonathan Lamb for his lively conversation on the topic of the garden, and most of all, Mark Schoenfield for his brilliant reading of Finch's poetry.

[2]   Anne Finch, "The Spleen," in *The Poems of Anne Countess of Winchilsea*, ed. Myra Reynolds (Chicago: University of Chicago Press, 1903), 248. Unless otherwise specified, Finch's poems are quoted from this collection.

[3]   When, in 1733, Lord Cobham, a member of Walpole's administration, twice thwarted his leader and suffered for it, he retired to Stowe to expand and embellish a garden already renowned for the improvements made to it by Sir John Vanbrugh. There he arranged triumphal arches, Chinese houses, temples, obelisks, temples, pillars, pyramids, statues, and so on to convene the inner circle of writers and politicians known as "Cobham's cubs," such as Gilbert West, James Thomson, William Pitt, George Lyttelton, Bubb Dodington, and the Grenvilles, and to refine the political expression of patriotic attitudes. See Jonathan Lamb, "The Medium of Publicity and the Garden at Stowe," *Huntington Library Quarterly* 59, no. 1 (1997): 53–72.

retirement to her country house, Eastwell Park in Kent, is, then, not just a personal issue but profoundly affected by the high politics of the print culture.

As the prototype of women writers to come, Finch anticipates and exceeds the binary logic of "Separate Spheres" as a dominant paradigm for imagining feminine and masculine power in the early Augustan period. At this time, the idea of the supposedly ideal woman emerges within the institutions of domesticity established by the construction of the patriarchal household. The house simultaneously expresses the individual subjects, locking them into spatial practices that define and reproduce the body. The exterior of the house serves as a male mask displaying the man's status to the world. Representing the unified self, protected by a seamless façade, the exterior of the house is masculine. A man's house and estate stand in his place as an extension of his propriety. On the other hand, the interior of the house is the scene of reproduction and femininity: the wife merely maintains this very hegemonic spatial order she is placed in. My critical perspective has been developed in a framework of feminist thought by thinkers such as Alice Friedman, Anne Bergren, Catherine Ingraham, Judith Butler, and Julia Kristeva, as well as informed by the literary criticism of Finch scholars such as Barbara McGovern and Charles Hinnant, among others. To think through the conceptual metamorphosis of feminism and geography, I engage myself in a critical way of investigating the links between space and gender, an innovative mode of analysis by which architecture becomes inextricably linked with a mirror reflecting and a stage reenacting the social distinctions between private experience and public writing. Finch destabilizes the division of labor between public and private by anticipating and exceeding the "functionalistic" division of architecture that Catherine Ingraham theorizes: "This [functional distribution of sexuality and space in architecture] consists of assigning certain spaces, usually in the residential or house project, to either women or men, depending on who most frequently uses or cares for these spaces. A functionalist account routinely leaves unquestioned a whole set of assumptions about what constitutes 'use' or 'occupancy' of an architectural space."[4] The functional division of gender topography as masculine and feminine defines the two disparate but interrelated positions Finch mediates in imagining who belongs to and uses the manor as a specific poetic locale enveloped by the reach and complexity of reconstruction and militarization.

In "Architecture, Authority, and the Female Gaze: Planning and Representation in the Early Modern Country House," Alice Friedman shows how the division of labor in the household shapes female visuality. By investigating the conceptual design of the country house, ranging from screening, sight lines, and contrast of scales, she traces the visibility and invisibility of women's behavior as a special focus of concern against the backdrop of the "ideological context in which domestic planning ordinarily took place and reconstructed the attitudes toward the

---

[4]　　Catherine Ingraham, *Architecture and the Burdens of Linearity* (New Haven: Yale University Press, 1998), 90.

family, sexuality, and the female body."[5] The plan of the ground floor in the early modern country house assumes an imbrication between the place of the home and the sphere of the feminine. The interior of the home contains a female sphere of emotion, immobility, and confinement within the female sphere of domesticity; its gender specificity is derived from and defined in opposition to a notion of masculine space: an outside, the sphere of the project, and movement. Friedman elaborates on the spaces that women occupied: "Her traditional activities took place in such areas as the nursery and kitchen, while her domestic and social responsibilities were fulfilled in the great chamber, parlor, and bed chambers, areas in which she might read, practice needlework, or entertain guests, shielded from the contact with most members of the household and with strangers." The visible public space is officially the realm of men and for men to venture for profit in exchange. For a woman to enter it entails unseen risks: "She was expected to play only a supporting role in the formal rituals of power, and she was generally excluded from the round of business meetings and especially business trips that her husband undertook."[6] A sense of interiority and its implied "inferiority" was a social construct marked on the functionally constituted body of sexuality.

For Friedman and Ingraham, the question of architecture is, in fact, also the question of the placement of body. Both analyze and question the conceptual pairs that were taken for granted as self-evident and natural, as if they hadn't been institutionalized at some precise point, as if they had no history. To recognize space is to recognize what takes place there and what it is used for. The inward-outward, internal-external, private-public exchange that architecture was part of provides a particular occasion for Ingraham to extend the intersection of space and sexuality into the eighteenth-century history of the functional body. Ingraham claims that since the eighteenth century, proper space has promised its inhabitants a normative life, which is, ideally and not accidentally, also a "clean" and "comfortable" life. She elaborates: "The idea of comfort, which is chiefly a functionalist idea in architecture, assumes that there is some compatibility between the body and space, but also that the spatial field within which we move is fully occupied by our (always generalized) daily functions." As far as Ingraham is concerned, the idea of full and continuous space as a representational problem has been codified as modern space in the eighteenth century. She argues, "Proprietary (spatial) identity is absolutely necessary to sexual identity and in complex ways, to sexual exchange. But sexual identity is also absolutely necessary to proprietary identity because spatial identity results from the action of 'difference.' This sexual-spatial equation influences every facet of our thinking about names, identity, property, and architecture."[7] The spectrum of spatial and gender categories has too often been conceptualized in the form of an all-inclusive experiential and epistemological

---

5   Alice Friedman, "Architecture, Authority, and the Female Gaze: Planning and Representation in the Early Modern Country House," *Assemblage* 18 (1992): 41–61.

6   Ibid., 44.

7   Ingraham, *Architecture*, 97.

dyad, and it produces deceptively illusory knowledge that embodies and nourishes gendered identity. The functional space is, then, the space of conventional gender roles. This functionalist "naturalization" has proceeded to the point where architecture performs a regulating (or generative) function for the body. Gender differentiation takes place in the literal and psychological space of home and the family, turning its domestic space into a complex terrain of literary, social, and sexual significance.

Not only does Finch intervene in this contemporary architectonics of gender politics, for the construction of gendered space as such cannot be separated from the construction of an ideology of gender difference, but she also makes Eastwell Manor a local center of influence in transit. Moving outward from her country seat, she forms a literary and social network of connections in various channels such as poetic writing, friendship with the three generations of Thynnes of Longleat and her Kent neighbor, Catherine Cavendish, Countess of Thanet, and also literary exchanges with Alexander Pope, Jonathan Swift, John Gay, and Nicholas Rowe. By extending her circle through writing and friendly exchange, Finch makes of her private and individual retreat a political and poetical artifact with a considerable degree of power and influence over the very public world from which she appears to be withdrawn.

While it is crucial to argue that Finch transforms her backward glance of retreat into a forward vision of print culture, it is equally important to ask, along the lines of Frederic Jameson, "If architecture wishes to dissent from the spatial order of things, how would it go about doing this?" When Jameson asks, "If architecture wishes to dissent from the status quo," he is giving space the active agency and power of political engagement. Insofar as space as architectural expression refuses to "underscore and reinforce whatever division of labor is active in the social order in question," Jameson views space as political when he suggests that

> The political relationship of works of art to the societies they reside in can be determined according to the difference between replication (reproduction of the logic of that society) and opposition (the attempt to establish the elements of a Utopian space radically different from the [previous or existing] one. At their extremes, both these stances raise some questions: for instance, can even the most undistinguished work still altogether replicate or reproduce the hegemonic spatial logic?[8]

Eastwell Park provides for Finch the poetic site of an alternative for oppositional (gender) politics, one at odds politically and poetically with the dominant division of both country life and the role of women in the early eighteenth century. Finch's work of art secures her the material conditions of dehiscence, as reopening or reflowering and of spacing and tracing, as well as deconstructing and destabilizing

---

[8]   Frederic Jameson, "Is Space Political?" in *Rethinking Architecture*, ed. Neil Leach (New York: Routledge, 1997), 259.

the standard hierarchy between "superior," "exterior," and "public" masculinity and "inferior," "interior," and "private" femininity.

Finch is deconstructive in the purest sense of the term; as Jacques Derrida states, "Architectural thinking can only be deconstructive in the following sense: as an attempt to visualize that which establishes the authority of the architectural metaphor. From this point, we can go back to what connects deconstruction with writing: its spatiality, thinking in terms of a path, of an opening up of a way in which it inscribes its traces."[9] Within the framework of deconstructionist thinking, Finch identifies architecture as a representational system, that is, as "a medium in which function and imagery are viewed not as separate but as overlaid aspects of a system, through which meaning is constituted."[10] By aligning my work with that of Friedman, I suggest that the geographical and social constructions that make it possible for the country house to function as a social agent of gender differentiation are transformed by the very interiority such constructions make visible. The form and force of writing reenacted by Finch's sense of displacement both depends on and assists in the cultural construction of the textured geography of interior, inferior, and therefore feminine spaces. My essay rests on the claim that Finch's withdrawal is inextricable from the materializing body of a figure, the figure both for imagining a society from the margins of society and for converting hindsight into an operative force at work in the destabilizing effects of cultural change.[11] It is a particular mode of Finch's poetic writing that spatial disjunctions accompany temporal disjoints, which intensify Finch's criticism of the court as her poetic career unfolds. By converting these spatial and temporal disjunctions into an event that calls attention to the form and force of her poetic writing, Finch redoubles the lines of gender (and) politics back into her poetry as if to translate her heightened circumstantial awareness into the mirror. This rhythmic tracing and retracing fluid connection between situations and events is what I call the *trajectivity* of the displaced female wanderer and writer in the name of Anne Finch. Finch does not have access to the elevation, the eminence, or the detachment of an idealized, usually male subject with political power. In the end, however, Finch crosses the boundaries of genre and gender, thus shaping and establishing a feminine structure of feeling in her poetry.

When critics have called attention to Finch as a significant participant in the political debates surrounding the Bloodless Revolution, her reflection becomes an enunciative method of evaluating her total experience of the Revolution, traversing her involvement in it. As Finch remarks in her poem, "Petition for Absolute Retreat," she finds herself thrown away, "Blasted by a storm of Fate,

---

9   Jacques Derrida, "Where the Desire May Live," in Leach, *Rethinking Architecture*, 321.

10   Friedman, "Architecture," 43.

11   We are not far from where Ingraham and Friedman intersect with Judith Butler's concept of the materializing bodies that matter. Judith Butler, *Bodies that Matter* (New York: Routledge, 1993), 9.

/ Felt thro' all British state."[12] Her feeling of personal and political deprivation is a sensitive register of an uncertain and unstable British history. Finch's "felt thought," which according to Raymond Williams is unpleasurable sensations of "disturbance, blockage, tension, emotional trouble," affects and redefines Finch's sense of the present, that is, the "this, here, and now" of the present British state.[13] By the 1680s, fears of a Catholic alliance between Louis XIV and James II gave rise to both the "Glorious Revolution" and its subsequent deposition of Britain's Catholic king and the selection of the Protestant William and Mary as joint monarchs. Many critics have already rehearsed the result of this regime change in Britain: Episcopalians and Catholics had to go into exile on the Continent. A trail of Jacobite soldiers and supporters ensued; the majority of them tried in vain to follow their king to France where they established a court in exile at Saint-Germaine-en-Laye. It was not surprising, therefore, that Heneage Finch, as Groom of the Bedchamber to the Duke of York, attempted to join this exodus, although he was captured on charges of Jacobitism at the coastal town of Hythe, Kent, in 1690. After the Catholic Finches, like other "non-jurors," refused to take the oath of allegiance to the Protestant King William III, Finch lost her position as one of Mary of Modena's Maids of Honor at the Stuart court. The Finches also lost their royal privileges at court. Thereafter, the Finches retired from London and the court to Kirby Hall in Northamptonshire during the first years of the Revolution, moving between Eastwell in Kent and Longleat and Lewston in Wiltshire and sojourning for a short period of time at Godmersham and also at Wye College. This complicated residential trajectory indicates that the Finches were tracing out a nation torn by split loyalties, involving those who supported the new regime of William and Mary against those who remained loyal to the deposed king, James II, and his successors. Finch's personal mode of feeling engages poetically in this historically unstable present of the Bloodless Revolution and its aftermath.

Without the security of position, property, estate, and inheritance, Finch took to the road in the intervening years, seeking a poetical and political framework for her displaced situation. Finch's Pindaric ode is marked by a nexus of sensations enabling the perception of warped space, much as in the interplay of images and words, through the visual components of language. Finch's poem "The Spleen" performs the double séance of reenacting her emotion in the infinite proliferation of objects equivalent to her mood:

---

[12]   Anne Finch, "The Petition for an Absolute Retreat," in Reynolds, *The Poems of Countess of Winchilsea*, 73.

[13]   Raymond Williams, *Politics and Letters* (New York: Schocken Books, 1979), 168. This reading of Williams is inflected by David Simpson, "Raymond Williams: Feelings for Structures, Voicing 'History,'" *Social Text* 30 (1992): 9–26; Kevis Goodman, *Georgic Modernity and British Romanticism: Poetry and the Mediation of History* (Cambridge: Cambridge University Press, 2004); and Mary Favret, *War at a Distance: Romanticism and the Making of Modern Wartime* (Princeton: Princeton University Press, 2010).

What art thou, SPLEEN, which ev'ry thing dost ape?
Thou Proteus to abus'd Mankind,
Who never yet thy real Cause cou'd find,
Or fix thee to remain in one continuous Shape.
Still varying thy perflexing Form,
Now a Dead Sea thou'lt represent,
A Calm of stupid Discontent,
Then, dashing on the Rocks wilt rage into a Storm.
Trembling sometimes thou dost appear,
Dissolv'd into a Panick Fear;
On Sleep intruding dost thy Shadows spread,
Thy gloomy Terrors round the silent Bed
And croud with boading Dreams the Melancholy Head.

By choosing a Pindaric mode, Finch visualizes the twists and turns of her emotion in the expansion and contraction of the poetic lines, also aligned spatially in the historical landscape of the Roman civil war:

Thy fond Delusions cheat the Eyes,
Before them antick Spectres Dance
Unusual Fires their pointed Heads advance,
And airy Phantoms arise.
....
Such was the monstrous Vision seen,
When Brutus (now beneath his Cares opprest,
And all Rome's Fortunes rolling in his Breast,
Before Philippi's latest Field,
Before his fate did to Octavius lead)
Was vanquish'd by the Spleen.

Instead of explicating her vision, Finch gives an historical example of another vision of the British Civil War:

I feel thy Force, whilst I against thee rail;
I feel my Verse decay, and my crampt Numbers fail.
Thro' thy black jaundice I all Objects see,
As Dark, and Terrible as Thee,
My Lines decri'd and my Employment thought
An useless Folly, or presumptuous Fault:
Whilst in the Muses Paths I stray,
Whilst in their Groves, and by their secret Springs
My hand delights to trace unusual Things,
And deviates from the known and common way ... .

Finch's cramped sentence moves along, adding to the next while aiming at irregularity. As it goes, like the spleen it describes, it moves across various strata of geography, sea or rocks, within its "perflexing Form," which Finch is obliged to take to be each of the objects and their accumulated sum as ending in her tumultuous brain "wreaking havoc with the senses" in the body. Finch exploits the spleen's capacity for distorting, deforming, disassociating, dislocating, or dismantling one image after another in its opening up for a way of "fond Delusions" and "fantastic" visions.

Finch returns to the Pindaric with "Upon the Hurricane in November 1703," referring to this text in Psalms 148:8, "Winds and Storms fulfilling the Word." As the title shows, this poem stages the divine will directed toward the human institutions via a textual system. The hurricane is a particularly bizarre event, which this poem seeks to naturalize:

> Throughout the Land, unlimited you flew,
> Not sought, as heretofore, with Friendly Aid
> Only, new motion to bestow
> Upon sluggish Vapors, bred below
> Condensing into Mists, and melancholy Shade
> No more such gentle Methods you pursue,
> But marching now in terrible Array.[14]

Three points merit attention. From the beginning of the poem, the short, fragmented sentences are set forward and piled one over the other, creating a rugged rhythm. This effect causes readers to wonder where they are going, to ask if the author, who herself is in the eye of the storm, prophesies or fulfills the divine will by setting in motion the word of God that Finch is quoting: "Fire, and hail; snow, and vapour: stormy wind fulfilling his word."[15] Secondly, while aligning herself with a psalmist, Finch is spacing and tracing the operative act of creation, an inspired breath of God, felt in atmospheric turbulence, in wind, in the swirl of storms. Here, Finch is translating John Donne's Holy Sonnet #14 into the sight and sound of the windstorm that happened on December 7th and 8th (November 26th and 27th on the old calendar still used in Finch's time):[16] "Batter my heart, three-personed God; for You / As yet but knock, breathe, shine, and seek to mend; / That I may rise and stand, o'erthrow me, and bend / Your force to break, blow, burn, and make me new."[17] At once an organic and inorganic force, Finch's hurricane moves ahead ceaselessly; it coils itself; it turns and breaks about; it arches in the direction of chaos. Thirdly, therefore, Finch historicizes and at the same time spatializes the 1703 windstorm as God's head of judgment and righteousness unfolding onto the bodily geography of human culture.

---

[14]   Anne Finch, "Upon the Hurricane in November 1703 …," in *Miscellany Poems, on several Occasions. Written by a lady.* (London: J. B., 1713), 230–47.

[15]   *The Bible*, King James Version, Ps. 148: 8.

[16]   Jan Golinski, *British Weather and the Climate of Enlightenment* (Chicago: University of Chicago Press, 2010), 45. While modern accounts of the storm rely largely upon Daniel Defoe's *The Storm*, I call scholarly attention to Finch's poetic engagement with a male and masculine "news journalism" surrounding the national disaster of 1703.

[17]   John Donne, "Holy Sonnet XIV," in *John Donne Poems*, ed. Sir Herbert Grierson (Franklin Center, PA: The Franklin Library, 1982), 358.

Finch spatially visualizes the disarray of a public world where nothing remains in place from the heaven-revealing storm of 1703: "The Earth agen one general Scene appears; / No regular distinction now, / Betwixt the Grounds for Pasture, or the Plough, / The Face of Nature wears" ("Hurricane," 194–97). A sense of identity based on proprietary properties, social distinctions, and geographic locales is being blotted out from the surface of the earth. The figure of the hurricane indicates the motions of sliding, bending, varying, twisting, jumping, undermining, loosening, yielding, and resigning; the author figure works to establish a continuity of reference to the winds and to the divine power that moves them, yet is distinguished from them. In other words, the author figure takes a third agency, by which her critical stance bears witness to the fact that she does not belong to the party agendas represented by Tory and Whig: "Contention with its angry Brawls / By Storms o'er clamour'd shrinks and falls; / Nor WHIG, nor TORY now the rash Contender calls" (172). All universalizing divisions bounded by any human contention, whatever they may be—for instance, brawls and storms or Whig and Tory—are erased without traces. And she is also located at an equal distance both from the deists' rational system that embodies divine purposes and from Hobbesian "*tertium super partes*," primarily concentrated in the hands of the brutish military.[18] "Free as the Men, who wild Confusion love, / And lawless Liberty approve," Finch writes, "Their Fellow-Brutes pursue their way, / To their own Loss, and disadvantage stray" (198–201). I suggest that the author's position is neutral to an extent, since she does not belong to either party or two competing philosophies of nature; she never ceases to circulate throughout, problematize, and intervene in the nation's dilemma:

> Whilst more the liquid Empire undergoes,
> More she resigns of her entrusted Shores,
> The Wealth, the Strength, the Pride of diff'rent Shores
> In one Devoted, one Recorded Night,
> Than Years had known destroy'd by generous Fight
> Or Privateering Foes. (259–66)

The hurricane brings forth a serious challenge to the state of international affairs in the Britain of 1703, questioning the very basis on which its commercial and naval empire stands. Finch's sentience is acute, for the motion and movement

---

[18]   In explaining Finch's stance in her animal fables, "The Eagle, the Sow, and the Cat," Thomas Hinnant suggests that "Finch's narrative projects a Hobbesian ideology whereby the eagle and sow are mere individuals and not members of an organic community—and whereby both exercise a right to all things and are enemies to one another." My reference to the term "*tertium super partes*" comes, however, from Michael Hardt and Antonio Negri's explanation of the two models of imperial power: the Hobbesian and the Lockean variants of power formation set into a global perspective. Thomas Hinnant, *The Poetry of Anne Finch* (Newark: University of Delaware Press, 1994), 195; Michael Hardt and Antonio Negri, *Empire* (Cambridge, MA: Harvard University Press, 2001), 7.

of the 1703 windstorm sweeps away the front line of the long-running War of the Spanish Succession. The track of the storm center passed over the English Midlands, across the North Sea into northern Denmark, moving at a steady 45 miles per hour, with the highest winds hitting southwest Wales at 3 A.M., London at 6 A.M., and Copenhagen around 11 A.M. (on December 8).[19] Drawing a vast sweep of time and space across the middle of England, Finch remaps the subtle lines of political coalition among England, France, Holland, and Spain in the cause of patriotism and privateering on the roads of the sea. Abruptly, Finch prizes a newly redrawn map from which new points can be made about the male regime of privateerings, maritime wars, piracies, and international jurisdictions.[20]

Finch also articulates radically differential gender relations. They are radical because her address of gender relations has the possibility of modifying and transforming the line of political debates. Insofar as views of gender did not exist as a codified, coherent entity in Stuart England, politics is a public arena in which ideas about gender, or relevant to the social construction of gender, are shaped and transformed.[21] Finch's poetical activity is definitely a political practice of subverting and destabilizing gender relations. Finch calls further into gendered question the matter and manner of writing:

> Did I, my lines intend for public view,
> How many censures, would their faults pursue,
> Some would, because such words they do affect,
> Cry they're insipid, empty, incorrect,
> ....
> Alas, a woman that attempts the pen
> Such an intruder on the rights of men. (1–10)

---

[19]   Risk Management Solutions, "The December 1703 Windstorm," <http://www.rms.com/Publications/ 1703_Windstorm.pdf, accessed 15 June 2011>.

[20]   Scott Murdoch provides a detailed study of privateering in relation to Scottish maritime warfare in *The Terror of the Sea? Scottish Maritime Warfare, 1513–1713* (Boston: Brill, 2010).

[21]   Rachel Weil, *Political Passions: Gender, the Family, and Political Argument in England, 1680–1714* (New York: Manchester University Press, 1999), 29. For a survey of the politics of the female writers in the early eighteenth century see, for example, Catherine Gallagher, "Embracing the Absolute: The Politics of the Female Subject in Seventeenth-century England," *Genders* (Spring 1988): 24–39; Anne K. Mellor, *Mothers of the Nation* (Bloomington: Indiana University Press, 2002), 69–84; Steven Pincus, *Protestantism and Patriotism: Ideologies and the Making of English Foreign Policy, 1650–1668* (Cambridge: Cambridge University Press, 1996), 441–52; Harriet Guest, *Small Change: Women, Learning, Patriotism* (Chicago: University of Chicago Press, 2000); Tim Dolin, *Mistress of the House* (Brookfield: Ashgate, 1997); Anita Levy, "Reproducing Urges," in *Inventing Maternity: Politics, Science, and Literature 1650–1865*, ed. Susan Greenfield and Carol Barash (Lexington: University Press of Kentucky, 1999), 193–214; Karen O'Brien, *Women and Enlightenment in Eighteenth-Century Britain* (New York: Cambridge University Press, 2009).

She testifies to the fact that a woman who writes, and especially a poet who writes as a woman, would perform an act of "transgression," insofar as writing is invoked as a kind of public property. If she spoke from a position of authority, the act would be stigmatized as a form of crime. At this juncture, Finch's poetical lines exemplify an act of political struggle for the new social ties among women; her poems not only "represent" and record the lived experience as a woman, but they also serve, more crucially, as practices to redefine and renegotiate the political line of public and private distinction.

Finch's withdrawal grounds her poetic turn from the public to private world as authoritatively female. She writes:

> She fights, she wins, she triumphs with a song,
> Devout, majestic, for the subject fit,
> And far above her arms, exalts her wit;
> Then, to the peaceful, shady palm withdraws,
> And rules the rescued nation, with her laws. (46–50)

Finch's predicament does not simply address "the constraint of being a woman" as a stratagem for an eccentric or versifying poet. Her strategy of working from an abject predicament takes a supplementary turn of the screw with regard to private and public dichotomy; that is, her writing as a "private" woman or her writing of women's privacy disrupts and subverts the standard convention between private interiority and public exteriority. The term "predicament" has also been synonymous with category, particularly as it denotes the basic system of classification that all knowledge can be compartmentalized. Insofar as male discourses and systems dream of dominion over the physical organization of space, especially the ordering of the political distinction of interiority and exteriority, femininity and masculinity, they cannot but perpetrate the violence of categorical concepts. In its concretization of inclusion and exclusion, architecture establishes the groundwork for society's so-called policing practices of the reductive reproduction of stable distinction between femininity and masculinity. Finch's act of retreat cannot be considered a passive capitulation to the naturalized, conceptual predicament of differentiation. If her writing "traces the unusual things and it deviates the known and common way,"[22] it means an activity of testifying to the management and organization of space in the early eighteenth century. The failure to consider the redistribution of space means, both for Finch and for the feminists I am drawing upon, to remain still in the conceptual predicament (category) of female abjection.

It is illuminating that Finch redefines private abjection in a critical mode. In "To the Nightingale," she says:

> Poets as thou were born,
> Pleasing best when unconfined,
> When to please is least designed,

---

[22]   Finch, "The Spleen," 248.

> Soothing but their cares to rest.
> Cares do still their thoughts molest,
> And still th' unhappy poet's breast,
> Like thine, when best he sings, is placed against a thorn. (7–13)

The nightingale as an emblem of female empathy is synonymous with the emotion it carries. It is arguable whether Finch records the lived experience of abjection or whether her poetic language manifests as the eighteenth-century "common way" of abject feeling. Regardless, she redefines the division between natural and abject, open and confined, natural authority and its studied "molestation." In so doing, she rethinks and reforms her abject retreat as a poetic and political practice to intervene in a naturalized labor of division and a stabilized division of labor, i.e., the political line of gender relations:

> Thus we poets that have speech,
> Unlike what thy forests teach,
> If a fluent vein be shown
> That's transcendent to our own,
> Criticize, reform, or preach,
> Or censure what we cannot reach. (30–35)

Finch reconfigures the relationship between the public and private spheres in reinventing the structure of feminine feeling.

Finch follows the tradition of strong upper-class women like Bess at Hardwick Hall, who, in coupling architecture and power, shapes the world visibly. Friedman explains:

> Bess had begun restoring and enlarging her ancestral manor house at Hardwick in the late 1580s; however, in 1590, after Shrewsbury's death, she turned her attention to another project, commissioning an enormous new house from Robert Smythson, builder of Longleat and Wollaton. Hardwick Hall represents a watershed in English architecture, not because its patron was a woman, but because it radically altered the typology of the English house through its most distinctive feature, the form and placement of the great hall. By situating the great hall at the center of a symmetrical plan and providing a means of direct visual and physical access to it, Smythson openly defied tradition, constituting both a new form and a new meaning for the country house.[23]

Bess's gender endows her with an alternative source of power to control the very grounds on which the social visibility of gender topography is inscribed: Bess "capitalizes on her ability to see and be seen [at the great hall], flaunting her power

---

[23]   Friedman, "Architecture," 50.

and undermining the challenge of others."[24] Bess's visuality stands in for her own manipulation of the terms of the social transaction in the great hall.[25]

So Finch intends Eastwell to combine two sorts of purpose, providing a space for gender reconfiguration of which the loophole, the aperture, and the trace are architectural expressions, insofar as they survey literary areas to plot as well as gender boundaries to cross. Eastwell Park is sublimated into what she calls "Poetry's native of the Place," or a cultural locus of educating the new taste for the garden:

> Whilst *Eastwell* Park does each soft gale invite,
> There let them meet and revel in delight,
> Amidst the silver beeches spread their wings
> Where ev'ry bird as in *Arcadia* sings.
> ....
> And Poetry's a native of the place.
> Those *Eastwell* hills let ev'ry breeze renew,
> Which from adjoining seats kind neighbours view;
> Pleas'd in the artful gardens which they boast .... . (88–104)

As the title of another poem, "Upon Lord Winchilsea *Converting* the Mount into a Terras," illuminates, Finch converts her retreat into a poetical artifact in the same way that Lord Winchilsea, her husband's nephew, converts the mount into an architectural artifact. Finch argues that Eastwell Manor conceals all the beauties of the park: it is, therefore, an error of the old to break the beauty of the landscape. Although rugged, striated lines of the natural mount are being changed now into a smooth view, just as the mount makes way for an architectural design to take place, Finch asks why there is no vision without the division of labor in man's sphere of architectural projects. While man's labor produces the glory of the seat from the same natural ground, woman is alienated and marginalized from the landscape. Finch laments the loss of the oak tree:

> When untimely fate
> Sadly prescribed it a too early date,
> The heavy tidings cause a general grief,
> And all combine to bring a swift relief.
> Some plead, some pray, some counsel, some dispute;
> Alas in vain, where power is absolute. (29–34)

---

[24]   Ibid, 53.

[25]   For more discussion of the significance of the country house, see Mark Girouard, *Life in the English Country House: A Social and Architectural History* (New Haven: Yale University Press, 1978); John Summerson, *Architecture in Britain 1530–1830* (Harmondsworth: Penguin, 1969); John Harris, *The Artist and the Country House: A History of Country House and Garden View Painting in Britain, 1540–1870* (London: Sotheby Parke Bernet Publications, 1979); and Christopher Ridgway and Robert Williams, eds., *Sir John Vanbrugh and Landscape Architecture in Baroque England 1690–1730* (Thrupp, Gloucestershire: Sutton Publishing, 2000).

The catastrophic event of an oak tree being cut down evokes the traumatic memory of the Bloodless Revolution, for she writes, "trees are sentenced to death," as if to suggest that the oak tree was the symbol of the king. The violence of paternal power is so absolute that it displaces communal speech acts into muffled whispers and unspeakable groans. Finch's practice of writing a poem about the male and masculine violence of power, however, does more than an ideological engagement, for she is layering up the strata for enacting power in poetry. The visibly enacted power in cutting down the oak tree provides an invisibly enacted literary power in educating a "futuristic" cultural logic of how to "read" the landscape garden:

> The new wrought gardens give a new delight
> Where every fault that in the old was found
> Is mended, in the well disposed ground.
> Such are th'effects, when wine, nor loose delights
> Devour the day, nor waste the thoughtless nights,
> But generous arts, the studious hours engage,
> To bless the present, and succeeding age.
> Oh, may Eastwell still with their aid increase,
> Plenty surround her, and within be peace.
> Still may her temperate air his health maintain,
> From whom she does such strength and beauty gain.
> Flourish her trees, and may the verdant grass
> Again prevail, where late the plough did pass:
> Still may she boast a kind and fruitful soil,
> And may someone with admiration filled
> In just applauses and in numbers skilled,
> Not with more zeal but more poetic heat,
> Throughly adorn bravely what we relate. (65–83)

Insofar as the capacity for aesthetic judgment identifies those most suited to rule the realms of both taste and politics, Finch teaches the significance of the newly "wrought" garden. As early as 1703, Finch's eye penetrates into the public function of the landscape garden. Later in the century, the country house provided a public space for tourists to supply the believing eye. In further complicity, armed with enthusiasm, the tourist represents the official view. In search of authentic sites of patriotism, the initial site, such as the country house's garden, struggles more often than not to resemble its representations, which is the case of the British gardens to come.[26] The issue of "forgery" in relation to landscaping has a double aspect:

---

[26] Jane Austen mocks this touristic enthusiasm with Catherine Morland's excessive response to Northanger Abbey. On a more theoretical note, however, Austen utilizes a viewer as an agent whose object is to discern the "shape" of a particular socioscopic practice. Peter de Bolla argues that because the regime of the picture (i.e., the map is representational, whereas the sentimental eye is self-organizing) the circulation of the eye demands a new inquiry into eighteenth-century visual culture. Peter de Bolla, "The Culture of Visuality" in *The Education of the Eye: Painting, Landscape, and Architecture in Eighteenth-Century*

first of all, in relation to language, which is old-fashioned, out of date, antique; and also in relation to its referent, which is made to seem ancient or ruinous, like follies and hermitages in landscape gardens. By refusing this forged landscape and official language, Finch fashions the green environment on which the new landscape, including the living practice of writing poetry, unfolds for the venue of a utopian community.

The country house supplies Finch with a medium of poetry; it serves, more significantly, as the material infrastructure of the new social and political ties among her female friends. Finch enjoyed recognition and friendship from other female friends through what McGovern describes as "an informal, loosely structured type of network."[27] In "To a Friend," Finch writes, "in Praise of the Invention of Writing Letters." "The Wings of Love were ... / ... shaped into a Pen, / To send in Paper-sheets, From Town to Town, / Words smooth were they, and softer than his Down. / ... / And hopt, from Bough to Bough, supported by the Wind" (11–16). The image of the letter as *anima*, the Latin word meaning breath, breeze, and spirit (as in the Latin word *pneuma*) shows that the author figure herself becomes a mode of address, just as her breath moves everywhere with the breeze. The power of words profoundly changes, and writing takes on unprecedented authority in a field of symbolic practices: "That the dark Pow'rs of distance cou'd subdue, / And make me See, as well as Talk to you; / That tedious Miles, nor Tracks of Air might prove / Bars to my sight, and shadows to my love" (33–36). Similar to what Julia Kristeva calls the semiotic mode of signification, Finch's epistolary writing functions to cut across the symbolic and masculine "bars" of communication, that is, the public postal services, to censure the letter: "The Charms / That under secret Seals in Ambush lie," and her letter extends across the scale of chorography, thereby securing her "the fond Engagements and the Ties" among her female friends.[28] The similarly invested structure of feminine feeling goes even further, anticipating the future control of an emerging British printing culture:

> Till time, which hastily advances,
> And gives to all new turns and chances,
> ....
> New Augustean days revive,

Britain (Stanford: Stanford University Press, 2003), 14–71. Within de Bolla's framework, Finch's "sentimental" eye serves as a cultural configuration of active looking in the new eighteenth century; therefore, it becomes a new map surveying gender topography. Lamb also notes that Cobham's plan seems to have embraced two different sorts of spectators— the inner circle of writers and politicians and a paying public, who paid for the printed guide and toured the garden. Lamb, "The Medium of Publicity," 62.

[27] Barbara McGovern, *Anne Finch and Her Poetry: A Critical Biography* (Athens: University of Georgia Press, 1992), 120.

[28] Finch, "An Epistle to Madam Deshouliers," 126. For Julia Kristeva's "The Semiotic and the Symbolic," see her *Revolution in Poetic Language* (New York: Columbia University, 1984), 19–45.

When wit shall please, and poets thrive.
Till when, let those converse in private,
Who taste what others don't arrive at;
Yielding that Mammonists surpass us,
And let the Bank out-swell Parnassus.[29]

The private means of communication becomes the feminine means of literary production.

Finch's poem titled "A Description of One of the Pieces of Tapestry at Longleat" concludes this discussion of Anne Finch. Finch's poetic voice comes from a particular feminine art of weaving, or writing the texture of, poetry. Finch's address to Raphael's tapestry cartoon moves along a continuous series of adjacent components from Sergius Paulus (the proconsul of Asia), through St. Paul, Elymas (the sorcerer who was struck blind by St. Paul), Lictors, and Barnabas, to Henry Theanor. Finch's practice of representation is an occasion of what Anne Bergren calls the *metis* practice:

> *Metis* works by continual shape-shifting, turning the morpe of defeat into victory's tool. Its method includes the trick or trap (*dolos*) … and the ability to seize the opportunity (*kairos*). Each of these exploits the essential forms of *metis*, the "*turning*" (*tropos*) that binds opposites, manifest in the reversal and the circle, in weaving, twisting, and knotting, and in every joint.[30]

Bergren's *metis* practice intersects with Finch's mode of converting her predicament into a strategically poetic and political activity. Not only does Finch establish the scene of collaborative feminine writing, but she also establishes her female friends as the surrogate writers and readers. She writes:

> Thus Tapestry of old, the Walls adorn'd
> Ere noblest Dames the artful Shuttle scorn'd:
> Arachne, then, with Pallas did contest,
> ....
> But all the Fame, that from the Field was brought,
> Employ'd the Loom, where the kind Consort wrought:
> Whilst sharing in the Toil, she shar'd the Fame,
> And with the Heroes mixt her interwoven Name. (1–9)

Finch identifies herself with Ovid's Arachne, who equips herself with a transformative force of tapestry she also envisions as feminine. "All Arts are by the Men engross'd / And Our few talents unimprov'd or cross'd" (12–13). But Finch attempts to shatter and subvert the very opposition of gender relations between feminine inferiority and masculine superiority. For this, she engages

---

[29]   Finch, "A Tale of the Miser and the Poet," 191.

[30]   Anne Bergren, "The (Re)Marriage of Penelope and Odysseus: Architecture, Gender, Philosophy," *Assemblage* 21 (1993): 8.

herself as if in a rhetorical competition: "My burden'd Thoughts, which labour for a Vent, / Urge me t' explain in Verse, what by each Face is meant" (22–23). Finch seeks the (productive) cause "why Nature acts not still by Natures Laws" or "why all Illumination quench'd or veil'd" in Raphael's tapestry cartoon. In other words, Finch is searching for the cause that gains its materiality in the effects, that is, "an absent cause" immanent in the structure of effects—"Deprivation," "the Negatives of life," "One important Want," uneven gender topography, or her political predicament:

> But to thy Portrait, Elymas we come
> Whose Blindness almost strikes the Poet dumb;
> And whilst She vainly to Describe thee seeks,
> The Pen but traces, where the Pencil speaks.
> Of Darkness to be felt, our Scriptures write
> Thro' all thy Frame such Stupefaction reigns,
> As Night it self were sunk into thy Veins:
> Not by the Eyes alone thy Loss we find,
> Each Lineament helps to proclaim thee Blind.
> An artful dimness far diffus'd we grant,
> And failing seem all Parts through One important want. (66–79)

By ascribing Elymas's blindness to "one important want," a lack of his faith in *Kyrios*, that is, the Crucified Lord, Finch convokes the question: "Who is, can be, and must be the real Sovereign?" Into the history of the Kingdom of Britain does Finch knead her poetry, a process of turning back (*kairos*) and, undeniably, a political act of intervening (*kairos*) in that which Finch's present state continues to lack. Finch's practice of *metis*, a weaving-together of the *topos* and trope of personal displacement, shifts the perspective of the poet's "speechless" predicament to the "traumatic" event of the Bloodless Revolution of 1688. Finch's poetic consciousness traces its cause retrospectively and casts it forward in her poems; the result is the anticipation of control and its converting force of address. The anticipation of control implies a critical stance from which Finch continues to engage politically and poetically with the displaced Stuarts in their absence. The practice of *metis* reconfigures the feminine means of communication as the means of feminine literary production. Finch forms a sense of community with the new social ties and allies, who are in one another's bodily presence and engage in a common enterprise that is an end in itself. Thus, the real and focal sense of feminine communication that takes place in Eastwell Park becomes a centering and radiating force to form the new public space for the communities of privilege that combine feminism and celebration.

Chapter 10
Masculinity, Space, and Late Seventeenth-Century Alchemical Practices

Laura Miller

Context: Space and the Scientist

Thomas Shadwell's theatrical satire *The Virtuoso* (1676) mocks a Restoration natural philosopher who, from his country estate, attempts to master too many talents for his intellectual capacity to support. At the end of the play, Sir Nicholas Gimcrack—the would-be virtuoso—shifts his focus to alchemical practice. He laments, "Am I deserted by all? Well, now 'tis time to study for use: I will presently find out the Philosophers Stone; I had like to have gotten it last year, but that I wanted May-Dew, being a dry season."[1] This ending mocks the false optimism of Gimcrack, who thinks he can solve the problem that centuries of alchemists had faced—finding the compound that would turn base metals into gold—with a single, ordinary ingredient. Gimcrack's interest in alchemy connects to his interest in philosophy: many natural philosophers were eager participants in alchemy, and it made an enticing subject for drama. Alchemy had also been satirized in Ben Jonson's *The Alchemist* (1610), in which the character of the alchemist is a charlatan who deals in false promises. Shadwell's play not only criticizes science, it also aligns scientific ineptitude with an inability to manage one's personal relationships. The same Gimcrack who is unable to achieve the intellectual feats of a true virtuoso is cuckolded: he is unable to control the women in his life because the play's male leads, Longvil and Bruce, outwit him.

Gimcrack's neglect of his marriage and family shows comedically how domestic obligations inhibit a person from engaging in the focused pursuit of knowledge, and vice-versa. In *The Virtuoso,* the spaces in which characters pursue marriage, socio-professional networking, and scientific experimentation overlap. The characters often engage in two different modes of interacting with the same space simultaneously, yielding comedy and farce. This chaotic setting prompts the play's audience to question the compatibility of philosophical pursuits and a traditional marriage, much as Sade's *La Philosophie Dans la Boudoir* (1795) would later juxtapose non-normative sexuality with libertine philosophy, forcing readers to reevaluate two scenes in which people commonly interact with private spaces: those of contemplation and of sex. Was private contemplation

---

[1] Thomas Shadwell, *The Virtuoso* (London: Henry Herringman, 1676), 100.

incompatible with heterosexual marriage, in which private spaces often competed with public, familial spaces? The central domestic problem with characters like Gimcrack was also central to the lives of late seventeenth-century alchemists: alchemy was a private practice connected to solitude and celibacy, and was performed by increasingly public men, many of whom were married and sociable. In *The Virtuoso*, removing the boundaries between the public and the domestic in turn removed the enclosures that separated semi-private scientific practices from public life, and thus facilitated criticism of these practices.

Alchemy and philosophy also challenge the way we view the intersections of gender, publicity, and privacy. Historian Lawrence Klein helped to recast definitions of gender and public and private spaces in his refutation of the "domestic thesis" that binary gender divisions mapped neatly onto the binaries of public and private.[2] Klein has argued that "there is no one 'public/private' distinction," much as there is no singular male/female division, and that "a closer examination of space and language" is necessary for situating gender within discussions of public and private.[3] Klein presents four contexts for reinterpreting publicity and privacy, including an "associative public sphere" fueled by cultural norms and sociability. In this sphere, he contends, "The 'public' and the 'private' were, thus, aligned with the difference between openness and secrecy, between transparency and opaqueness. ... 'Public' referred to those matters that were open to participation by some others or by people in general, while 'private' matters were, in some respect, restricted or closed."[4] During the late seventeenth century, alchemy sat at this crossroads "between openness and secrecy" as scientific practices became more embedded in public social life.

This essay examines alchemy at the intersection of gender, space, and publicity, investigating the uses of language to evoke alchemical space and practices that overlapped with domestic spaces. Like the practitioners of everyday life Michel de Certeau identifies, those who practiced alchemy in the late seventeenth century had to work against the strategies governing domestic and public space. Examining the varied tactics alchemists adopted in the pursuit of alchemy within spaces planned by others reveals important connections between space, identity, and gender during a time of transition. Alchemists attempted to reconcile the contradictory definitions of the philosopher and the public man of science during a time when the conflicts of terrain for both were spatial as well as philosophical ones. Practitioners such as Robert Boyle were relatively open about participating in the formerly secretive practice of alchemy, whereas other alchemists, such as Isaac Newton, remained secretive. I show how this associative public sphere posed problems to the identity of the alchemist, as alchemists struggled to reconcile the idealized identity of

---

[2]   Lawrence E. Klein, "Gender and the Public/Private Distinction in the Eighteenth Century: Some Questions about Evidence and Analytic Procedure," *Eighteenth-Century Studies* 29, no. 1 (1995): 97.

[3]   Ibid., 99, 102.

[4]   Ibid., 104.

the celibate and private philosopher with emerging societal pressures for men to participate in public and sociable scientific circles. These conflicting identities were often worked out in the written traces that alchemists left.

Alchemy alters understanding of the spatial and gendered practices associated with scientific knowledge making, in particular the scholarly narrative that too neatly aligns publicity, masculinity (in the form of the "gentleman"), and truth. Although scholars of early modern science have paid more attention to alchemy in recent years, the study of alchemical practices requires us to reevaluate established narratives of late seventeenth-century science, including the narrative of "gentlemanly sociability" as a component of scientific credibility. The concepts of "gentlemanly sociability" and "scientific credibility" initially described by Steven Shapin and Simon Schaffer have been understood to be aligned with one another and united in the semi-public places where scientific experiments occur. However, the semi-private and enclosed alchemical practices of Restoration scientists were not isolated, even though they were confined. The gender negotiations in alchemical practice cannot be glossed under a vague term such as "gentlemanly" or "sociable"—which means that we must reexamine the role of masculinity in social histories of seventeenth-century science.

Associative Masculinity and Diversified Alchemical Practices

The emerging bourgeois gentleman whom Jürgen Habermas identifies is a new type of male figure whose domestic life is oriented toward the public sphere.[5] Philip Carter and other recent critics have written about the ways such men circulated in enclosed public spaces, such as theatre boxes and coffeehouses.[6] However, these same transformations in British society were at odds with the private lives of natural philosophers. As Schaffer and Shapin write, late seventeenth-century philosophers were often pressured to be sociable—not just to royal patrons, but to one another.[7] One's public reputation as a philosopher could become tied to one's gentlemanly status, a tension between public and private that was difficult to uphold.

This tension between publicity and privacy meant that the semi-public practice of scientific experimentation and the largely private pursuit of alchemical knowledge were also changing. The changing domestic priorities of the natural philosopher necessitated an altered understanding of domestic space as well as

---

[5]   Jürgen Habermas, *The Structural Transformation of the Public Sphere: An Inquiry into a Category of Bourgeois Society,* trans. Thomas Burger and Frederick Lawrence (Cambridge, MA: MIT Press, 1991).

[6]   Philip Carter, *Men and the Emergence of Polite Society: Britain 1660–1800* (New York: Longman/St. Martin's Press, 1997).

[7]   Steven Shapin and Simon Shaffer, *Leviathan and the Air-Pump: Hobbes, Boyle, and the Experimental Life. Including and Translation of Thomas Hobbes*, Dialogus Physicus de Natura Aeris, *by Simon Shaffer* (Princeton: Princeton University Press, 1989).

the gendering of that space. Michael McKeon describes paintings by Thomas Wijck and Richard Brakenburgh showing wives cooking alongside alchemists working, the laboratory sharing space with the kitchen. McKeon writes that "the conventionality of the alchemist paintings militates against reading them ... as representations of laboratory space." Rather, such paintings reveal "a household in which work and housework enjoy a harmonious coexistence."[8] Some alchemists were caught between the demands of philosophy and domesticity, however, rendering this harmony more of a compromise. Alchemy was connected to gender as well as to ideals of celibacy, as my analysis of the complicated domestic spaces of Robert Boyle and Isaac Newton will show. Although Newton and Boyle were not the only practitioners of alchemy, Boyle was so well known as an alchemist that it is likely that his model inspired others, while Newton presents a socially withdrawn alternative to understanding the connections between science and sociability. I will focus primarily on Newton, but will indicate the ways that his and Boyle's trajectories intersected.

Like the associative public sphere that Klein describes, masculinity had its own associative characteristics. D. Christopher Gabbard describes the relational qualities of masculinity in Aphra Behn's *The Dutch Lover* (1673), linking the masculinities in Behn's play to the second Anglo-Dutch War.[9] The military contact zones of Behn's play allowed for masculinity to diversify along a spectrum in which the Spanish were "macho," the Dutch were effeminate, and the English occupied the middle—strong and manly, but also civilized. This associative definition of ideal masculinity could be translated to British science: alchemy and natural philosophy involved both intellectual and physical work, so a person needed to be physically healthy, civil, and intelligent. It is also provocative that the English stage changed from a male space to a mixed-gender space during the Restoration, so other public male spaces became mixed-gender spaces.

In addition to exploring masculinity in constructive ways, the theater influenced laboratory space. John Shanahan describes the influence of *The Alchemist* on seventeenth-century laboratory space. "Laboratories and stages, then, share important physical and conceptual features consequent on being boundaries both virtual and real," he writes. "By means of physical practices and mental representations, both labs and stages can link together local and distant places and employ a mix of fixed and mobile architectures."[10] Much as the semi-public laboratory used representation and practice to yoke the local and the distant in one space, more secretive alchemical practice allowed for representational fluidity in terms of gender, space, and time. So, while *The Alchemist* may have influenced

---

    8   Michael McKeon, *The Secret History of Domesticity: Public, Private, and the Division of Knowledge* (Baltimore: The Johns Hopkins University Press, 2006), 213.

    9   D. Christopher Gabbard, "Clashing Masculinities in Aphra Behn's *The Dutch Lover,*" *SEL Studies in English Literature 1500–1900* 47, no. 3 (2007): 557–72.

    10   John Shanahan, "Ben Jonson's *The Alchemist* and Early Modern Laboratory Space," *JEMCS* (Spring/Summer 2008): 38.

seventeenth-century laboratory space, it is unclear whether it influenced alchemical space, which was not standardized.

Alchemical practice lacked standardization, in part because of its focus on secrecy, but many alchemists nonetheless imposed their own rigorous standards. Alchemical publications sought to differentiate proper alchemical practice from amateur pursuit: there were attempts to classify alchemists as of a superior class, even though alchemy was not costly. One seventeenth-century treatise, "The Practice of Lights: or an Excellent and Ancient Treatise of the Philosophers Stone" (1683), reprinted in a 1684 collection, defended alchemists: "I advise every man not to meddle with this science unless they be well learned and practised. Many men do boldly meddle and clatter therein saying, it is a thing cast in the street, and costeth nought, and every man hath it, as well the poor as the rich, and every time and place, as it is in every hill and in every dale, and the value at the beginning costeth not past fifty pence."[11] In these lines, publicity, or "being cast in the street," challenges the legitimacy of alchemy as a historical, gentlemanly, and covert practice.

Bruce Janacek's work has shown that Elias Ashmole had an individualistic approach to alchemical practice that intersected with his antiquarian interests; the diversity of alchemical pursuits meant that a practitioner could adapt his alchemy to his other philosophical strengths, including activities like antiquarianism that were more costly than the 50 pence alluded to previously. Janacek writes that "Some alchemists attributed vast, even cosmological significance to their work, believing they were purging the natural world of its impurities, redeeming a natural world that had fallen as surely as Adam and Eve had fallen. The philosophers' stone was therefore often associated with explicitly theological themes of redemption and restitution."[12] Even the motives of alchemists, and their interpretations of alchemical substances, varied.

Newton and Boyle pursued alchemy individualistically as well, marrying their scientific (and in Boyle's case, social) strengths to their alchemical work. Much as Newton was methodological, private, and suspicious, the alchemical space he evoked seemed secretive and policed. Newton was continually interested in discovering systemic truths from alchemy. As Dobbs writes, "he attempted to bring order out of the chaos" and labored intensely at both writing and experimentation to find the unity he sought.[13] Boyle, by contrast, offered a permeable alchemical

---

[11]   "The Practice of Lights: or an Excellent and Ancient Treatise of the Philosophers Stone" (1683), rpt. in *Collectanea Chymica: A Collection of Ten Several Treatises in Chymistry, Concerning the Liquor Alkahest, the Mercury of Philosophers, and other Curiosities worthy the Perusal* (London: Printed for William Cooper, at the Pelican in Little Britain, 1684), 37.

[12]   Bruce Janacek, "A Virtuoso's History: Antiquarianism and the Transmission of Knowledge in the Alchemical Studies of Elias Ashmole," *Journal of the History of Ideas* 69, no. 3 (2008): 398.

[13]   Betty Jo Teeter Dobbs, *The Janus Faces of Genius: The Role of Alchemy in Newton's Thought* (Cambridge: Cambridge University Press, 1992), 117.

space where gentlemanly sociability could reign, however much that space overlapped symbolically with other spaces.

Shapin and Schaffer write that the "uses of terminology such as 'experimental space' or 'philosophical space' [are] twofold: we have referred to space in an abstract sense, as a cultural domain. This is the sense customarily intended when one speaks of the boundaries of disciplines or the overlap between areas of culture."[14] The cultural domain of the celibate philosopher, who might answer to a royal patron or university, overlapped with that of the gentleman, who was more widely networked and who could be a scientist or philosopher as an option rather than a calling. Experimentation, then, like the common space in which different activities occur, linked hermetic philosophers to sociable city dwellers.

Of Hearths and Sperm: Domestic Conventions and Alchemical Practices

The private, enclosed nature of alchemical experimentation also enabled the exploration of gender among men commonly thought to fit the loose category of "gentleman." The writings that described alchemical practices had their own coded, figurative language. In "Praecipiolum: or the immature mineral-electrum. The first metal, which is the minera of mercury," alchemist Jean Baptiste Van Helmont writes that alchemists nickname common substances "to deceive the people."[15] Modern critic Allison B. Kavey connects the freedom to imagine gender reconfigurations with the possibilities for chemical change that alchemy enabled.[16] Kavey describes the interest in spontaneous generation in alchemy, noting its fostering of male-male couplings and other non-normative gender configurations. She finds that "alchemical discourse that lends itself to sexual description dismantles a natural world made of binaries in favor of one constructed by systems of sympathy."[17] The new possibilities for imagining gender could liberate men who wanted same-sex sexual relationships as well as those who aimed at the ideal of the celibate philosopher. These alchemists also occupied a world in which homosocial relationships were the norm. Such philosophers ideally refrained from carnal desires in the pursuit of knowledge. The private and semi-private nature of alchemical practices in England allowed for greater freedom to redefine one's gender than the easy alignment of gentlemanly sociability and public display in discussions of masculinity imply. In private, alchemists could manipulate substances with names like "the Doves of Diana" and "spiritual semen" to change gender or fuse gendered objects together.

---

[14]   Shapin and Shaffer, 333.

[15]   Jean Baptiste Van Helmont, "Praecipiolum: or the immature mineral-electrum. The first metal, which is the minera of mercury," rpt. in *Collectanea Chymica*, 50.

[16]   Allison B. Kavey, "Mercury Falling: Gender Flexibility and Eroticism in Popular Alchemy," in *The Sciences of Homosexuality in Early Modern Europe*, ed. Kenneth Borris and George S. Rousseau (New York: Routledge, 2007), 221–41.

[17]   Ibid., 222–23.

Kavey writes that "alchemists frequently used male and female labels for metals to encourage readers to think about the qualities generally associated with human males and females."[18] Some examples from "The Practice of Lights" confirm how gendered the language of alchemy was; it often focused on terms associated with generation. "After this preparation done," the author advises, "put the man and the woman in their bed and keep them close, and in the egg shall be brought forth a child."[19] Later in the text, the author writes that "it appeareth, that meat and drink is the first substance of sperm, and sperm is the very true substance and matter to bring forth man: so likewise in mercury of white matter, and of white substance cometh that mercury … the sperm of metals" (39). Alchemy even offered experimenters a chance to play a masculine, godlike role, using chemicals to create the net Vulcan employed to trap Venus and Mars in an embrace. In "The Practice of Lights," the secret of the philosopher's stone is told as if he who finds it can repopulate the earth. The author writes that "the very truth of this secret is more worth and richer than man can devise; for of his own sperm or seed he shall evermore encrease and multiply to the worlds end" (43). Descriptions like these indicate that the physical space in which alchemists experimented was a procreative one in which the tools of domesticity were used for generative purposes. The consistently deployed metaphors of domestic sexuality and reproduction likewise imply that alchemists' experiments belied the celibate stereotypes of philosophical asceticism. Even though there were no homes designed around the structural needs of alchemists, they found ways to accommodate domestic spaces to fit their needs and rich possibilities for manipulating systems of sexual metaphor.

As provocative as the metaphorical names for alchemical substances were, alchemy also required ordinary domestic tools. An important element of alchemical space that was also central to domestic space was the hearth, a functional space often associated with home and family. In alchemy, the hearth did not just provide heat and warmth, it allowed for the heating of different chemicals in experimentation. An alchemical text from the 1680s offers a description of an oven and custom-made pan: "G. H. M. made an iron pan a foot and half long, and a foot broad, the brims two inches deep, and made an oven in a chimney with bars of iron in the bottom, whereon he placed the pan, and a place under to make fire, and it will after this manner sooner be burned (viz half a day) the smoak will not hurt it."[20] Images of alchemical labs and of eighteenth-century kitchens show the prominence of the fireplace or hearth in each. An alchemist could be intrigued by fire beyond having an interest in the heat that could alter matter; Boyle and Newton, for example, explored the use of fire in ancient religions. Newton's interests in the origins of the world included the prytaneum, the "fire for offering sacrifices [that] burned perpetually in the heart of a sacred place."[21] He

---

[18]   Kavey, "Mercury falling," 237.

[19]   "The Practice of Lights," 35.

[20]   "Aurum potabile: or the receipt of Dr. Fr. Antonie," rpt. in *Collectanea Chymica*, 73.

[21]   Qtd. in Dobbs, *Janus Faces*, 151.

admired this ancient "fire at the heart of the world"[22] and studied the architecture surrounding it.[23] Newton's image of the sacred fire of Solomon's Temple in Israel, connected to his alchemical experiments, would eventually be published after his death. In spite of Newton's solitary, unsociable reputation, his interests in the ingredients of domestic space corresponded with a more sociable philosopher's curiosity. Similarly, Boyle's *Sceptical Chymist* (1661) used philosophical curiosity to develop an understanding of the products of alchemical experimentation.

Tensions between Sociability and Privacy in Newton's Alchemical Practice

Although the career of scientists such as Boyle seemed to trend toward the sociable, sociability itself was a loose term that was not wholly positive during the seventeenth century. It was possible to be excessively sociable or excessively formal. Philip Carter writes that "more and more people sought, and could afford to seek, a reputation for refinement cultivated by involvement in polite social spaces" during the eighteenth century.[24] As Carter writes, the more sociable public spaces were not honest spaces that accurately reflected an individual's true opinions: "theorists were conscious that the desire to appear sociable brought with it pressures for the would-be fashionable individual to assume a polite persona at the expense of other personality traits."[25] Perhaps de Certeau had this kind of narrative in mind when he described stories themselves as "spatial trajectories" because "every day, they traverse and organize places; they select and link them together; they make sentences and itineraries out of them."[26] The narrative of cultivated refinement in sociable circles, in which people are always linked to one another, contrasted to the untidy allegorical narrative of alchemy, which, because of its explicit sexual metaphors and references to bodily fluids such as semen and urine, did not always conform to expectations for civilized conversation.

The narratives loved by practitioners of alchemy allowed the possibility of material transformation and changes in identity—including gender changing—that a non-alchemist might find confusing or distasteful. Alchemists could even reconfigure the spatial trajectory of one story into an alchemical narrative, much as they responded to Ovid's *Metamorphoses*. Because of its allusions to shape-shifting and change, Ovid's *Metamorphoses* were important to practicing alchemists like Boyle, Newton, and Robert Hooke, and the *Metamorphoses'* free explorations of

---

[22]   Dobbs, *Janus Faces*, 150.

[23]   Ibid., 152–53.

[24]   Philip Carter, "Men About Town: Representations of Masculinity and Foppery in Early Eighteenth-Century Urban Society," in *Gender in Eighteenth-Century England: Roles, Representations and Responsibilities*, ed. Hannah Barker and Elaine Chalus (New York: Longman/St. Martin's Press, 1997), 48.

[25]   Ibid., 51.

[26]   Michel de Certeau, *The Practice of Everyday Life* (Berkeley: University of California Press, 2002), 115.

gender did not escape their attention. For Hooke and Boyle, and later Newton, the physical transformations described in the *Metamorphoses* served a more practical purpose—that of actually using the materials mentioned in the text for alchemical recipes. Because the *Metamorphoses* could be useful in alchemical practice, alchemists read them differently than a person who was reading for their literary merit or for entertainment. Thomas Willard proposes that "the answer to the question 'Why look for answers in Ovid?' seems to be that [Ovid] knew about almost everything ... if the poet knew the answers, they could be found in the poetry, no matter how much he hid them."[27] The story of Diana and Actaeon was a popular one for alchemists; Newton, for instance, annotated it in one of his copies of *Metamorphoses*. The phrase "Diana's Doves" was used as a code phrase for the metal silver in George Starkey's *Marrow of Alchemy* (1654–1655), which Newton cites in an alchemical manuscript. The branched silver compound the "Philosopher's Tree" is also referred to as the "Tree of Diana." Although gender was part of the practice of alchemy, it was also connected to chemical experiments and recipes, rather than to the stories of physical love that the *Metamorphoses* celebrated.

In her analysis of Newton's alchemical works, Dobbs describes Newton's use of the *Metamorphoses* for alchemical experiments, such as the fusion of Mars (iron) and Venus (copper) into a blue alloy called "the net."[28] But beyond the possible alchemical applications of the *Metamorphoses,* they could provide a linguistic screen for alchemists to discuss experimentation openly. Using the *Metamorphoses* could bridge alchemy with sociability and popular culture in a form of double-coding. Alchemists were participating in a literary discourse with a shared metaphorical language as well as a secretive chemical practice. Beyond the use of alchemical recipes in the *Metamorphoses*, the use of metaphor and allegory provided a bridge between publicity and private experiment.

Reevaluating a figure like Newton in the context of alchemical practice offers a different narrative of his masculinity than those commonly presented in the history of science. Newton was a reclusive and irritable scholar, yet his publications, especially the *Principia*, gave him a reputation as a superman among men, a reputation he did not discourage. This same Newton rented London rooms to conduct alchemical experiments with his close friend Nicolas Fatio de Duillier, known as Fatio. Newton's exchange of letters with Fatio reveals a need for secrecy and privacy in alchemical practice. As an alchemist who also challenged orthodox theological views, Newton encoded or concealed some of his communications. Some of Newton's most intimate correspondence that connected to alchemy was kept private. For a period, Newton and Fatio were fast friends, with a common interest in alchemy and an intense personal interest in one another. Fatio

---

[27]   Thomas Willard, "Ovid and the Alchemists," in *Metamorphosis: The Changing Face of Ovid in Medieval and Early Modern Europe*, ed. Alison Keith and Steven Rupp (Toronto: Centre for Reformation and Renaissance Studies, 2007), 153.

[28]   Ibid., 161–64.

helped Newton with translations of French alchemical texts and Newton shared scientific and mathematical knowledge with Fatio. Compared to Newton's other correspondence, his exchanges with Fatio were emotional: the letters confirm Newton's ambivalence toward community and his desire for privacy. Newton wrote to Fatio shortly after their meeting in 1689. The letter survives, but with carefully cut holes. Places where several written words have been physically cut out of the letter are indicated with empty brackets [ ]:

> Sir, I am extremely glad that you [ ] friend and thank you most heartily for your kindness to me in designing to bring me acquainted with him. I intend to be in London the next week and should be very glad to be in the same lodgings with you. I will bring my books and your letters with me. Mr. Boyle has divers times offered to communicate and correspond with me in these matters but I ever declined it because of his [ ] and conversing with all sorts of people and being in my opinion too open and too desirous of fame. Pray let me know by a line or two whether you can have lodgings for us both in the same house at present or whether you would have me take some other lodgings for a time till [ ] I am Yours most affectionately to serve you Is. Newton[29]

The content is relatively straightforward, even given the missing passages. Newton arranges to meet Fatio in London, where the two will meet a third party for some covert activity. Newton prefers Fatio to Boyle because of Boyle's indiscretion and even wishes to lodge with Fatio, presumably to facilitate the secrecy of this activity. He avows his affection to Fatio as he closes the letter. Alchemy is the secretive activity described, and Newton's aims in coming to London are at least partly to conduct some experiments with Fatio and to meet another unnamed person who is also connected to alchemy in some way. A different letter of Fatio's mentions his desire to acquaint Newton with a friend in London who has extra alchemical supplies and needs to dispose of them, so the person in the letter may have been a supplier.

The three places where words are cut from the letter break down as follows: The first describes the friend of Fatio with whom Newton wishes to be acquainted. The second refers to Robert Boyle, whose openness about alchemy was well known. Regardless of Boyle's candor, Newton's letter had the words removed to prevent his own identification with alchemy. The final section where words have been removed poses more problems. This section offers a rare discussion of the space where alchemy would be practiced. Here, Newton discusses the possibility of his lodging with Fatio. There appears to be no reason for these words to be removed, as they ostensibly relate to the finalization of living arrangements. Several factors may account for these words' omission. Newton could have mentioned alchemical experiments briefly in this passage because the location refers to the place of experimentation. Alternatively, the three removed lines may

---

[29]   Isaac Newton, October 10, in *Correspondence*, 1689, III, ed. H. W. Turnbull. Cambridge: Cambridge University Press for the Royal Society, 1959.

have been an encoded message between the two men that was cut out once the meaning of the lines had been deciphered.

As it stands, it is a warm note from one man to another with common interests during a developing friendship. It is noteworthy, however, that the words were physically removed from the letter rather than blotted out in ink. The actual removal of the words meant that no one could decipher them, in contrast to effacing or blacking out words, where a reader could possibly glean what was written. The holes resemble an external representation of the methodological problems germane to studying alchemy: even though there is material that one can study, the many gaps are tantalizing. The words of alchemical treatises remain, although few physical images of alchemical experiments, especially ones conducted in urban spaces like the rooms Newton would have rented, endure. The importance to Newton and Fatio of secrecy and private space—including lodging together—remains in spite of the holes.

Newton had many different kinds of letter from Fatio over the years, suggesting that the men's relationship was a complicated one. Their relationship, even though few letters survive, was important enough in Newton's life that he kept some seemingly inconsequential letters from Fatio. Newton burned many of his private papers before his death, so it is difficult to know how long the men stayed in contact. Fatio was significant enough in Newton's life that, following Newton's death in 1727—nearly 40 years after the men's meeting—Newton's nephew-in-law, John Conduitt, corresponded with him about the epitaph for Newton's memorial in Westminster Abbey.

Reflections on Alchemy, Masculinity, and Domestic Space

It was often considered abnormal for philosophers to marry; marriage was incompatible with the life styles of many men who chose a philosophical career, including Galileo (who had a mistress instead) and Descartes. However, some of the records of Newton and Boyle show a discomfort with living lives of philosophical and most likely physical celibacy. Elizabeth Potter unites Boyle's interest in science with the ways that gender informed his scientific practices. Potter argues that Boyle "worked to produce a new form of masculinity conducive to the new science as he envisioned it, and he did so by reinforcing a traditional form of femininity, one necessary for the new man of science."[30] Even though Boyle wrote privately that men bore partial responsibility for women's lack of education, he did not seek publicly to redress this gap.

According to Potter, Boyle's new definition of masculinity was that "the new man of science be a chaste, modest heterosexual who desires yet eschews a sexually dangerous yet chaste and modest woman."[31] This definition contrasts to

---

[30]   Elizabeth Potter, *Gender and Boyle's Law of Gases* (Bloomington: Indiana University Press, 2001), 3.

[31]   Ibid., 4.

the lives of celibacy idealized by the medieval scholastics, in that this new man of science lived in a comparatively secular, usually urban setting and circulated among men and women. Boyle's definition also contrasts to the masculinity in Behn's *The Dutch Lover*, in which the Englishman is valued because he rests between two extremes of behavior. The tension between wanting and refusing to participate in a fully consummated domestic relationship seemed to be very real to Boyle, and I propose that this tension was strong because in the late seventeenth century, it revealed the changing relations between the married patriarch and the unencumbered philosopher, who were brought into contact with one another professionally. For example, fellows of the Royal Society such as Henry Oldenburg and Samuel Pepys were married and contributed to scientific knowledge. William and Margaret Cavendish, the Duke and Duchess of Newcastle, shared interests in natural philosophy as part of their marriage. The duchess even made a controversial visit to the Royal Society, something that would only have been possible for someone of her social rank. The duchess was not, however, highly regarded in scientific circles, and was often dismissed as an eccentric. The ideas I have outlined in this essay illuminate why she was treated this way: a woman entering a masculine space that was already vulnerable and in flux would be hard to incorporate or respond to positively.

Apart from marriage's perceived incompatibility with philosophy, the practice of alchemy was also incompatible with the demands of a traditional heterosexual marriage—especially with regard to sex. Both Newton and Boyle were reluctant to marry and claim to have remained chaste, and both demonstrated a fear of what women's sexuality could do to men. During his nervous breakdown in the 1690s, Newton once accused John Locke of attempts to "embroil [him] with woemen."[32] Some of Newton's theological papers also reveal concerns with men's unhappiness in marriage, including his lengthy correspondence with John Locke on marital unhappiness and the marginalia in Newton's Bible. As Potter writes, "the necessity of chastity for undistracted devotion to God is deeply connected in Boyle's texts to its necessity for proper investigation of nature."[33] For Boyle, "serving God through experimental philosophy is best done by a celibate man."[34] The conflicts between devotion and desire in Boyle's life stemmed from the very exposure to public life that the experimental philosophy he espoused produced.

Neither Boyle nor Newton ever married, and both enjoyed the vicarious benefits of housekeeping and hosting by women to whom they were related, but not married: in the case of Boyle, by his sister Lady Katherine Ranelagh, and in the case of Newton, by his niece Catherine Barton Conduitt. Both Boyle and Newton, then, enjoyed domestic spaces in which someone who was not a wife fulfilled a wife's role. Significantly for Boyle, this meant that the woman who lived closest

---

[32]   Isaac Newton, September 16, in *Correspondence*, 1693, III, ed. H. W. Turnbull. Cambridge: Cambridge University Press for the Royal Society, 1959.

[33]   Potter, *Boyle's Law*, 8.

[34]   Ibid.

to him would not excite the "illicit male desire" he feared from women.[35] After Newton died, those who inherited his personal and professional legacy were not the children of a wife, but Catherine and her husband, John Conduitt, who would later succeed Newton as Master of the Mint. During the latter years of his life, Newton lived in a domestic space in which public and private collided: his nephew-in-law was also his would-be biographer. Both Newton and Boyle lived the public functions of a marriage without the physical embodiment, because in spite of the social transformation through which they lived, they were deeply grounded in celibate philosophical traditions. However, they were not without the opportunity to think freely about gender and sexuality. Alchemy offered a contained space for the natural philosopher to think about gender and a metaphorical space for him to think about sexuality while still remaining celibate.

---

[35]   Ibid., 9.

Chapter 11

Invaded Spaces in Charlotte Smith's
The Banished Man (1794)

Heather Ann Ladd

The prologue to Charlotte Smith's *The Banished Man,* a fictionalization of recent events on the Continent and Britain's response to the people and ideas flowing out of France, pointedly ushers a work composed in private into the public world of print. Smith intends her audience to pause in the novel's paratextual vestibule— to borrow Gérard Genette's architecturally inspired image—before entering the world of her Romantic novel; in this vestibule, readers are acquainted with the private factors that shaped a text now open to public scrutiny. Humbly introducing her audience into the imperfect confines of her literary imagination, Smith is not only self-conscious about this movement of her private writing into the public sphere, but also acutely aware that it is as a female author that she negotiates this movement of her work. We see these concerns reflected in her writing as Smith both echoes and individuates the apologetic rhetoric characteristically used by eighteenth-century professional authors. Cataloguing the "great disadvantages"— including a frustrating legal battle over her late husband's inheritance—that affected her writing, Smith carefully details how her authorial energies have been sapped by family obligations, financial pressures, and the other menial "inconveniences " of her existence.[1]

Images of seizure dominate Smith's prologue as she refers to her family's dispossession and the thieves, those *"weazles* [sic], *wolves,* and *vultures,"* who have "plundered" her property and who are admittedly portrayed in her work.[2] Her defensive strategy against those who might metaphorically invade (that is, misinterpret or cut down) the words and characters of her novel is to make a personal appeal to their sympathy, inviting them into her domestic/discursive space. The author preemptively resists the unsympathetic and censorious among her readers, critics, and booksellers, diffusing their censure by predicting and articulating it. Smith's imagery of aggression and physical encroachment here is evocative, given that the author was herself concerned about invasions of a more literal nature: when she lived in Bath, she received mail from her booksellers under an assumed name so her creditors would not find her. This prologue's evocative

---

[1]   Charlotte Turner Smith, *The Banished Man,* in *The Works of Charlotte Smith,* ed. M. O. Grenby, vol. 7 (London: Pickering & Chatto, 2006), 106.

[2]   Ibid., 108.

imagery of invaded spaces—coupled with its intense scrutiny of the boundaries between private and public expression—heralds some of the major thematic concerns of Smith's novel. As this essay argues, *The Banished Man* is a text that foregrounds spatial intrusions, ranging from the onslaught of revolutionary armies (in the case of the novel's French emigrants) to intrusive booksellers (in the case of the author-character Mrs. Denzil).

Questions about the invasion, occupation, and ownership of space are inseparable from questions about gender because of the ways in which patriarchal society regulates the relationship between women and their environment. Space is intimately connected to the gendered self as it is conceived and charted from both the inside and the outside: by family, society, and the individual.[3] The lives of many of the fictive female (and feminized male) characters that people *The Banished Man*, like the life of Smith herself, are teeming with restrictions, inconveniences, and violations, whether legal, economic, or artistic in nature. Moreover, Smith's resistance to such invasive forces, as articulated in her prologue, is restated— or, more precisely, ventriloquized and embodied—by the cast of infringed-upon characters who appear throughout the novel. Through a close examination of Smith's fictional portrayals of invaded domestic and artistic interiors and her attendant foregrounding of resistant feminine spaces, I demonstrate that invaded space is used by the novelist to signal the female/feminized subject's social vulnerabilities and limitations. The analysis of the novel begins with a discussion of the literal invasion that occurs at its beginning, focusing on the threatened Castle Rosenheim and the Baroness Rosenheim, a figure of resistance against the might of the revolutionary armies. Moving into increasingly abstract concepts of invasion, I subsequently examine the novel's protagonist, D'Alonville, who, feminized by displacement, experiences the discomforts of invasion and exile, which are both physical and social. Finally, I discuss the invasions—economic and artistic—endured by the female author-character Mrs. Denzil, an Englishwoman whose trials as a writer highlight commerce as an invasive force, counteracted by sympathetic communities and the Romantic imagination.

As a novel of the revolutionary period, *The Banished Man* would initially seem to be interested in space as a public, national issue; in this sense, space is implicitly gendered masculine. Set amongst the political upheavals of the 1790s, Smith's work depicts the geopolitics of violently contested territories, and abstractions like political and national ideologies are realized through war and its immediate consequences. The action of the novel's early chapters occurs in Austria, near the French border at the soon-to-be besieged Castle of Rosenheim. The French army,

---

[3]   Recall that in the eighteenth century, property and titles—formal indicators of spatial dominance—conferred social status. Eighteenth-century women, single or married, were often accustomed to less (and less stable) personal space, contingent as it was on the magnanimity of the owners of the property they occupied, usually their husbands, brothers, or fathers. The nation's laws guaranteed them no personal freedoms, as they were not legally considered persons.

according to reports, is following the retreating Austrian and Prussian forces and nearing this stronghold. Despite such early accounts of military movements and machinations, however, the reader quickly perceives that Smith is less interested in representing the battlefield than the home and its inhabitants. This focus is reflected even in the novel's opening sentences: although exile is conceptually significant in a story that revolves around perilous acts of emigration and repatriation, setting— as it conveys either comfort or discomfort—is often a vital consideration in the novel, which begins with a "storm which had never ceased the whole day."[4] This tempest "howl[s] round the castle of Rosenheim," presaging the other threatening forces—invading troops, fire, revolutionary ideas—that act on this domestic structure and the people within.[5]

The castle, a symbol of the past as it vies, futilely, with the present and future, is "situated on an eminence, and once strongly fortified, could make but a feeble resistance now against the troops."[6] A medieval holdover, this castle has no power against a besieging radical force with its new ideas and warfare technologies. The titled owner of this archaism, the Baron de Rosenheim, is a general in the Austrian army. Drawn away to Vienna by his military duties, he cannot act on the imminent "danger to his private property."[7] Nonetheless, his wife, the Baroness de Rosenheim, confidently takes on the role of leader, bravely facing the threats of invasion, and is "unwilling ... to abandon the castle to the care of servants."[8] The Baroness, who refers to the property as "*her* little garrison," exhibits a subversive relationship to this space, for she exercises a dominance and control over the castle that is traditionally associated with male leadership.[9] Her independent reign over this space brings about a key social change, as well: while the Baron is away, a community consisting of the baroness, her daughter Madame D'Alberg, and a French stranger named Armand D'Alonville forms within the walls of Rosenheim.

In the opening chapters of Smith's novel, D'Alonville and his father, the mortally wounded Viscount de Fayolles—two aristocratic French soldiers fighting in the counterrevolutionary army—appear outside of Castle Rosenheim. These Frenchmen are initially taken to be revolutionary invaders rather than victims and resistors of the Terror. But the anxieties of the castle-bound are unfounded as D'Alonville, a modern Aeneas who carries his parent to safety, is no ruthless revolutionary but an aristocrat possessing conservative views. This pseudo-siege by foreigners is thus a false invasion, as D'Alonville offers equalizing friendship rather than physical dominance or ideological tyranny. In these early chapters, then, we see the persecuted French aristocrat being absorbed, albeit temporarily,

---

4   Smith, *Banished*, 111.

5   Ibid.

6   Ibid., 112.

7   Ibid, 110.

8   Ibid.

9   After the Baroness and her party surrender the castle and flee to Vienna, the castle is plundered, turned into a French army hospital, and finally deliberately destroyed by fire.

into the domestic space of Rosenheim, where he enjoys the society of the Baroness and Madame D'Alberg. D'Alonville, receiving a surrogate parent through the bonds of sympathy rather than blood, is grateful for the space the Baroness makes in her home for him.

The novel's early chapters are not the only ones in *The Banished Man* to highlight the social and spatial possibilities—however temporary they might prove to be— opened up by invasion and absence. Several others are similarly afflicted in Smith's novel, in which revolution, war, and private causes separate family members. The De Touranges (French) and the Denzils (English) are, like the Rosenheims, families with missing patriarchs. These "banished men" cannot exert the influence that proximity would give them and are prevented from extending their protection and their authority to their dependents. Like the Rosenheims, the De Touranges women are separated from their patriarchs by the threat of political violence and military invasion. As aristocrats and French royalists they flee the continent and live for a time in England, where they find friends in the Denzil family: Mrs. Denzil, a middle-aged author, and her children, including Angelina, the young woman who captures the heart of D'Alonville. The De Touranges' difficulties mirror those of the Denzils, who are similarly disadvantaged and rootless, but as a result of a much more localized problem: a seemingly interminable lawsuit. In a letter from Mrs. Denzil to D'Alonville, who has returned to the Continent, the authoress relates that "They are, like us, expelled from the quiet scenes of heath and copse that surrounded us at Northfellbury."[10] The exiled De Touranges and Denzils experience both physical and psychological discomfort as a result of political, economic, and social disruption. They benefit only temporarily from the tranquility and natural beauty of the countryside. Nonetheless, a new space is forged by the female community of exiles, despite the uncertainty that pervades their lives in England.

Eleanor Ty has observed that in *Desmond* (1792) and in *The Young Philosopher* (1798), Smith "makes connections between domestic and political oppression by male figures of authority."[11] These tyrants contract or invade either the "borrowed" female spaces of the home or the "disputed" spaces of national and international conflict. Smith also envisions ways around this subjugation and "celebrates female energy and the feminine powers of connection, sympathy, and faith."[12] Ty's reflections on *Desmond* apply equally to *The Banished Man*. Reconstituted social and familial groups continue to operate, with some difficulty, when dispossessed of their lands and fortunes. Together, they are able to mitigate the new vulnerabilities, chiefly material, created by patriarchal absence. The De Touranges are impoverished by their flight from France but the Denzils, although

---

[10]   Smith, *Banished*, 344.

[11]   Eleanor Ty, "Revolutionary Politics: Domesticity and Monarchy in *Desmond*," in *Women, Revolution and the Novels of the 1790s*, ed. Linda Lang-Peralta (East Lansing: Michigan University Press, 1999), 130.

[12]   Ibid., 141.

likewise economically disadvantaged, assist the De Touranges in England. In all of these instances, it is female helping hands—or those feminized by the sympathetic powers of the imagination—that alleviate suffering. These unconventional family units are much more accepting and outward-looking than the traditional, masculine-governed family. Significantly, women and feeling men see beyond national identities to forge meaningful social ties.

Although Smith's novel follows the movements of a number of female exiles, émigrés, and outcasts like the Rosenheim and De Tourange women, D'Alonville is the focalizer of *The Banished Man*. Even simply as a prominent exile in a novel of exiles, he is a necessary topic of scrutiny in an essay about space and the outcast, as well as gender, because of his feminization. In this section I examine how spatial concerns manifest themselves in the novel's central character, whose experiences with invasion and exile parallel those of the author-character Mrs. Denzil later in the novel. D'Alonville is also important as he operates as a literary nexus of sorts, because of the way his story intersects with others, creating links between characters and narrative threads that highlight the existence of a "shared state of banishment" in the novel.[13] This sense of communal dispossession is connected to gender, as the young Frenchman is aligned with the feminine via his status as a landless asylum-seeker. The narrator terms him "the unhappy, persecuted wanderer,"[14] a label which is just as appropriate for Mrs. Denzil, as I will discuss later in this essay. In her representations of D'Alonville, Smith carefully underscores the fact that his sufferings, the personal consequences of political and economic forces, involve spatial dynamics. And despite his sex, D'Alonville is affected by the gender politics of space, which become increasingly apparent in *The Banished Man* as multiple characters find themselves marginalized and impinged upon by stronger material or ideological forces.

When D'Alonville arrives in England, his nationality and position as an exile from an enemy country changes his relationship with space, public and private. On British soil, he is the intruder, regardless of his anti-revolutionary politics; consequently, he becomes subject to incursions and confinements which divest him of his prescribed male autonomy. At best a guest and at worst a prisoner, Smith's hero must endure either the horrors faced by a Gothic heroine or the hassles of a dependant, e.g., a lady's companion. Though no longer threatened with the guillotine, the aristocrat finds that there is little room for him across the Channel. The narrator reports that the "common people of England" during this period were engaged in a "universal condemnation" of the French.[15] This English xenophobia limits the hero's movements in the metropolis. His discomfiture in London's public spaces extends to the more private spaces he also must negotiate as a socially inferior visitor; he is especially conscious of propriety, knowing

---

[13]   Amy Garnai, *Revolutionary Imaginings in the 1790s: Charlotte Smith, Mary Robinson, Elizabeth Inchbald* (New York: Palgrave McMillan, 2009), 41.

[14]   Smith, *Banished*, 341.

[15]   Ibid., 227.

that his words and movements are subject to scrutiny. This exposure to a more invasive societal gaze feminizes Smith's hero; women are accorded less freedom and anonymity than their male counterparts, who had, and debatably still have, fewer social expectations and obligations to fulfill. While a guest of the Ellesmere family, D'Alonville declines an invitation to a ball, "not thinking it proper for a native of France to appear at a place of public entertainment, while so many of his countrymen were exposed to the greatest distress, and his sovereign arraigned before a tribunal of his subjects."[16] When the family leaves, D'Alonville retires to Ellesmere's "little book-room":

> It was the first time he had been alone for some weeks, for he could hardly fancy himself so in the noise and hurry of London, where, though nothing amused him, everything distracted his attention. He felt relieved by being now for a few hours left to his own reflections: for the extreme civility of Sir Maynard, the questions of the ladies, and even the attentions of his friend, were sometimes oppressive to him.[17]

His emigration from France feminizes him by divesting him of privacy, freedom, and physical space, traditionally masculine privileges. The "book-room" is a version of the more explicitly feminine "closet," the tiny allotment of private space accorded to an eighteenth-century lady. As an emigrant in England, d'Alonville's space is circumscribed and invaded, his movements in both public and private space being self-conscious because they are influenced by surveillance.

While D'Alonville experiences social discomforts in England, on the Continent he endures much bodily discomfort. Traveling between cities, often with several other exiles, such as the Abbé de St. Remi and the De Touranges, D'Alonville is forced to accept inadequate shelter, periodically spending the night in "wretched" lodgings. Again and again, Smith emphasizes the party's physical discomfort on the road. On the way to Berlin, for example, an approaching storm compels them to take shelter at an alehouse with no beds, where they meet the Polish radical Carlowitz, who becomes their friend, and his daughter, Alexina, whom Ellesmere eventually weds. In this case and in others, suffering causes the productive breakdown of social and national barriers and facilitates the intimate connections that dampen the effects of public strife.

The social and personal discomforts that D'Alonville endures with his travel companions, though wearying, are mere vexations next to the solitary trials he faces when he returns to France. D'Alonville finds himself in mortal danger when he attempts to return to his homeland. He is captured and, becoming a political prisoner, is only saved from the guillotine by his brother's timely intervention. Space—both mental and physical—closes in on him in a dramatic way when he is incarcerated and witnesses the Terror first-hand. D'Alonville's mind is invaded by images of the horrors he has beheld, the "spectacles, which continually haunt

---

[16]   Ibid., 236.
[17]   Ibid., 237.

[his] imagination" and "embitter [his] existence so entirely, that it is hardly worth having."[18] Smith uses images of the natural landscape invaded and perverted by violence, using Voltaire's words to express D'Alonville's revulsion for "des fleuves de sang" (rivers of blood) and "ces champs de carnage" (fields of carnage).[19] Overrun by bloodthirsty, power-hungry revolutionaries, France is to the nauseated hero now a "polluted country," ruined by self-mutilating internal invasion.[20] As D'Alonville's experiences and politics prompt him to minimize his self-identification as French, his ebbing of national identity is indicative of a more stereotypically feminine relationship with space, one less concerned with forceful occupation, ownership, and other institutional, rather than intuitive, bonds; space is to be shared between liberal individuals tied together by sympathy—personal as well as political.

Smith's author-character in *The Banished Man*, a novelist and mother, articulates a similar ambivalence about her national identity, embittered as she is by her experiences as a British subject. Like D'Alonville, she is alienated on several levels, robbed of her property and social position and the respect she could command, and shunned for her politics, which are too liberal for reactionary England. Mrs. Denzil recognizes her kinship with the French aristocrat, an outsider, and she and her immediate family befriend D'Alonville. A seemingly endless legal battle has impoverished and demoralized her and she has endured the indifference of friends, relatives, and her bookseller. With no permanent domicile or steady income as a buttress against poverty's advances, Mrs. Denzil has a relationship to space that is representative of those of the novel's other female or feminized emigrants: her social status is tenuous, her gentility unmoored by land or money, her gender impeding the acquisition of both, and, like D'Alonville, she finds herself needy and therefore imposed upon, denied the liberty and privacy these assets would secure.

Katherine Binhammer, in her incisive examination of revolutionary domesticity in Charlotte Smith's Desmond, analyzes the complexities of politics, gender, and space and the merging and demarcation of spheres of influence. "The boundaries between the domestic and the political," Binhammer argues, are "drawn, paradoxically, through their very integration."[21] I also consider the collapse of these spacial categories, considering invaded space as a political and domestic crisis; the concept of the home as battleground comes to the fore with the introduction of Mrs. Denzil into the narrative. Despite the repeated evocation of the revolutionary wars, as well as Gothic castles and dungeons, a number of significant scenes in the second half of the book occur in England, and in particular in the private environs of this genteel authoress of reduced circumstances, clearly

---

[18] Ibid., 225.

[19] Ibid.

[20] Ibid., 352.

[21] Katherine Binhammer, "Revolutionary Domesticity in Charlotte Smith's *Desmond*," in Lang-Peralta, *Women, Revolution and the Novels of the 1790s*, 27.

modeled after Smith herself.[22] Autobiographical elements aside, Smith makes a case against recurrent spatial oppression, the curtailment of female space as it occurs on an almost day-to-day basis. As a woman without a husband, Mrs. Denzil cannot exercise adequate control over her physical environment, and the family's legal troubles have an impact on the amount and kind of space allowed to Mrs. Denzil and her children. She inhabits a permeable space which is infiltrated by public marketplace economics, namely by importuning creditors and booksellers, as well as their letters and their agents. She lives in a state of besieged domesticity, invasive encounters occurring in the contested familial space of her home, where the opposing demands of work and personal life are expressed *vis-à-vis* space.

Like other proto-feminist British women writers of the 1790s, Smith highlights living space as a contentious issue, the apportionment of space being fraught with ideological implications, even when it seems to be a private matter concerning private individuals. As an impoverished woman, Mrs. Denzil is personally affected by the humiliations and concessions involving space. Her psychic distress is evoked not only through abstract expostulations against "the spectre Poverty," which haunts her imagination, but by telling details about how she responds to her habitat.[23] Worries involving space are shown to be psychologically taxing, as shadowy duns; her creditors even invade her dreams in the moments of sleep she can get despite work and insomnia. Mrs. Denzil possesses a Romantic susceptibility to setting that is tried by her difficult living situation, as the material realities of yielded space are insistently forced upon her consciousness. Mrs. Denzil's uninvited guests remind her that her literary powers are constrained, fettered by a financial dependence that precludes genuine self-expression.

Space does not simply mean land or rooms, but mental space, the peace born of privacy, freedom, and tranquility. In the Romantic text, space is, of course, not limited to topical geographies, but includes mental ones, the cartographies of art, sympathy, and the imagination. It is hardly surprising, then, that space and creativity are intimately linked in *The Banished Man,* which, as a Romantic text, is deeply invested in liberty (physical and mental space) as a powerful catalyst for artistic creation. Mrs. Denzil's literal interior spaces—the rooms in which she lives and writes—are in interesting ways analogous to the compositions she produces, her figurative interior spaces. Her interiors, when invaded by commercial agents, are connected to the production of mediocre novels. When they remain inviolate, however, these spaces result in the production of more inspired work. Romantic verses "written" by the author-character and embedded within the larger prose text can be viewed as a kind of ideal and seemingly impermeable interior space, an intimate milieu of subjective, personal revelation. Yet her other works, chiefly

---

[22]   Jacqueline M. Labbe, writing about the thematically similar poem "The Emigrants" (1793), argues that "Smith uses the situation of the emigrants to construct a case detailing her own sense of exile." *Charlotte Smith: Romanticism, Poetry and the Culture of Gender* (Manchester: Manchester University Press, 2003), 118.

[23]   Smith, *Banished*, 397.

novels, possess no such immutability and are subject to the unwelcome editorial incursions of a bookseller-character and to the disheartening effects of her financial troubles. The blunt intrusion of commercial intermediaries into her household impels her to foster a community that assuages her distressing circumstances. The reader's interest is focused on interiors, the space of the small society that develops around the authoress. The shift from the plight of the émigré to that of the struggling author is appropriate, all the same. Mrs. Denzil herself articulates the connection between the persecution of French aristocrats and her own private trials. She is sympathetic to the émigrés of the revolution because, as she claims, "in every species of humiliation and mortification, none of the unhappy exiled French have suffered, perhaps, more than I have done."[24] In her view, political oppressions are comparable to the economic and artistic oppressions faced by the professional author.

These oppressions are made apparent in the depictions of the invasion of interior spaces, trespasses occurring within both the author-character's domestic sphere and this putative writer's texts. The image of the besieged writer harassed by impertinent agents of the book trade is not a new one, recurring in eighteenth-century imaginative literature and visual culture—for example, in William Hogarth's "The Distrest Poet" (1737–1741). The reader, urged to sympathize with Mrs. Denzil (and, by extension, with Smith, as she is engaged in an act of self-doubling) is given an unromanticized glimpse into the life of the overworked novelist. Though physically and mentally exhausted, Mrs. Denzil still

> leaves her bed in a morning, when her health permits, to go to her desk; from whence she rises only to sit down to a dinner she cannot eat, waited upon by an awkward boy, or a strapping country-girl, who stare at madam 'bin [sic] as how she writes all them there books that be on the shelf.[25]

The reaction of her servant points to the general lack of understanding that is extended to her. Instead, as a singular sufferer, she finds herself under the intrusive gaze of others, and the sympathy of others rarely runs deep enough for them to commit to action. The impoverished author's life is circumscribed and her distress evoked not only through vague expostulations, but also by telling details about the physical space she inhabits and accounts of her personal discomforts. Smith's author-character candidly lists the indignities and nuisances that stem from her precarious financial position. She complains that "the small beer is almost out" and the neighbor's pigs have run into her garden and destroyed her flowers because she cannot afford to build a protective wall around her plants.[26]

The incident involving the pig in the garden signals more than bad luck; the destruction of her flowers also reminds us of Mrs. Denzil's tenuous position as a temporary tenant and the fleeting nature of her moments of happiness. Her

---

[24]   Ibid., 344.

[25]   Ibid., 275–76.

[26]   Ibid., 276.

flowerbed, "on which she depended for the amusement of a few solitary moments in the spring," is a cherished private space, somewhere she can be alone and indulge in her love of natural beauty.[27] The event of its destruction, then, underlines the authoress's powerlessness, the extent to which her domestic space is subject to interruption. Moreover, she does not sleep well, and when she does slumber, "the figure of that animal, 'hateful to gods and men', a Dun, appears before her disturbed imagination."[28] Even that intensely private interior space—her dreaming mind—is invaded by the spectres of financial insecurity. Her dreams reiterate the economic woes that plague her daylight hours, visited as she is by corporeal creditors.

The material conditions that impact Mrs. Denzil's physical and mental health are magnified by the intrusion of commercial intermediaries into her household. Smith shows her wrangling with her bookseller and dealing directly with aggressive creditors. Smith stages a conversation between her authoress and Mr. Thomas Tough, who has called to demand a sum of money. These kinds of intrusive agents, like the trespassing pigs, can rudely enter her residence because she lacks the protective barrier, financial stability, which would keep them at arm's length. Following this unpleasant exchange, Mrs. Denzil resumes writing and recognizes, with some bitterness, that pragmatic concerns rather than a transcendent mood of inspiration incite her to composition; she sarcastically calls these circumstances a "precious recipe to animate the imagination and exalt the fancy!"[29] The interiority of her creative consciousness is invaded by this intruder, for whom she is writing "safe" imitations of bestselling books—commodities for which her market-driven bookseller might advance her money. Mrs. Denzil's novels contain nothing of herself; they reflect neither her own literary tastes nor her values and life experiences. This alienation is apparent in the dichotomy in tone between the author's heated tête-à-tête with her creditor, who treats her to "rude threats and boisterous remonstrances," and the stock scenes which she must pen after this harsh treatment. In the evening after this interview, "she must write a tender dialogue between some damsel, whose perfections are even greater than those 'Which youthful poets fancy when they love,' and her hero; who, to the bravery and talents of Caesar, adds the gentleness of Sir Charles Grandison, and the wit of Lovelace."[30] The scenes she is compelled to compose bear no traces of the events occurring around her. When a nearby family is afflicted with scarlet fever, Mrs. Denzil interrupts her literary drudgery to extend charity to them, despite her own poverty. She arranges to send them the necessities they might require and then resumes her work, which—replete with the sentimental agonies and ecstasies—is far removed from the reality of the sufferings of her neighbor. She notes that "[t]he rest of the day is passed as before; her hero and her heroine

---

[27]   Ibid.
[28]   Ibid.
[29]   Smith, *Banished*, 275.
[30]   Ibid., 275–76.

are parted in agonies, or meet in delight."[31] Communities of active benevolence alter the dynamics of space, sympathy creating inroads into the domestic milieu: concern for her neighbors "invades" her consciousness in a socially, though not economically, productive way.

The disconnect between the real events of Mrs. Denzil's life and the artificial narratives of her commercial writing suggests the extent to which the demands of English readers and, by extension, the bookseller, colonize her artistic output. But invading financial agents remind her that her creative powers are constrained, fettered by a financial dependence that precludes self-expression. An inviolate and secure, that is, masculine space would help her realize her true potential as a writer; intrusions of space reaffirm her lesser literary status. She is a "lady novelist" producing generic works.

Mrs. Denzil's interactions with her bookseller, Joseph Clapper (probably based on Joseph Bell, a prominent bookseller in Smith's time), whom Smith characterizes as mercenary and insensitive, are as disheartening as those involving her duns. Clapper first invades the author-character's "interiors" or spaces of literary creation (her home and her works in progress) by sending an unpleasant letter in which he demands that she submit the rest of her manuscript. He reminds her—needlessly— that he paid her in advance for her work, telling her that he is "much surprised at your not sending up, as promised, the end of the third novel purchased by me."[32] The relationship between the author and this commercial intermediary is governed solely by economics; the bookseller evinces no sympathy or personal regard for his author, whom he must know is already working herself—quite literally—to death. His impatience is palpable when he informs her: "The trade expects it the time I notified to them it would be ready; and the printer informs me he shall stand still if not supplied immediately."[33] Clapper bullies and threatens Mrs. Denzil, his intrusive letter jarring her with its content and style, its exaggerated, "businesslike" tone, and its formal yet unlettered phrasing. He coldly ends his missive: "Hopin [sic] to receive the manuscript (as you have had money thereon,) at the time before-named."[34] The profession of writing, as a topic of business in Clapper's letter to Mrs. Denzil, is reduced to its most quotidian essence, the author simply one of the many participants engaged in the endless manufacture of saleable books. More concerned with attractive packaging, titles, and page counts than he is with literary content, Clapper gives Mrs. Denzil an exact quota to fill, telling her that he "[m]ust insist on having a hundred page at least by Saturday night; also the Ode to Liberty."[35] The irony of the latter part of his request is unmistakable. His demands make Mrs. Denzil a veritable slave in the service of the literary marketplace; working within her bookseller's time constraints, she is

---

[31] Ibid., 277.
[32] Ibid.
[33] Ibid.
[34] Ibid.
[35] Ibid.

supposed to pen verses celebrating liberty, an ideal of human existence to which, in her pecuniary situation, she has little access. Mrs. Denzil's lack of aesthetic liberty and artistic agency as a writer are revealed further when her bookseller mentions that he "shall change the title of that."[36]

Mrs. Denzil and her bookseller interact directly later in the novel, when he pays an unexpected visit to the author after she misses her deadline because of an illness brought on by overexertion and exacerbated by anxiety. The bookseller uses her economic dependence on him to justify his boorish intrusion into personal space. "With the rudest threats," the bookseller "demanded the completion of her engagement, declaring that he would prosecute her if this was not fulfilled by the day which he had named."[37] Clapper cruelly exacerbates Mrs. Denzil's suffering by sabotaging her character: "he took an opportunity of telling the people who belonged to [the house], that they would do well not to trust their lodgers, for to his certain knowledge they would not be paid."[38] This is a particularly unpleasant tactic, ensuring that not only her home but also her identity is breached, Mrs. Denzil being painted as both insolvent and untrustworthy. This encounter, as the bookseller intends, serves to increase the already severe pressure on the overtaxed novelist to complete her work. Shortly thereafter, Mrs. Denzil's landlady follows suit and also demands money owed by the author, as "the precaution thus given, and from a man who was supposed to know, had an immediate effect on the behaviour of the people."[39] Invasions of the domestic space continue, Angelina reporting in a letter that

> during my absence the woman of the house had brought in a lawyer's clerk, and a sheriff's officer, and had taken an inventory of my mother's books, the musical instruments that belonged to my sister, and what little plate and linen we had, and had given my mother notice, that the ruffian to whom this inventory was given would remain in the house in order to take care that none of the effects were removed, till the money due to Mrs. Capern, the landlady, was paid.[40]

The novelist's daughter stresses the toll that that these events have taken on her beleaguered mother's health. The bookseller's visit to her household is a pivotal scene in Mrs. Denzil's narrative, underlining the extent to which her household, like Castle Rosenheim, is a vulnerable space, invaded by forces which appear to precipitate ruin.

Mrs. Denzil, an Englishwoman, also finds her nationalistic sentiments dampened by her experiences as a social outcast and a target for discursive attack. Her peace of mind, like her home, is invaded by the harsh judgments of not only those with whom she does business, but even her so-called friends. She

---

[36] Ibid.

[37] Smith, *Banished*, 397.

[38] Ibid.

[39] Ibid.

[40] Ibid., 398.

receives a letter from one such friend, "who remonstrated with her on the restless temper she had lately evinced, which had induced her more than once to change her residence."[41] Mrs. Denzil's correspondent incorrectly ascribes internal rather than external motivations to her "frequent removals," blaming the victim rather than recognizing the systemic oppressions contributing to her plight. Her friend sermonizes to her, dropping "proverbs of great authority" into a letter laden with unhelpful advice.[42] Unfairly judged by her countrymen, many of whom have not experienced or witnessed great hardship, she turns away from the complacent English and toward the emigrants, who are reeling from their devastating losses.

The dislocations and relocations of the Denzils align them with the nomadic French, who are likewise "victims of injustice," both individually and collectively as a disempowered group. Mrs. Denzil's friendship for the emigrants is animated by her own personal mortification:

> Mrs. Denzil, herself a veteran in calamity, and who had gone through, and not without many severe struggles, the hard task of learning to submit to adversity, and all its train of humiliation, was only impressed with a deeper sense of compassion for the unfortunate family of De Touranges, and grew more solicitous to serve and assist them, though her power to do so became every day less.[43]

Significantly, when Mrs. Denzil describes herself as "banished," Smith aligns her authoress with D'Alonville, the title character. Both she and the French hero are "banished from the rank of life where fortune originally placed us," using a term for physical exile to describe the social exile from the class into which she was born.[44] Neither Mrs. Denzil nor D'Alonville find England to be "the country where such a change of fortune is much softened to the sufferer."[45] The word "softened" would suggest the alleviation—material or psychological—of poverty's discomforts by a supportive community; in an ideal world, something Mrs. Denzil as a writer of fiction is accustomed to envisioning, the sufferer would be succored rather than shunned for her misfortunes. Conjuring up an illusory space of utter freedom— an alternative to English society, remote from this invasive marketplace—the authoress articulates her desire "to pack up my children and my books, in which consist all my riches, and, like a female Prospero, set forth for some desert island, or any island but this dear England of ours."[46] Mrs. Denzil, vocal in her criticism of the state of English society, ironically praises its merits and fantasizes about extricating herself from its injustices. The physical irritants of a "desert island" are

---

[41] Ibid., 271.
[42] Ibid.
[43] Smith, *Banished*, 403–4.
[44] Ibid., 268.
[45] Ibid.
[46] Ibid., 272.

preferable to poverty, which is compounded, as it is for D'Alonville and the other exiles, by social discomfort.

In *The Banished Man,* Mrs. Denzil enacts a retreat from the aggressive and impersonal intrusions of commerce when she visits a friend in Bristol and, from there, relocates her family to Wales, where she lives for a time in a remote cottage. This first picturesque spot proves to be "the very scene of inspiration."[47] She resists the tedious, unsatisfying pragmatism of an existence as a hack writer and engages with the sublime landscape around her as a Romantic poet, a dignified and gifted individual able to feelingly appreciate the natural world. While there, she composes a short autobiographical piece, *Written at Bristol Hot-Wells, in answer to a friend, who recommended a residence there to the author.* These Romantic verses, embedded within the larger prose text, can be viewed as a kind of ideal and impermeable interior space, an intimate milieu of subjective, personal revelation. Through lyricism, the writer is able to reassert the identity threatened by her patriarchal intruders. As Elizabeth A. Dolan avers, "with her depiction of woman's melancholic suffering, Smith [and Mrs. Denzil, her inscribed self] also claims literary authority. She wishes, that is, to make visible both her suffering and her poetic talent."[48]

In her mournful sonnet, Mrs. Denzil characterizes herself with gendered language as a "languid sufferer" and alludes to her "broken heart."[49] Her work, despite its elevated diction, is effortlessly produced as she obtains physical and mental space when breaking from her routine of prose composition. Unlike the novels that Mrs. Denzil mechanically churns out at a desk, these lines are spontaneously inscribed "after a moment's further conversation, in a blank leaf of her pocket book."[50] There is a smooth, near-seamless movement between the sentiments of the verse and those expressed in the framing dialogue in which they were produced. In this sense, the close relationship between her poem and her life stands in stark contrast to the divisive relationship between the stylized world portrayed in Mrs. Denzil's novels and her domestic situation. She alludes, in this episode, to a supportive community sustained by the feminine ties of empathy. The poem, part of a conversation between two friends, is a reply to Mrs. Armitage's suggestion that the writer extend her stay in Bristol. In this instance, writing encourages social bonding and genuine communication, rather than limiting them by unrealistic deadlines and unrealistic expectations of prolific output.

For the outcast, be it émigré, woman, author, or some combination of the three, dispossession can be productive in unexpected ways for male and female subjects in *The Banished Man.* Inclusive domestic yet cosmopolitan spaces come out of the traumas of disenfranchisement, and new bonds are created with the withdrawal

---

[47]   Ibid., 444.

[48]   Elizabeth A. Dolan, *Seeing Suffering in Women's Literature of the Romantic Era* (Burlington, VT: Ashgate, 2008), 22.

[49]   Smith, *Banished,* 444.

[50]   Ibid.

of the patriarch and the reallocation of power. National identities retreat into the background without dissolving entirely, while gender demarcations are likewise softened in the transnational spaces carved out by Smith's characters. United by their mutual suffering and sympathy, along with their sensitivity to the beauties of nature, her characters are also brought closer together in "Romantic androgyny," to use Diane Long Hoeveler's phrase. Smith, who self-consciously deploys Gothic tropes like the castle and the dungeon, can be considered alongside the "women writers of Gothic [who] were engaged in polemical revision of gender expectations."[51] She acknowledges these expectations in her depiction of female characters as victimized, confined, intruded upon, and exiled. Nonetheless, she also engages in a revision of these expectations, as individuals transcend the self and respond with feeling and grace to others' suffering even as such suffering encroaches on their own space.

As this essay has argued, Smith deals with the problem of space, not simply as clashes between the public and the private, but as tensions between collective concerns and individual ones. Space is both a domestic and a national issue, men and women laying claim to space in their homes as well as their countries. Smith depicts space in *The Banished Man*, particularly feminine spaces brought about by social upheaval, as often disturbingly porous, but not always unproductively so. Mrs. Denzil and the female/feminized characters in the novel are by turns oppressed and (self-) liberated by their spatial dispossession. The banished characters in Smith's text, though deeply and tangibly affected by their material circumstances, are able to rise above these circumstances, banishment becoming about escape and the promise of new beginnings, not just victimization. Constrained spaces of penury, powerlessness, and discomfort suppress but do not permanently occlude the writer's Romantic artistry, which surfaces regardless of the woes and banalities that plague their days. Uncertain spaces stimulate the imaginative sympathies that bind communities of political and economic exiles, which are comprised of individuals, who, like Smith, are receptive to the "social passions which were hailed as the forces of progress."[52] With gender and nation diluted as forces of conformity, new unities are made possible and agencies realized. Invasions—be they physical or mental—oppose, yet inadvertently engender different kinds of inclusive, egalitarian private space. This new space, which can be described as domestically cosmopolitan, welcomes rather than rejects the incursions of the sufferer into its midst. That incursion creates an opportunity for empathy and charity in *The Banished Man,* and these are embraced with enthusiasm by Smith's women and men alike.

---

[51] E. J. Clery, *Women's Gothic from Clara Reeve to Mary Shelley* (Horndon: Northcote House, 2000), 7.

[52] Chris Jones, *Radical Sensibility: Literature and Ideas in the 1790s* (New York: Routledge, 1993), 183.

Chapter 12
Seeking Shelter in
Charlotte Smith's *Emmeline*

Kathleen M. Oliver

The England depicted in Charlotte Smith's 1788 novel *Emmeline, the Orphan of the Castle* consists of institutions, edifices, and interiors that privilege the masculine to the exclusion and/or detriment of the feminine. Within these gendered spaces, male guardians treat their young female wards with disdain and neglect, nor are they above denying them their rightful inheritances; husbands are cruel, profligate, or debauched, and male lovers seduce, then abandon, or harass and intimidate, the women they profess to love. Legal and banking systems assure that female independence and security are thwarted at every possible turn, while self-serving lawyers and bankers utilize the utmost arts of their professions to deprive, even to cheat women out of what few rights and assets they possess. While interior spaces offer protection in terms of feminine reputation, women must surrender all freedoms and submit to arbitrary, restrictive, and often abusive control in order to secure this protection. In contrast, exterior spaces offer freedom and self-discovery for women, but with substantial risk in regards to physical virtue and feminine reputation. In this essay, I argue that Smith utilizes space as a means to articulate women's (lack of) place in late eighteenth-century English society, and that, as a solution, Smith offers idealized, though liminal, sites wherein interior space and nature are integrated, and which, in turn, provide women with security in terms of their physical bodies and their reputations, while also procuring women the rights of subjectivity and the pleasures of self-possession.

The essay is organized into three parts. The first section examines domestic spaces such as castles, houses, and cottages, arguing that Smith's novel repeatedly depicts domestic interiors as domains of masculine authority and privilege. The second section explores exterior spaces, which, in Smith's novel, are almost always natural spaces. This section asserts that Smith renders the natural world as a bi-gendered space which proves simultaneously liberating for women and potentially dangerous in regards to female virtue and feminine reputation. The final section analyzes Smith's proposed solution to the spatial dilemma encountered by women—interior spaces that integrate the natural world as fully as possible, theoretically allowing for both freedom and security.

An Englishman's Home is His Castle: Women and Domestic Spaces

In the past 20 years, scholars such as Amanda Vickery have questioned the hard division between the "separate spheres" of home and work, as well as the assumption that feminine domestic life was necessarily enervating and oppressive. In addition, they have shown that during the latter part of the eighteenth century, the ideology of "separate spheres" was only at its nascent stage, and that the concept held little practical meaning for members of the landed gentry, who generally did not "work" for a living. Nonetheless, during this time period, domestic interiors were considered the proper domain of women from the gentry and the upper-middle station, as women were principally responsible for household management and child-rearing. With only rare exceptions men held rights to, ownership of, and authority over interior spaces. English common law precluded women from owning freehold land;[1] social customs such as primogeniture and entail privileged male inheritance of land and buildings; and hierarchical ideology—predominant in religion, government, and the culture as a whole—still insisted that "the female is by a law of nature put under the dominion of the male."[2]

If "women and men experience spaces and places differently and ... these differences themselves are part of the social constitution of gender as well as that of place,"[3] then even if gentlewomen in eighteenth-century England were predominantly associated with domestic interiors, the fact that men retained ultimate control over the home suggests the vulnerability of women in relation to domestic space, something that men from these same social stations either would not experience or would experience in substantially different ways. As Mona Domosh and Joni Seager note, "it is within the home that most violence against women is committed."[4] For eighteenth-century English women, the space that is "home" is always at risk of being lost (lack of ownership precluding feminine agency), and/or it exists as a possible site of abuse. In addition, the fact that a woman's relationship to home is always fraught with some measure of potential peril or loss serves to perpetuate and naturalize cultural ideas of "feminine" vulnerability and weakness. The space that is "home" is imbued with contradictions, for it simultaneously exists as feminine space (the central site for women's work and the principal location for the protection of feminine reputation and the female body) and as masculine space (a site controlled and owned by men). If, as the old

---

[1]   Anne Laurence, *Women in England, 1500–1760: A Social History* (London: Weidenfeld and Nicolson, 1994), 228.

[2]   J. R. Dinwiddy, "Bentham's Transition to Political Radicalism, 1809–10," *Journal of the History of Ideas* 36, no. 4 (October/December 1975): 683–700, 698. Dinwiddy quotes from Jeremy Bentham, Bentham MSS, box 125, folios 138–41 (London: University College).

[3]   Linda McDowell, *Gender, Identity and Place: Understanding Feminist Geographies* (Minneapolis: University of Minnesota Press, 1999), 12.

[4]   Mona Domosh and Joni Seager, *Putting Women in Place: Feminist Geographers Make Sense of the World* (New York: The Guilford Press, 2001), 34.

adage goes, an Englishman's home is his castle, then woman's place within this proverbial castle is subject to the whims of its lord and master.

Consistent with its times, its author's social station (born into the gentry and married into the middle station), and its author's personal experiences (a profligate husband), Smith's novel depicts the instability of the notion of "home" for women. While "home" ostensibly offers women some semblance of protection—in terms of food, shelter, and feminine reputation—even these basic needs prove uncertain, tenuous, and conditional when the home itself is ruled by a careless or cruel master. Smith's domestic interiors are rarely the sites of domestic bliss, and the protection provided to women in such an environment more often than not is mere cultural pretense and illusion. Again and again in *Emmeline*, a woman is forced "to quit her home,"[5] either because the physical abode itself has been forfeited through male imprudence, or because the home exists as the site of emotional abuse or sexual threat.

The novel opens at Mowbray Castle, the ancestral home of Emmeline Mowbray, the presumed natural daughter and sole offspring of the late Edward Mowbray. Because of her illegitimacy, Emmeline possesses no legal entitlement to the only home she has ever known, as illegitimate children were considered *filius nullius* (nobody's son) under English law. In consequence, her father's only brother, Lord Montreville, is "proprietor," "possessor," and "master" (45) of the castle, which has fallen into ruin and disrepair under his management. Lord Montreville is Emmeline's guardian, but it is evident from the start that, for him, she exists merely as an insignificant piece of household inventory, unwanted, but of insufficient interest or value to warrant much notice: "Lord Montreville, on taking possession of Mowbray Castle, *found* there his [brother's] infant daughter" (45); the child is "*suffered* to remain" (46) [emphases are mine]. As Diane Long Hoeveler notes, Smith's novel demonstrates "how precarious it is for women to navigate and negotiate a social system that defines them always as appendages, dependents, ornaments, or incidental accoutrements to the 'main chance,' the patriarch."[6] Within the ruined confines of Mowbray Castle, the orphaned child is provided with the basics of food and shelter, yet receives nothing more from the lord and master of Mowbray Castle. Emmeline experiences Mowbray Castle as home, responding to it in terms of memory and emotions—it is the site wherein "she had passed her early infancy, and had known, in that period of unconscious happiness, many delightful hours" (75). In contrast, Lord Montreville experiences Mowbray Castle solely in terms of entitlement and possession, and, as Loraine

---

5   Charlotte Smith, *Emmeline, the Orphan of the Castle*, ed. Loraine Fletcher (Peterborough: Broadview Press, 2003), 95. All quotations are from this edition of the text, and all subsequent quotes are noted parenthetically.

6   Diane Long Hoeveler, *Gothic Feminism: The Professionalization of Gender from Charlotte Smith to the Brontës* (University Park: The Pennsylvania State University Press, 1998), 43.

Fletcher notes, neither Montreville nor his son "has earned the privilege that they take for granted."[7]

Such is Emmeline's existence at Mowbray Castle until the deaths of the elderly steward and housekeeper who have raised her. When their replacements arrive, Emmeline's spatial relationship to the castle begins to change; specifically, the range of interior space available to Emmeline suddenly and radically narrows. Whereas before, only "one end of the castle [was] habitable" (47), the entirety of the castle—habitable and uninhabitable—was available for Emmeline to roam. Now, however, the new steward, Maloney, treats her with an "assured and forward manner" (49), and, in order to avoid his "insulting familiarity" (49) and "troublesome civilities" (51), Emmeline must confine herself to her room, pleading "ill health" (51). She realizes the improper nature of his attentions, and finds herself physically and sexually threatened by him: "The freedom of his behaviour … might now, she feared, approach to more insulting familiarity; to be exposed to which, entirely in his power, and without female companion, filled her with the most alarming apprehensions" (49). Although this male is not her guardian, he exists as his surrogate, and his easy presumption of ownership—over the castle and Emmeline—renders the preponderance of interior space inhospitable to its sole female inhabitant.

Next, the arrival of the "dirty, tawdry, and disgusting" new housekeeper, Mrs. Garnet, chases Emmeline from her accustomed room, forcing her to take refuge in "the only unoccupied room not exposed to the weather" (53)—a small room in one of the turrets of the castle. Because Mrs. Garnet gives herself social airs, hierarchically privileging her London upbringing over the rural upbringing of her Welsh charge, and because she appears highly interested in "the gallantries of Maloney" (54), aligning herself with his interests, her intrusion into the castle functions as further encroachment of the masculine into the domestic space. Despite all this, for Emmeline, the castle remains a refuge, if only because to leave it is potentially to forfeit all rights to protection: "By abruptly leaving the asylum Lord Montreville had hitherto allowed her, she feared she might forfeit all claim to his future protection" (50), and, as dubious as that protection has been, it is Emmeline's sole source of security from hunger and want.

When Lord Montreville finally arrives at Mowbray Castle after a 12-year absence, it becomes clear how tenuous an asylum Mowbray Castle truly is, how masculine its interior spaces. In preparation for the visit of Lord Montreville and his lordship's only son, Frederic Delamere, the "whole end of the castle which was yet habitable" is repaired and "furniture from London" is sent (55), merely to transform the castle into a hunting lodge for a few weeks for Delamere and two of his friends. However, with the arrival of Lord Montreville, Delamere, and Delamere's boon companions, Emmeline's true spatial relationship to the castle is revealed: within its interiors, she exists as part inventory, part prisoner. Delamere,

---

    [7]   Loraine Fletcher, *Charlotte Smith: A Critical Biography* (Basingstoke: MacMillan, 1998), 97.

heir to Mowbray Castle, evinces a violent romantic interest in Emmeline that initially expresses itself in terms of property ownership. Offered the castle by his father in advance of his inheritance, Delamere muses, "I already begin to see great capabilities about this venerable mansion. I think I shall take to it, as my father offers it to me; especially as I suppose Miss Emmeline is to be included in the inventory" (61). Delamere's interest in his fair cousin results in his father's attempts to separate the two, which in turn results in further restrictions on Emmeline's spatial use of the castle. Lord Montreville refuses to "send for her down to supper" and desires that "she would remain in her own apartment; where every thing necessary should be sent to her" (61, 67). Her cousin Delamere demands of his father to know if Emmeline is "always to remain a prisoner in her own room?" (69), and though he says this to protest his cousin's absence, it is nonetheless true that, within the confines of the castle, Emmeline exists as a prisoner, not free to enjoy the interior spaces of the castle precisely because they exist as masculine spaces over which she holds no authority or control. Even the relative safety and freedom of her locked turret room is taken from her, as Delamere kicks in the door at night seeking access to Emmeline—"the metaphoric correlative of rape."[8]

With no space available to Emmeline within the castle, she must leave the only home she has ever known, yet all future "homes" and residences are also at risk, as Lord Montreville has made his economic support of Emmeline contingent upon the "condition of her concealing her abode from Delamere" (67). In contrast, her "persecutor" (72), Delamere, remains free to enjoy the castle—and to pursue Emmeline elsewhere. Emmeline's relationship to "home" is always tentative, as her cousin relentlessly pursues her wherever she goes, and as any residence she chooses is always at risk of forfeiture if her uncle chooses to lessen or revoke his financial support. The façade of "home" as a place of safety and security, a site for the protection of feminine reputation and the female body, is shown to be that—mere façade. Kate Ferguson Ellis argues, "It is when the home becomes a 'separate sphere,' a refuge from violence, that a popular genre [the Gothic] comes into being that assumes some violation of this cultural ideal."[9] In Smith's *Emmeline*, with its Gothic overtones, the domestic sphere is repeatedly violated, with the violence and violation almost always perpetrated by the very individuals (guardians or husbands) whose job it is to protect the home and its inhabitants.

It is not merely because of Emmeline's illegitimate and orphaned status that she is without agency in terms of space; other women within the novel suffer similar experiences of displacement from and/or persecution within domestic interiors. Mrs. Stafford, a married woman who befriends Emmeline, finds her home constantly under threat due to the foolish, insensitive, and often cruel behavior of her husband. Upon their first meeting in Swansea, Mrs. Stafford informs Emmeline that she has temporarily fled her home of Woodfield "at Mr.

---

8   Ibid.

9   Kate Ferguson Ellis, *The Contested Castle: Gothic Novels and the Subversion of Domestic Ideology* (Urbana: University of Illinois Press, 1989), 3.

Stafford's request, who is fond of improvements and alterations, and who intends this summer to add considerably to our house; which is already too large, I think, for our present fortune" (81). As we learn later, Mr. Stafford has impoverished Woodfield and made his home a site of suffering for his wife:

> he dissipated that property [Woodfield] ... in vague and absurd projects which he neither loved nor understood; and his temper growing more irritable in proportion as his difficulties encreased, he sometimes treated his wife with great harshness; and did not seem to think it necessary, even by apparent kindness and attention, to excuse or soften to her his general ill conduct, or his "battening on the moor" of low and degrading debauchery. (192)

Unnecessary and ill-advised architectural additions and whimsical financial schemes—"manuring land with old wigs" (203), for example—place Woodfield at economic risk, and eventually Stafford forfeits Woodfield to creditors, having "scorned and even resented her [Mrs. Stafford's] efforts to keep them [his financial difficulties] at a distance" (289). The entire family, including five small children, must flee to France. However, during the time that he remains master of Woodfield, Mr. Stafford engages in behavior that makes the home a dubious sanctuary for his wife and his children: he invites inappropriate guests to Woodfield, he conceals his amours in neighboring cottages, and he treats his wife "with reproach, with invective, with contempt." As Mrs. Stafford notes, the entire "burthen of affairs" experienced by her family must be laid at her husband's doorstep, yet he "but adds to their weight by cruelty and oppression" (420). For Mrs. Stafford and her children, domestic interiors should provide safety, security, and protection, but, due to the carelessness and cruelty of the man who holds authority over the space known as "home," this interior becomes the site of oppression—and then the home itself is lost.

One final example of the masculine domination of interior domestic space may be found in relation to the character of Lady Adelina Trelawney, whom Mrs. Stafford and Emmeline discover in a remote cottage in Woodbury Forest. The married Lady Adelina is pregnant by Colonel Fitz-Edward—not by her husband—yet we are given to understand that her moral lapse is largely due to the conditions that existed within her marital abode. Mr. Trelawney indulges in a life of dissipation and waste, with his days and nights spent in a blur of booze. When he is not sitting in "sullen silence," his conversation consists of "tiresome details of adventures among jockies, pedigrees of horses, or scandalous and silly anecdotes" (225). He invites into his home "young men of fashion, who ... would have relieved him from the affections of his wife, if he had ever possessed them." Lady Adelina notes, "They made love to me with as little scruple as they borrowed of him" (222), yet she remains faithful to her husband despite her disgust. Still obedient to her husband, Lady Adelina finds herself suddenly displaced when her drunken husband gambles away the entirely of their freehold estate (227), their various residences, and their personal effects, leaving her to the dubious protection of Fitz-Edward. It is only then, when home in all its various meanings has been lost to her, that she sexually transgresses. Once pregnant, she flees to the woodland cottage, desperate "To remain, and to die here unknown" (231).

Two female characters in Smith's novel do possess some rights and agency in regards to domestic interiors. Mrs. Ashwood, a widow, owns a residence outside of London, yet her home is constantly overrun by "a great number of single men" (109), whom Mrs. Ashwood invites and, indeed, welcomes into her home precisely because she wishes to remarry, a goal which she achieves midway through the novel. Her home, although her own, is populated by men and later becomes the property of her grasping new husband, Mr. James Croft. Why would Mrs. Ashwood deliberately seek to shed herself of property and agency? I would suggest that, as femininity itself is constructed by and within domestic spaces, Mrs. Ashwood's femininity appears at risk precisely because of her control over her house. Prior to her remarriage, the constant parade of male visitors remakes Mrs. Ashwood's home into a masculine space, as she caters to their wishes and whims; in turn, the daily transformation of Mrs. Ashwood's home into a masculine space restores her femininity and desirability in her own eyes. In addition, possessed of "an almost equal share of vanity and ambition," Mrs. Ashwood believes marriage will procure her admission "into a higher line of life," so she is willing to "sell" her house through marriage in order to secure a higher social status (109). The other female character with agency and control over domestic places and interiors is Lady Montreville, wife of Lord Montreville and mother of Delamere. The sole inheritor of a substantial family fortune, Lady Montreville treats interior spaces—and their female occupants—in a domineering masculine fashion, at one point attempting to detain and confine Emmeline within her ladyship's London townhouse. Lady Montreville has so internalized patriarchal ideology that, although she is female, her relationship to space reinforces and reproduces the cultural norm—that is, interior domestic space as masculine space. Yet significantly, all Lady Montreville's patriarchal ambitions are centered on her only son, Delamere, in whom she beholds "the last male heir of a very ancient and illustrious house" (68) and who will inherit the combined wealth and property of her and her husband. For Lady Montreville, then, interior spaces are valued principally for the fact that her son will ultimately own them; she views "home" in terms of patrilineage, primogeniture, and entail. As Linda McDowell notes, "The term 'the home' must be one of the most loaded words in the English language—indeed in many languages,"[10] and Smith's novel demonstrates the ideological tension—the cultural tug-of-war between feminine domesticity and masculine ownership—inherent in domestic spaces.

Friends and Lovers: Women and Natural Spaces

In Western thought, nature is often aligned with the female and the feminine, through the hierarchal dualisms of nature-woman and culture-man; yet, in late eighteenth-century England, the vast majority of writers and thinkers viewed the

---

[10]   McDowell, *Gender, Identity and Place*, 71.

natural world as bi-gendered, frequently in accordance with Burkean aesthetic. In his highly influential treatise *A Philosophical Enquiry into the Origin of Our Ideas of the Sublime and Beautiful* (1757), Edmund Burke characterizes the sublime and the beautiful in specifically gendered ways. The sublime evokes awe or terror through a display of power, privation, vastness, magnitude, obscurity, and so on; in contrast, the beautiful engenders "Love, or some passion similar to it," through smallness, smoothness, delicacy, and the like. In his musings on the beautiful, Burke explicitly refers to the "beauty of women."[11]

Yet if late eighteenth-century English writers thought of nature in gendered aesthetic terms, their responses differed widely. Anne K. Mellor, in *Romanticism and Gender*, suggests two disparate responses to the sublime on the part of female Romantic writers: one response accepts the pairing of masculinity and sublimity, the other "domesticates" the masculine sublime, refashioning it as "feminine." As Mellor writes, the former response "accepts the identification of the sublime with the experience of masculine empowerment," yet it "explicitly equate[s] this masculine sublime with patriarchal tyranny ... expos[ing] the dark underside of the doctrine of separate spheres, the sexual division of labor, and the domestic ideology of patriarchal capitalism." In contrast, the second type of response domesticates the sublime as "the location of blissful childhood memories" within which "characters experience heightened sensibility" and "loss of ego or consciousness-of-self ... ." In this latter instance, although nature is gendered as feminine, "this female nature is not an overwhelming power, not even an all-bountiful mother. Instead nature is a *female friend* ... ."[12]

For Mellor, writers from the Romantic era generally choose one response to the sublime or the other, not both. However, in *Emmeline*, Smith does choose both and, while Smith's feminine sublime functions in ways similar to that described by Mellor—nature as friend—Smith's masculine sublime is not expressive of patriarchal tyranny and oppression, but, rather, is expressive of a violent, often sexual commingling of the masculine with the feminine, which Smith shows as both natural and necessary. Smith restricts the depiction of patriarchal tyranny to domestic interiors and to public institutions; any patriarchal oppression that exists within a natural setting generates from men, not from nature. In addition, within either masculine or feminine settings, a character may "lose" herself—or find herself.

Consistent with notions of the feminine sublime as delineated by Mellor, as a young child Emmeline experiences the natural world surrounding Mowbray Castle as friend: "[S]he delighted to wander among the rocks that formed the bold and magnificent boundary of the ocean ... . Simply dressed, and with no

---

[11]   Edmund Burke, *A Philosophical Enquiry into the Origin of our Ideas of the Sublime and Beautiful,* in *A Philosophical Enquiry into the Origin of Our Ideas of the Sublime and Beautiful and Other Revolutionary Writings,* ed. David Womersley (London: Penguin, 2004), 128, 150.

[12]   Anne K. Mellor, *Romanticism and Gender* (New York: Routledge, 1993), 91, 97.

other protection than Providence, she often rambled several miles into the country, visiting the remote huts of the shepherds, among the wildest mountains" (48). Nature is viewed as non-threatening, a place where protection of any sort is not required; the shepherds exist as an integral part of this natural, safe, femininely pastoral world. The feminine landscapes in Smith's novel combine restrained and/or muted elements of the sublime—for instance, "restless waves" (58) and rocky shores—with near-human expressions of "feminine" sympathy: the tides speak in "low murmurs" (58), the winds sigh, and the rays of sun caress. Feminine landscapes are safe spaces, offering solace and temporary forgetfulness. Gazing out to sea, Emmeline is thrown into "a profound reverie," "a sort of stupor" taking "possession of her senses." She forgets time, and she becomes "unconscious of the surrounding objects." As with a dear friend, Emmeline forgets "all her apprehended misfortunes" (58). Similarly, at the beach in Swansea, Emmeline engages in "walks along the shore or among the rocks … indulg[ing] that contemplative turn of mind which she acquired in the solitude of Mowbray Castle" (79). Although it is true that "nature cannot cure human misery" in Smith's world, as Katherine M. Rogers notes, I would argue against Rogers's assertion that Smith's characters can "never count on finding consolation"[13] in the natural world, as again and again, characters in *Emmeline* seek and find within nature a source of recuperation, inspiration, and contemplation.

Feminine landscapes promote female friendship and provide protection for women. At the beach at Swansea, Emmeline first meets Mrs. Stafford and, as both women view nature as friend, it follows that the two women will become friends as well. In Woodbury Forest, which adjoins Mrs. Stafford's home of Woodfield, Emmeline and Mrs. Stafford first encounter Lady Adelina Trelawney, and they befriend her, as well. The forest possesses muted elements of the sublime—"the deep shade of the beech trees … is broken by wild and uncultured glens [covered with] the broom, hawthorn and birch of the waste"—but magnanimity is also part of its persona, offering "fewel, so amply afforded by the surrounding woods" (212), to the poor of the community, unlike the human owners of neighboring estates. Lady Adelina finds within the forest's refuge safety, friendship, and protection, as Mrs. Stafford and Emmeline, during their many trips to Woodbury Forest, become intimate friends with Lady Adelina and eventually find the means to secure her life, child, and reputation.

Even within the relatively safe spaces of the feminine sublime, female reputation is at risk, but this is only so if the woman is viewed by an individual with an adversarial relationship to nature itself. Ecofeminism argues for "a connection between the exploitation and degradation of the natural world and

---

[13]   Katherine M. Rogers, "Romantic Aspirations, Restricted Possibilities: The Novels of Charlotte Smith," in *Re-Visioning Romanticism: British Women Writers, 1776–1837*, ed. Carol Shiner Wilson and Joel Haefner (Philadelphia: University of Pennsylvania Press, 1994), 72–88, 74.

the subordination and oppression of women,"[14] and in *Emmeline*, characters who treat nature as a site for colonization and subjugation, such as hunting the wildlife, also treat women poorly, while those characters who view nature in terms of communion, solace, and inspiration, such as admiring the scenery, also treat women respectfully. Of course, feminine reputation is a social construct, but because ideas of "home" and "nature" are also socially constructed, a female found outside masculine-dominated domestic space—which, in patriarchal ideology, posits itself as the principal site for the protection of women in terms of physical safety and personal reputation—must necessarily, in this viewpoint, have no reputation to protect. Those men who subscribe to patriarchal norms and who engage in oppressing nature are also the ones who view a woman alone in a natural setting as sexually available or compromised.

Once Lord Montreville and his son lay claim to Mowbray Castle, Emmeline's innocent and carefree relationship with the natural world alters. Previously, she wandered far and wide, safely and securely; now, her usual morning walk is subject to reinterpretation and misinterpretation. While it is unclear whether Delamere himself believes that Emmeline planned their outdoor meeting, it is evident that, when he sees her seated by herself within the woods, he views it as an invitation for importunities and lovemaking. When his father appears, Delamere claims that he has been "making love to my cousin, who was so good as to sit and wait for me under a tree" (65), encouraging his father in the belief that Emmeline has engineered this meeting. Lord Montreville automatically assumes that his niece is at fault: "Your having been brought up in retirement, Miss Mowbray, has, perhaps, prevented your being acquainted with the decorums of the world and the reserve which a woman should ever strictly maintain. You have done a very improper thing in meeting my son" (65). Note that both Lord Montreville and Delamere are at Mowbray Castle for the hunting season; Delamere, in particular, is associated with guns and hunting, and his entry into the castle is always preceded by the discharge of his gun (67), a particularly phallic and sexually suggestive act. Another example of a male with an adversarial relation to nature is Mr. James Crofts, who is "more at home in the cabinet than the field" (247). While Crofts is no hunter of animals, he is a hunter of gossip and human misfortune. Curious about Emmeline's frequent woodland walks, Crofts believes her to be engaged in a romantic liaison with Colonel Fitz-Edward, and, following her, finds "evidence" that she is sexually compromised. A later woodland visit from Delamere, during which he discovers Emmeline holding Lady Adelina's infant son, confirms his belief in Emmeline's sexual transgressions.

If a woman's reputation is at risk within the feminine sublime merely by being found out-of-doors and unaccompanied by other women, then the masculine sublime offers itself as a site for the awakening of realized sexual desire. In

---

[14]   Mary Mellor, *Feminism and Ecology* (New York: New York University Press, 1997), 1.

Emmeline, stormy seas prove the prelude to heterosexual love.[15] Lady Adelina's illicit love affair with Colonel Fitz-Edward begins on shipboard during a powerful storm at sea. Expectations that the ship will "be driven back on the [sand]bar, and beat to pieces" (226), that all will be killed, force Lady Adelina and Fitz-Edward below decks. Although she and Fitz-Edward do not consummate their love until some weeks later, it is at that moment, during the storm, that her "partiality" for Fitz-Edward becomes fixed. A similar stormy scene sets the stage for Emmeline and Godolphin's awakening romance. At Godolphin's home on the Isle of Wight, Emmeline takes pleasure in "the heavy gloom of an impending storm, the great and magnificent spectacle afforded by the sea." When the storm arrives, the hurricane-force winds blow "with astonishing violence ... the gust grew more vehement, and deafened her with its fury; while the mountainous waves it had raised, burst thundering against the rocks and seemed to shake their very foundation" (301). Godolphin watches Emmeline watch the sea, and although Emmeline and Godolphin—uncertain about the future—refrain from openly acknowledging their mutual desire, it is clear that it exists.

The masculine sublime, then, presents itself as a space of sexual desire. Ecofeminists Maria Mies and Vandana Shiva view this sexual energy as an expression of the "female principle" or "connecting principle," which in essence is the creative life force shared by women and nature.[16] Smith's presentation of the masculine sublime is more complex, as the sexual energy associated with the masculine sublime comes from the intermingling of the masculine with the feminine, a sort of spatial insemination of the landscape that brings with it the possibility for (pro)creation and which, in turn, inspires in its human spectators similar procreative energies. As the scenes of sexual desire always take place during a storm at sea, I would suggest that the sea functions as the feminine element and the storm as the masculine element; the violent encounter between these opposing elements intermixes the two, generating the possibility of birth (metaphorically and through sexual encounter).

The (pro)creative force expressed within the masculine sublime is coupled with a destructive element: in *Emmeline*, sexual desire seems provoked by the specter of death. As Burke writes, "the passions belonging to the preservation of the individual, turn wholly upon pain and danger; those which belong to *generation*, have their origin in gratifications and *pleasures*; the pleasure most directly belonging to this purpose is of a lively character, rapturous and violent, and confessedly the highest pleasure of sense."[17] What sexual activity and physical danger have in common, then, are the violence of the passions inspired and the fact that these two actions (death and sex)—although they provoke disparate emotions

---

[15]   Smith very much views the world in heteronormative fashion and her depiction of the natural world and human sexuality is founded upon the notion of heterosexual normativity.

[16]   Maria Mies and Vandana Shiva, *Ecofeminism* (London: Zed Books, 1993), 17.

[17]   Burke, *Sublime and the Beautiful*, 87.

(pain and pleasure)—are nonetheless complementary acts, as one concerns "self-preservation" and the other "propagation";[18] both acts center on life, whether the preservation of it or the creation of it. Thus, when Lady Adelina and Colonel Fitz-Edward hurry below decks, fearful that their ship will "be driven back on the [sand]bar, and beat to pieces" (226), the violent passions inspired by fear of death find an outlet in the violent passions of sexual desire. Similarly, the storm that Emmeline watches inspires her with trepidation, fear, and pleasure: "Could she have divested her mind of its apprehensions that what formed for her a magnificent and sublime scene brought shipwreck and destruction to many others, she would have been highly pleased with a sight of the ocean in its present tremendous state" (302). Once Emmeline becomes aware of Godolphin watching the storm as well, she expresses concern for his preservation, and at that moment, both become aware of their mutual attraction and desire.

Fear of destruction—whether for self or others—is a principal component of the Burkean masculine sublime, yet it is important to note that in *Emmeline* the storms threaten both men and women. In *Emmeline*, the natural world may comfort or it may kill, but it never singles out women as its chosen victims; the masculine sublime is not a source of patriarchal tyranny, but merely a force that potentially holds destruction for all humans, regardless of sex. In addition, as she did when contemplating more feminine landscapes, Emmeline "loses" herself while gazing upon the storm. She finds herself "lost in contemplating the awful spectacle," she is "so extremely absent" (302). Thus women—in this case, Emmeline—may experience "loss of ego or consciousness-of-self"[19] as easily in a masculine landscape as in a feminine landscape, but why? First, Smith views the masculine and feminine aspects of nature as complementary. In her discussion of Smith's poem *Beachy Head*, Kandi Tayebi argues that Smith engages with "a revolutionary idea—that nature is a combination of dynamically opposed forces and that true art, like nature, must be composed of oppositions that work together."[20] While Smith portrays and denounces patriarchal oppression, particularly within the domestic sphere, she is by no means adverse to masculinity in and of itself; rather, she sees men as having a responsibility to protect women and to befriend them, particularly in a culture that does so much to disenfranchise them. As Mrs. Stafford bitterly complains, "Others have, in their husbands, protectors and friends" (420), while she does not. I would also suggest that Smith views the natural world in all its gendered displays as greater and more powerful than the world constructed by humans; subsequently, to become one with it, to lose oneself within it, is to become part of something greater than oneself. In the world

---

[18]   Ibid., 86, 87.

[19]   Anne K. Mellor, *Romanticism and Gender*, 97.

[20]   Kandi Tayebi, "Undermining the Eighteenth-Century Pastoral: Rewriting the Poet's Relationship to Nature in Charlotte Smith's Poetry," *European Romantic Review* 15, no. 1 (March 2004): 141–42.

of *Emmeline*, masculine sublimity in nature does not oppress women, but rather provides a necessary complement to the feminine sublime.

In the end, bi-gendered nature provides Emmeline with the means to establish her legitimacy and gain personal agency. While in France, traveling between Marseilles and Toulon, Emmeline and her companions enter a region of "steep crags and the sky ... huge masses" of "mountainous rocks" hang over them (330). Alighting from the carriage and transfixed by the landscape surrounding her, Emmeline wanders ahead, coming across "a transparent stream, which bursting with some violence out of the rock, is received into a small reservoir of stone" (330). The masculine elements of the setting (the craggy tors, the massive boulders, and the violently tumultuous waterfall) are countered by the feminine and the maternal: the spring is "beautiful" and "transparent" (331, 330), and the reservoir magnanimously provides the water for a small "village at some distance" (330); Emmeline and her traveling companions feel as if they have entered into "the bosom of the rock" (330), a strikingly maternal image. Nearing the spring, Emmeline discovers an old Frenchman, who (in the wondrous coincidental manner of the sentimental novel) turns out to be her father's former manservant and who reveals the truth regarding her parents' marriage and the legitimacy of her own birth. The bi-gendered setting, combining the masculine and feminine sublime, demonstrates the compatibility of opposites and metaphorically (re)joins the orphaned Emmeline with her father and mother. Arguably, if Emmeline were not a lover of nature, such an important encounter could never have occurred.

The setting also foreshadows other couplings. Just prior to meeting with Le Limosin (as the old Frenchman calls himself), Emmeline has conjured up thoughts of Godolphin: "[S]he had brought Godolphin before her, and was imagining what he would have said had he been with her; with what warmth would he enjoy, with what taste and spirit point out the beauty of the scenes so enchanting" (330). Mental and emotional union with Godolphin occur, and it is through Godolphin's brother and surrogate, Lord Westhaven, with whom Emmeline has been traveling, that Emmeline's claim to the Mowbray fortune will be defended against the interests of Lord Montreville, Lord Westhaven's own father-in-law. Nature in this instance inspires spiritual union between the feminine and masculine, and provides a model of masculinity that never oppresses or overwhelms women, but rather acts in their best interests, inspiring similar behavior from men.

In Smith's novel, the natural world in and of itself is not oppressive for women: it may storm and rage and it may take lives, but it does not persecute women, and more often it offers comfort, nurturing, inspiration, and example. Nonetheless, the natural world—in both its masculine and feminine manifestations—offers very real risks to feminine reputation and female chastity. The question, then, is "Where can women find both safety and freedom?" Troubled by the attentions of the Chevalier Bellozane, Emmeline finds her options limited: "to go a great distance from the house, alone, Emmeline had not courage; to stay near it, subjected her to the intrusion and importunity of the Chevalier" (354). Charlotte Smith offers this answer: homes "embosomed" within nature offer themselves as sites of feminine agency, security, and desire.

The Edge of the World: Women and Women's Space

The characters whom we, as readers, are expected to admire within Smith's novels are those who love nature, and these nature-lovers all share specific characteristics, as Carrol L. Fry notes:

> Characters who follow nature are sentimentalists similar to those of the persona in Smith's poems: They have powerful feelings; prefer simplicity in lifestyle to the "ton"; have natural talents rather than "learned accomplishments"; respond to the distress of others; share a congenital sadness and love of what the language of the period calls a "pleasing melancholy" or an "interesting languor" in another person; bond after meeting on a perception of share sensibilities; and feel a sense of alienation from "the world" that fails to follow their values.[21]

Not all nature lovers in Smith's novels enjoy domestic bliss or marital happiness (for instance, Mrs. Stafford), but when they do, it is always within abodes that integrate the natural world and that are remote from urban environments. As Henri Lefebvre writes, "the more a space partakes of nature, the less it enters into the social relations of production,"[22] and, in *Emmeline*, this distancing from socially produced space appears critical to any form of feminine agency. By fusing the natural with the domestic, Smith imagines liminal spaces that simultaneously partake of and resist the dominant social relations (of patriarchy), and in doing so, Smith creates spaces wherein women experience both safety and freedom.

In a novel teeming with desperately unhappy married couples, the first truly happy married couple presented to the readers is Lord and Lady Clancarryl. Sister to Lady Adelina and Godolphin, Lady Clancarryl lives with her husband in Ireland, somewhere in the countryside beyond Dublin, on the banks of the fictitious Lough Carryl. Lady Adelina describes its merits: "I attended my sister therefore to Lough Carryl, on the beautiful banks of which her Lord had built an house, which possessing as much magnificence as was proper to their rank, was yet contrived with an attention to all their domestic retirement. Here Lady Clancarryl chose to reside the whole year; and my Lord never left it but to attend the business of Parliament at Dublin" (224). The house with its estate integrates nature (water and land) and domesticity, and it functions as the site of domestic and marital felicity for both Lord Clancarryl and his wife. Similarly, Lord Westhaven (brother to Lady Clancarryl, Lady Adelina, and Godolphin) and his wife (younger sister to Delamere) enjoy conjugal harmony at their country estate in Kent. Because Lord Clancarryl and Lord Westhaven—both rational, compassionate men—must, as lords, serve their country in Parliament, their country estates are located within reasonable distances of Dublin and London, respectively, although Smith makes it clear that any time spent in these urban locales is of short duration and based purely on duty.

---

[21]　　Carrol L. Fry, *Charlotte Smith* (New York: Twayne, 1996), 48.

[22]　　Henri Lefebvre, *The Production of Space*, trans. Donald Nicholson-Smith (Malden, MA: Blackwell, 1991), 83.

The sole remaining couple in the novel who experience connubial happiness—Emmeline and Godolphin—enjoy a much more complex spatial arrangement: both Mowbray Castle and East Cliff will become "home" to the happy couple, and Emmeline and Godolphin will presumably alternate time spent in each location. In addition, each site is liminal, existing on the very "edges" of Great Britain. Mowbray Castle, located in "a remote part of the country of Pembroke" (45), sits snugly between the coastline of Wales and "a chain of mountains"; the castle lies "almost embosomed" within a wood (75). It should be noted that, by the conclusion to the novel, Mowbray Castle has become the rightful possession and home of Emmeline, whose legitimacy has now been proved. Godolphin's estate of East Cliff lies on the Isle of Wight, five miles from the principal town of Cowes; to reach East Cliff, one must travel by open boat from Southhampton, then by cart, then by foot. Like Mowbray Castle, East Cliff is situated between the sea and a "hill," enclosed within a wood that similarly "embosom[s] the house" (295).

We are assured of the domestic bliss of Emmeline as Godolphin is proclaimed "the tenderest of husbands, the best, the most generous and amiable of men" (476). Smith displays real spatial equality between husband and wife: the conclusion to the novel implies that the two abodes, castle and house, will function equally as "home." (If a castle trumps a house in terms of spatiality, then Emmeline may even be said to have bested Godolphin in terms of space). Unlike the relationships between the other couples, the one between Emmeline and Godolphin is most equal in terms of property ownership and spatial dominance—and we are led to believe it will be the most rewarding of all the marriages.

The problem, of course, is that this display of spatial equality occurs at the edges and peripheries of England and Wales, which suggests the impossibility or the implausibility of such an arrangement being enjoyed by the vast majority of King George III's subjects. Sites wherein women may experience safety and self-possession are liminal spaces which, in order to exist, must remain physically, psychically, and metaphorically remote from the gendered masculine world of hegemonic culture, paradoxically rendering these spaces, by their very definition, always liminal, always marginal. Ultimately, Smith does offer one other possible solution in regards to women's spatial displacement—the displacement of men. While Emmeline and Godolphin unite to restore Woodfield and some measure of happiness to Mrs. Stafford, the novel assures the continuance of this happiness for her and her children at Woodfield, as Lord Westhaven has arranged "lucrative employment in the West Indies" (460–461) for Mr. Stafford.

Conclusion

Charlotte Smith's *Emmeline* offers an extended meditation on the (dis)placement of women in eighteenth-century English society. Through her depiction of the masculine domination of interior spaces, Smith highlights the fact that the domestic sphere can never truly be the site of feminine safety and identity as long as it exists as masculine space; and, while the natural world offers women freedom from social constraints, it can also serve as the site of women's ruin, whether real or rumored. However, spaces where women truly enjoy safety and personal freedom exist only on the borders of the masculine, patriarchal country that is England or in the fictional world of the novel, never in the reality of eighteenth-century England itself.

Bibliography

Adams, Percy. *Travel Literature and the Evolution of the Novel*. Lexington: University Press of Kentucky, 1983.

Addison, Joseph. "The Spectator No. 15" (March 17, 1711). In Bond, 66–69.

———. "The Spectator No. 37" (April 12, 1711). In Bond, 152–59.

Alliston, April. "Transnational Sympathies, Imaginary Communities." In *The Literary Channel: The Inter-National Invention of the Novel*, edited by Margaret Cohen and Carolyn Dever, 133–48. Princeton: Princeton University Press, 2002.

Al-Rawi, Ahmed K. "The Portrayal of the East vs. the West in Lady Mary Montagu's *Letters* and Emily Ruete's *Memoirs*." *Arab Studies Quarterly* 30 (2008): 15–30.

Anderson, Benedict. *Imagined Communities: Reflections on the Origin and Spread of Nationalism*. New York: Verso, 2006.

Anzaldua, Gloria and Cherrie Moraga, eds. *This Bridge Called My Back: Writings by Radical Women of Color*. New York: Kitchen Table, Women of Color Press, 1983.

Aravamudan, Srinivas. "Lady Mary Wortley Montagu in the Hammam: Masquerade, Womanliness, and Levantinization." *ELH* 62 (1995): 69–104.

———. *Tropicopolitans: Colonialism and Agency, 1688–1804*. Durham: Duke University Press, 1999.

Ardener, Shirley. "Ground Rules and Social Maps for Women: An Introduction." In *Women and Space: Ground Rules and Social Maps*, edited by Shirley Ardener, 1–30. New York: St. Martin's Press, 1981.

Astell, Mary. *Political Writings*. New York: Cambridge University Press, 1996.

———. *Some Reflections Upon Marriage, Occasion'd by the Duke & Dutchess of Mazarine's Case; Which is also consider'd*. London, 1700.

Athey, Stephanie, and Daniel Cooper Alarcon. "Oroonoko's Gendered Economies of Honor/Horror: Reframing Colonial Discourse Studies in the Americas." *American Literature* 65, no. 3 (September 1993): 415–43.

Aubin, Penelope. *The Life of Madame de Beaumont, a French Lady* (1721). *Foundations of the Novel Series*. Compiled and edited by Michael F. Shugrue. New York: Garland, 1973.

"Aurum potabile: or the receipt of Dr. Fr. Antonie." In *Collectanea Chymica: A Collection of Ten Several Treatises in Chymistry, Concerning the Liquor Alkahest, the Mercury of Philosophers, and other Curiosities worthy the Perusal*. N. p. London: William Cooper, 1684.

Austen, Jane. *Mansfield Park*. Edited by Claudia L. Johnson. New York: W. W. Norton, 1998.

Ayyash, Mark Muhannad. "Edward Said: Writing in Exile." *Comparative Studies of South Asia, Africa and the Middle East* 30, no. 1 (2010): 107–18.

Bachelard, Gaston. *The Poetics of Space*. New York: Orion, 1964.

Backscheider, Paula R. and John J. Richetti, eds. *Popular Fiction by Women, 1660–1730: An Anthology*. New York: Oxford University Press, 1996.

Bandele, 'Biyi. *Aphra Behn's* Oroonoko*: In a New Adaptation*. Oxford: Amber Lane Press, 1999.

Barash, Carol. *English Women's Poetry, 1649–1714: Politics, Community, and Linguistic Authority*. New York: Oxford University Press, 1996.

Barbour, John D. "Edward Said and the Space of Exile." *Literature & Theology* 21, no. 3 (September 2007): 293–301.

Batsaki, Yota. "Exile as the Inaudible Accent in Germaine de Staël's *Corinne, ou l'Italie.*" *Comparative Literature* 61, no. 1 (Winter 2009): 26–42.

Beach, Adam. "Behn's Oroonoko, The Gold Coast, and Slavery in the Early-Modern Atlantic World." *Studies in Eighteenth-Century Culture* 39 (2010): 209–27.

Beattie, J. M. "The Criminality of Women in Eighteenth-Century England." *Journal of Social History* 8 (1975): 80–116.

Begnal, Michael H. "Molly Bloom and Lady Hester Stanhope." In *Joyce and Popular Culture*, edited by R. B. Kershner, 64–73. Gainesville: University Press of Florida, 1996.

Behn, Aphra. *Love Letters between a Nobleman and his Sister* (1684–7). London: Virago, 1987.

———. *Oroonoko: An Authoritative Text, Historical Backgrounds, Criticism.* Edited by Joanna Lipking. New York: Norton, 1997.

Benhabib, Seyla. "Models of Public Space: Hannah Arendt, the Liberal Tradition, and Jurgen Habermas." In *Habermas and the Public Sphere*, edited by Craig Calhoun, 73–98. Cambridge, MA: MIT Press, 1999.

Bentham, Jeremy. Bentham MSS, box 125, folios 138–41. London: University College.

Bergren, Anne. "The (Re)Marriage of Penelope and Odysseus: Architecture, Gender, Philosophy." *Assemblage* 21 (1993): 8–46.

Bhabha, Homi, ed. *Nation and Narration.* New York: Routledge, 1990.

Bhabha, Homi and W. J. T. Mitchell. *Edward Said: Continuing the Conversation.* Chicago: University of Chicago Press, 2005.

Binhammer, Katherine. "Revolutionary Domesticity in Charlotte Smith's *Desmond.*" In *Women, Revolution and the Novels of the 1790s*, edited by Linda Lang-Peralta, 25–46. East Lansing: Michigan University Press, 1999.

Blake, Reverend J. L. Preface to *Conversations on Natural Philosophy*, by Jane Marcet, iii-iv. 8th American ed.. Boston: Lincoln and Edmonds, 1826.

Blunt, Alison, and Gillian Rose. *Writing, Women and Space: Colonial and Postcolonial Geographies*. New York: The Guilford Press, 1994.

Bohls, Elizabeth. "The Gentleman Planter and the Metropole: Long's *History of Jamaica* (1774)." In *The Country and the City Revisited: England and the*

Politics of Culture, 1550–1850, edited by Gerald MacLean, Donna Landry, and Joseph P. Ward, 180–96. Cambridge: Cambridge University Press, 1999.

———. *Women Travel Writers and the Language of Aesthetics: 1716–1818*. New York: Cambridge University Press, 1995.

Bond, Donald F., ed. *The Spectator*. Oxford: Oxford University Press, 1965.

Bourdieu, Pierre. *Distinction: A Social Critique of the Judgement of Taste*. Cambridge, MA: Harvard University Press, 1984.

Bowers, Toni. "Collusive Resistance: Sexual Agency and Partisan Politics in *Love in Excess*." In *The Passionate Fictions of Eliza Haywood: Essays on her Life and Work*, edited by Kristen T. Saxton and Rebecca P. Bocchicchio, 48–68. Lexington: University Press of Kentucky, 2000.

Brady, Mary Pat. *Extinct Lands, Temporal Geographies: Chicana Literature and the Urgency of Space*. Durham: Duke University Press, 2002.

Brathwaite, Edward. *The Development of Creole Society in Jamaica 1770–1820*. Oxford: Clarendon, 1971.

Brewer, Daniel. "Lights in Space." *Eighteenth-Century Studies* 37, no. 2 (Winter 2004): 171–86.

Brown, Laura. *Ends of Empire: Women and Ideology in Early Eighteenth-Century English Literature*. Ithaca: Cornell University Press, 1993.

Brück, Mary T. *Women in Early British and Irish Astronomy*. Dordrecht: Springer, 2009.

Bryan, Margaret. *A Compendious System of Astronomy, in a Course of Familiar Lectures*. London: Leigh and Sotheby, 1797.

———. *Lectures on Natural Philosophy*. London: John Murray, 1806.

Buell, Lawrence. *The Future of Environmental Criticism: Environmental Crisis and Literary Imagination*. Malden, MA: Blackwell, 2005.

Burke, Edmund. *A Philosophical Enquiry into the Origin of our Ideas of the Sublime and Beautiful*. In *A Philosophical Enquiry into the Origin of Our Ideas of the Sublime and Beautiful and Other Revolutionary Writings*, edited by David Womersley, 49–200. London: Penguin, 2004.

Burnard, Trevor. *Mastery, Tyranny, and Desire: Thomas Thistlewood and His Slaves in the Anglo-Jamaican World*. Chapel Hill: University of North Carolina Press, 2004.

———. "Passengers Only: The Extent and Significance of Absenteeism in Eighteenth-Century Jamaica." *Atlantic Studies* 1 (2004): 181–83.

Burney, Frances. "Brief Reflexions Relative to the Emigrant French Clergy" (1793). Project Gutenberg, 2009. http://www.gutenberg.org/cache/epub/29125/pg29125.txt.

———. *Journals and Letters*. Edited by Peter Sabor and Lars E. Troide. London: Penguin Books, 2001.

———. *The Wanderer; or, Female Difficulties*. Edited by Margaret Anne Doody, Robert L. Mack, and Peter Sabor. Oxford: Oxford University Press, 2001.

Burton, Robert. "The Anatomy of Melancholy." In *Race in Early Modern England: A Documentary Companion*, edited by Ania Loomba and Jonathan Burton, 201–3. New York: Palgrave Macmillan, 2007.

Butler, Judith. *Bodies that Matter.* New York: Routledge, 1993.

Carey, Daniel and Lynn Festa, Introduction. In *The Postcolonial Enlightenment: Eighteenth-Century Colonialism and Postcolonial Theory*, edited by Daniel Carey and Lynn Festa, 1–33. Oxford: Oxford University Press, 2009.

Carter, Philip. "Men About Town: Representations of Masculinity and Foppery in Early Eighteenth-Century Urban Society." In *Gender in Eighteenth-Century England: Roles, Representations and Responsibilities*, edited by Hannah Barker and Elaine Chalus, 31–57. New York: Addison Wesley Longman, 1997.

———. *Men and the Emergence of Polite Society: Britain 1660–1800.* New York: Longman/St. Martin's Press, 1997.

Chard, Chloe. "Women Who Transmute into Tourist Attractions: Spectator and Spectacle on the Grand Tour." In *Romantic Geographies: Discourses of Travel, 1775–1844*, edited by Amanda Gilroy, 109–26. Manchester: Manchester University Press, 2000.

Cheah, Pheng, Bruce Robbins, and the Social Text Collective. *Cosmopolitics: Thinking and Feeling beyond the Nation.* Minneapolis: University of Minnesota Press, 1998.

Chedgzoy, Kate. *Women's Writing in the British Atlantic World: Memory, Place and History, 1550–1700.* Cambridge: Cambridge University Press, 2007.

Cheek, Pamela. *Sexual Antipodes: Enlightenment Globalization and the Placing of Sex.* Stanford: Stanford University Press, 2003.

Clerke, Agnes M. *The Herschels and Modern Astronomy.* London: Cassell and Co., 1895.

Clery, E. J. *Women's Gothic: From Clara Reeve to Mary Shelley.* Horndon: Northcote House, 2000.

Cohen, Margaret. "Sentimental Communities." In *The Literary Channel: The Inter-National Invention of the Novel*, edited by Margaret Cohen and Carolyn Dever, 106–32. Princeton: Princeton University Press, 2002.

———. *The Sentimental Education of the Novel.* Princeton: Princeton University Press, 1999.

Colley, Linda. *Britons: Forging the Nation 1707–1837.* London: Pimlico, 2003.

Colomina, Beatriz, ed. *Sexuality and Space.* New York: Princeton Architectural Press, 1992.

Corbin, Alain. *The Lure of the Sea: The Discovery of the Seaside in the Western World 1750–1840.* Translated by Jocelyn Phelps (1994). London: Penguin, 1995.

Craciun, Adriana. *British Women Writers and the French Revolution: Citizens of the World.* New York: Palgrave MacMillan, 2005.

———. "Citizens of the World: Émigrés, Romantic Cosmopolitanism, and Charlotte Smith." *Nineteenth-Century Contexts* 29, no. 2–3 (June-September 2007): 169–85.

Crane, Mary Thomas. "Illicit Privacy and Outdoor Spaces in Early Modern England." *The Journal for Early Modern Cultural Studies* 9, no. 1 (2009): 4–22.

Crang, Mike and Nigel Thrift, eds. *Thinking Space*. New York: Routledge, 2000.

Craton, Michael. "Reluctant Creoles: The Planters' World in the British West Indies." In *Strangers Within the Realm: Cultural Margins of the* First *British Empire*, edited by Bernard Bailyn and Philip D. Morgan, 314–62. Chapel Hill: University of North Carolina Press, 1991.

Craveri, Benedetta. *The Age of Conversation*. New York: New York Review of Books, 2005.

Cresswell, Tim. *Place: A Short Introduction*. Malden, MA: Blackwell Publishers, 2004.

Curran, Stuart. "Romanticism displaced and placeless." *European Romantic Review* 20, no. 5 (December 2009): 637–50.

Dainotto, Roberto M. *Place in Literature: Regions, Cultures, Communities*. Ithaca: Cornell University Press, 2000.

Daniels, Christine and Michael V. Kennedy, eds. *Negotiated Empires: Centers and Peripheries in the Americas, 1500-1820*. New York: Routledge, 2002.

Davys, Mary. *The Reformed Coquet*. In Backscheider and Richetti, *Popular Fiction by Women, 1660–1730*, 251–322.

De Bolla, Peter. *The Education of the Eye: Painting, Landscape, and Architecture in Eighteenth-Century Britain*. Stanford: Stanford University Press, 2003.

de Certeau, Michel. *The Practice of Everyday Life*. Berkeley: University of California Press, 2002.

Deleuze, Gilles and Guattari, Félix. "Kafka: Toward a Minor Literature." In *The Norton Anthology of Theory and Criticism*, edited by Vincent B. Leitch, et al., 1598–1601. New York: W. W. Norton, 2001.

Derrida, Jacques. "Where the Desire May Live." In *Rethinking Architecture*, edited by Neil Leach, 319–23. New York: Routledge, 1997.

Dinwiddy, J. R. "Bentham's Transition to Political Radicalism, 1809–10." *Journal of the History of Ideas* 36, no. 4 (October-December 1975): 683–700.

Dobbs, Betty Jo Teeter. *The Janus Faces of Genius: The Role of Alchemy in Newton's Thought*. Cambridge: Cambridge University Press, 1992.

Dolan, Elizabeth A. *Seeing Suffering in Women's Literature of the Romantic Era*. Burlington, VT: Ashgate, 2008.

Dolin, Tim. *Mistress of the House*. Brookfield: Ashgate, 1997.

Domosh, Mona and Joni Seager. *Putting Women in Place: Feminist Geographers Make Sense of the World*. New York: The Guilford Press, 2001.

Donne, John. "Holy Sonnet #14." *The Poems of John Donne*, edited by Sir Herbert Grierson, 358. Franklin Center, PA: The Franklin Library, 1892.

Doody, Margaret Anne. "Burney and Politics." In *The Cambridge Companion to Frances Burney*, edited by Peter Sabor, 93–110. Cambridge: Cambridge University Press, 2007.

———. *Frances Burney: The Life in the Works*. New Brunswick, NJ: Rutgers University Press, 1988.

———. "Missing Les Muses: Madame de Staël and Frances Burney." *Colloquium Helveticum: Cahiers suisses de littérature générale et comparée* 25 (1997): 81–117.

The Dutchess of Mazarine's Farewell to England." London: Langley Curtis, 1680.

"The Dutchess of Portsmouths and Count Coningsmarks Farwel to England." London: J. Bayly, 1682.

Durand, Gilbert. *The Anthropological Structures of the Imaginary*. Translated by Margaret Sankey and Judith Hatten. Brisbane: Boombana Publications, 1999.

Ekirch, A. Roger. *Bound for America: The Transportation of British Convicts to the Colonies 1718–1775*. Oxford: Clarendon Press, 1987.

Ellis, Kate Ferguson. *The Contested Castle: Gothic Novels and the Subversion of Domestic Ideology*. Urbana: University of Illinois Press, 1989.

Ellis, Kirsten. *Star of the Morning: The Extraordinary Life of Lady Hester Stanhope*. New York: HarperPress, 2008.

Faroqhi, Suraiya. *The Ottoman Empire and the World Around It*. New York: I. B. Tauris, 2004.

Favret, Mary. *War at a Distance: Romanticism and the Making of Modern Wartime*. Princeton: Princeton University Press, 2010.

Ferguson, Margaret. "Juggling the Categories of Race, Class and Gender: Aphra Behn's *Oroonoko*." *Women's Studies* 19 (1991): 159–81.

Festa, Lynn. "Sentimental Bonds and Revolutionary Characters: Richardson's *Pamela* in England and France." In *The Literary Channel: The Inter-National Invention of the Novel*, edited by Margaret Cohen and Carolyn Dever, 73–105. Princeton: Princeton University Press, 2002.

Finch, Anne. *The Anne Finch Wellesley Manuscript Poems*. Edited by Barbara McGovern and Charles Hinnant. Athens: University of Georgia Press, 1998.

———. "An Invocation to the southern Winds." In *Poems on Several Occasions, By His Grace the Duke of Buckingham ... And other eminent Hands*, 172–79. London: Bernard Lintot, 1717.

———. *The Poems of Anne Countess of Winchilsea*. Edited by Myra Reynolds. Chicago: University of Chicago Press, 1903.

———. "To a Friend," in *Miscellany Poems, on Several Occasions*, 215–17. London: John Barber, 1713.

Flather, Amanda. *Gender and Space in Early Modern England*. Woodbridge, UK: Boydell Press, 2007.

Fletcher, Lorraine. *Charlotte Smith: A Critical Biography*. Basingstoke: Macmillan, 1998.

Foucault, Michel. "Of Other Spaces." *Diacritics* 16, no. 1 (Spring 1986): 22–27.

Fraser, Nancy. "Rethinking the Public Sphere: A contribution to the critique of Actually Existing Democracy." In *Habermas and the Public Sphere*, edited by Craig Calhoun, 109–42. Cambridge, MA: MIT Press, 1999.

Friedman, Alice. "Architecture, Authority, and the Female Gaze: Planning and Representation in the Early Modern Country House." *Assemblage* 18 (1992): 41–61.

Fry, Carrol L. *Charlotte Smith*. New York: Twayne, 1996.

Fulk, Mark K. "Mismanaging Mothers: Matriarchy and Romantic Education in Charlotte Smith's *The Young Philosopher*." *Women's Writing* 16, no. 1 (May 2009): 94–108.

Fuss, Diana. *The Sense of an Interior: Four Writers and the Rooms that Shaped Them*. New York: Routledge, 2004.

Fyfe, A. *Science for Children*. Vol. 1. Bristol: Thoemmes Press, 2003.

Gabbard, D. Christopher. "Clashing Masculinities in Aphra Behn's *The Dutch Lover*." *SEL Studies in English Literature 1500–1900* 47, no. 3 (2007): 557–72.

Gallagher, Catherine. "Embracing the Absolute: The Politics of the Female Subject in Seventeenth-Century England." *Genders*, March 1988, 24–39.

Garnai, Amy. *Revolutionary Imaginings in the 1790s: Charlotte Smith, Mary Robinson, Elizabeth Inchbald*. New York: Palgrave MacMillan, 2009.

Gates, Barbara T. *Kindred Science*. Chicago: University of Chicago Press, 1998.

Gates, Barbara T. and Ann B. Shteir, eds. *Natural Eloquence: Women Reinscribe Science*. Madison: University of Wisconsin Press, 1997.

Genand, Stéphanie. *Romans de l'émigration* (1797–1803). Paris: Honoré Champion, 2008.

Ghazi-Walid Falah, and Caroline Nagel, eds. *Geographies of Muslim Women: Gender, Religion, and Space*. New York: The Guilford Press, 2005.

Gibb, Lorna. *Lady Hester, Queen of the East*. London: Faber & Faber, 2006.

Gilroy, Paul. *Postcolonial Melancholia*. New York: Columbia University Press, 2005.

Girouard, Mark. *Life in the English Country House: A Social and Architectural History*. New Haven: Yale University Press, 1978.

Goldsmith, Elizabeth. *Publishing Women's Life Stories in France, 1640–1720*. Aldershot: Ashgate, 2001.

———. "'Savoir la carte': Travel, Self-Advancement, and Survival in Letters by Women." In *Formes et formations au dix-septième siècle*, edited by Norman Buford, 15–34. Tübingen: Narr, 2006.

———. "Thoroughly Modern Mazarin." In Shifrin, "*The Wandering Life I Led*," 2–30.

Golinski, Jan. *British Weather and the Climate of Enlightenment*. Chicago: Chicago University Press, 2010.

Goodman, Kevis. *Georgic Modernity and British Romanticism: Poetry and the Mediation of History*. Cambridge: Cambridge University Press, 2004.

Greer, Donald. *The Incidence of the Emigration During the French Revolution*. Cambridge: Harvard University Press, 1951.

Grubb, Farley. "The Transatlantic Market for British Convict Labor." *Journal of Economic History* 60, no. 1 (2000): 94–122.

Grundy, Isobel. *Lady Mary Wortley Montagu*. New York: Oxford University Press, 1999.

Guest, Harriet. *Small Change: Women, Learning, Patriotism*. Chicago: Chicago University Press, 2000.

———. "The Wanton Muse: Politics and Gender in Gothic Theory after 1760." In *Beyond Romanticism: New Approaches to Texts and Contexts, 1780–1832*, edited by Stephen Copley, 127–28. London: Routledge, 1992.

Guffey, George. "Aphra Behn's Occasion and Accomplishment." In *Two English Novelists: Aphra Behn and Anthony Trollope: Papers read at a Clark Library*

Seminar, May 11, 1974. Los Angeles: William Andrews Clark Memorial Library, 1975.

Gutwirth, Madelyn. *Madame de Staël, Novelist.* Urbana: University of Illinois Press, 1978.

Habermas, Jürgen. *The Structural Transformation of the Public Sphere: An Inquiry into a Category of Bourgeois Society.* Translated by Thomas Burger and Frederick Lawrence. Cambridge, MA: MIT Press, 1991.

Hall, Catherine. *Civilising Subjects: Metropole and Colony in the English Imagination, 1830–1867.* Cambridge: Polity Press, 2002.

Hardt, Michael and Antonio Negri. *Empire.* Cambridge, MA: Harvard University Press, 2001.

Harris, John. *The Artist and the Country House: A History of Country House and Garden View Painting in Britain, 1540–1870.* London: Sotheby Parke Bernet Publications, 1979.

Harrow, Sharon. *Adventures in Domesticity: Gender and Colonial Adulteration in Eighteenth-Century British Literature.* New York: AMS Press, 2004.

Hartmann, Cyril Hughes. *The Vagabond Duchess: The Life of Hortense Mancini Duchesse Mazarin.* New York: E. P. Dutton, 1927.

Harvey, David. *Justice, Nature and the Geography of Difference.* Cambridge, MA: Blackwell, 1996.

Harvey, Karen. *Reading Sex in the Eighteenth-Century: Bodies and Gender in English Erotic Culture.* Cambridge: Cambridge University Press, 2004.

———. "Spaces of Erotic Delight." In *Georgian Geographies: Essays on Space, Place, and Landscape in the Eighteenth Century,* edited by Miles Ogborn and Charles W. J. Withers, 131–53. New York: Palgrave, 2004.

Haslip, Joan. *Lady Hester Stanhope: The Extraordinary Life of the "Queen of the Desert."* Charleston, SC: The History Press, 2006.

Hayden, Dolores. *The Power of Place.* Cambridge, MA: MIT Press, 1995.

Haywood, Eliza. *The British Recluse.* In Backscheider and Richetti, *Popular Fiction by Women,* 153–226.

———. *The History of Miss Betsy Thoughtless.* Edited by Christina Blouch. Peterborough: Broadview, 1998.

———. *Love in Excess, or, The Fatal Inquiry.* Edited by David Oakleaf. Peterborough: Broadview, 2000.

———. *Philidore and Placentia: or, L'Amour trop Delicat* (1722). In *Four Before Richardson: Selected English Novels, 1720–1727,* edited by William H. McBurney, 153–232. Lincoln: University of Nebraska Press, 1963.

Heffernan, Teresa. "Feminism against the East/West Divide." *Eighteenth-Century Studies* 33 (2000): 201–15.

Hellegers, Desiree. *Handmaid to Divinity: Natural Philosophy, Poetry, and Gender in Seventeenth-Century England.* Norman: University of Oklahoma Press, 2000.

Hesse, Carla. *The Other Enlightenment: How French Women Became Modern.* Princeton: Princeton University Press, 2003.

Higonnet, Margaret R. and Joan Templeton, eds. *Reconfigured Spheres: Feminist Explorations of Literary Space*. Amherst: University of Massachusetts Press, 1994.

Hilbish, Florence. *Charlotte Smith, Poet and Novelist, 1749–1806*. Philadelphia: University of Pennsylvania Press, 1941.

Hinnant, Charles. *The Poetry of Anne Finch*. Newark: University of Delaware Press, 1994.

Hitchcock, Peter. *The Long Space: Transnationalism and Postcolonial Form*. Stanford: Stanford University Press, 2010.

Hoeveler, Diane Long. *Gothic Feminism: The Professionalization of Gender from Charlotte Smith to the Brontës*. University Park: The Pennsylvania State University Press, 1998.

Hoeveler, Diane Long and Jeffrey Cass, eds. *Interrogating Orientalism*. Columbus: Ohio State University Press, 2006.

Hogle, Jerrold E. "Introduction." In *The Cambridge Companion to Gothic Fiction*, edited by Jerrold E. Hogle, 1–20. Cambridge: Cambridge University Press, 2002.

Holden, Edward S. "The Three Herschels." *The Century Magazine* 39, no. 2 (1885): 179–85.

Hope, Quentin M. *Saint-Evrémond and His Friends*. Geneva: Droz, 1999.

Hoskins, Michael. "Caroline Herschel as an Observer." *Status*, June 2006, 1–6. http://www.aas.org/cswa/status/2006/JUNE2006/CarolineHerschel.html.

———. "Caroline Herschel as Observer." *Journal for the History of Astronomy* 36 (2005): 373–406.

Hubbard, Phil, Rob Kitchin, and Gill Valentine, eds. *Key Thinkers on Space and Place*. 2nd ed. Thousand Oaks: Sage Publications, 2004.

Hunt, John Dixon. *The Figure in the Landscape: Poetry, Painting, and Gardening during the Eighteenth Century*. Baltimore: The Johns Hopkins University Press, 1976.

Hunt, Margaret. *The Middling Sort: Commerce, Gender, and the Family in Early Modern England*. Berkeley: University of California Press, 1996.

Ingraham, Catherine. *Architecture and the Burdens of Linearity*. New Haven: Yale University Press, 1998.

Issitt, John R. "Jeremiah Joyce: Science Educationist." *Endeavour* 26, no. 3 (2002): 97–101.

Jackson, Peter. *Maps of Meaning: An Introduction to Cultural Geography*. London: Routledge, 1992.

———. "Why I am a Foucauldian." *SOJOURN: Journal of Social Issues in Southeast Asia* 21, no. 1 (2006): 113–23.

Jackson, Shona N. "Subjection and Resistance in the Transformation of Guyana's Mytho-Colonial Landscape." In *Caribbean Literature and the Environment: Between Nature and Culture*, edited by Elizabeth M. DeLoughrey, Renee K. Gosson, and George B. Handley, 85–98. Charlottesville: University of Virginia Press, 2005.

The Jamaica Lady: or, the life of Bavia. Containing an account of her intrigues, cheats, amours in England, Jamaica, and the Royal Navy. London, 1720.

Jameson, Frederic. "Is Space Political?" In *Rethinking Architecture*, edited by Neil Leach, 255–70. New York: Routledge, 1997.

Janacek, Bruce. "A Virtuoso's History: Antiquarianism and the Transmission of Knowledge in the Alchemical Studies of Elias Ashmole." *Journal of the History of Ideas* 69, no. 3 (2008): 395–417.

Jenkins, Hugh. *Feigned Commonwealths: The Country House Poem and the Fashioning of the Ideal Community.* Pittsburgh: Duquesne University Press, 1998.

Johnson, Claudia L. *Equivocal Beings: Politics, Gender and Sentimentality in the 1790s; Wollstonecraft, Radcliffe, Burney, Austen.* Chicago: The University of Chicago Press. 1995.

Jones, Chris. *Radical Sensibility: Literature and Ideas in the 1790s.* New York: Routledge, 1993.

Jordan, Nicolle. "Eastern Pastoral: 'Female Fears' and 'Savage Foes' in Montagu's 'Constantinople'." *Modern Philology* 107 (2010): 400–420.

Joyce, Reverend Jeremiah. *Scientific Dialogues.* London: Knight and Son, 1852.

Justice, George. "Burney and the Literary Marketplace." In *The Cambridge Companion to Frances Burney*, edited by Peter Sabor, 147–62. Cambridge: Cambridge University Press, 2007.

Kahf, Mohja. *Western Representations of the Muslim Woman: From Termagant to Odalisque.* Austin: University of Texas Press, 1999.

Kaplan, Caren. "Deterritorializations: The Rewriting of Home and Exile in Western Feminist Discourse." In "The Nature and Context of Minority Discourse." Special issue, *Cultural Critique* 6 (Spring 1987): 187–98.

Kaul, Suvir. "Reading Literary Symptoms: Colonial Pathologies and the *Oroonoko* Fictions of Behn, Southerne, and Hawkesworth." *Eighteenth-Century Life* 18, no. 3 (November 1994): 80–96.

Kavey, Allison B. "Mercury Falling: Gender Flexibility and Eroticism in Popular Alchemy." In *The Sciences of Homosexuality in Early Modern Europe*, edited by Kenneth Borris and George S. Rousseau, 221–41. New York: Routledge, 2007.

Kay Dian Kriz. "Marketing Mulatresses in the Paintings and Prints of Agostino Brunias." In *The Global Eighteenth Century*, edited by Felicity Nussbaum, 195–210. Baltimore: The Johns Hopkins University Press, 2003.

Kinsley, Zoë. "'In moody sadness, on the giddy brink': Liminality and Home Tour Travel." In *Mapping Liminalities: Thresholds in Cultural and Literary Texts*, edited by Lucy Kay, Zoe Kinsley, Terry Phillips and Alan Roughley, 41–67. Bern: Peter Lang, 2007.

Kirby, Kathleen. *Indifferent Boundaries: Spatial Concepts of Human Subjectivity.* New York: Guilford Press, 1996.

Klein, Lawrence E. "Gender and the Public/Private Distinction in the Eighteenth Century: Some Questions about Evidence and Analytical Procedure." *Eighteenth-Century Studies* 29: 1 (1995): 97–109.

Knapen, Johan H. "Scientific Collaborations in Astronomy Between Amateurs and Professionals." In *Stellar Winds in Interaction*, edited by Thomas Eversberg and Johan H. Knapen, 77–83. Arràbida: International ProAm Workshop, 2010. http://www.stsci.de/pdf/arrabida.pdf.

The Koran. Translated by N. J. Dawood. New York: Penguin, 1999.

Kraft, Elizabeth. "Encyclopedic Libertinism and 1798: Charlotte Smith's *The Young Philosopher*." *Eighteenth-Century Novel* 2 (2002): 239–72.

Krise, Thomas W. *Caribbeana: An Anthology of English Literature of the West Indies 1657–1777*. Chicago: University of Chicago Press, 1999.

Kristeva, Julia. *The Revolution in Poetic Language*. New York: Columbia University Press, 1984.

Kroll, Richard. "'Tales of Love and Gallantry': The Politics of *Oroonoko*." *Huntington Library Quarterly* 67, no. 4 (2004): 573–605. http://www.jstor.org. ezproxy.lib.usf.edu/stable/3817945.

Labbe, Jacqueline M. *Charlotte Smith: Romanticism, Poetry and the Culture of Gender*. Manchester: Manchester University Press, 2003.

Lamb, Jonathan. "The Medium of Publicity and the Garden at Stowe." *Huntington Library Quarterly* 59, no. 1 (1997): 53–72.

Lamb, Susan. *Bringing Travel Home to England: Tourism, Gender, and Imaginative Literature in the Eighteenth Century*. Newark: University of Delaware Press, 2009.

Landes, Joan. *Women and the Public Sphere in the Age of the French Revolution*. Ithaca: Cornell University Press, 1988.

Landry, Donna. "Horsy and Persistently Queer: Imperialism, Feminism and Bestiality." *Textual Practice* 15, no. 3 (2001): 467–85.

———. "Love Me, Love My Turkey Book: Letters and Turkish Travelogues in Early Modern England." In *Epistolary Histories: Letters, Fiction, Culture*, edited by Amanda Gilroy and W. M. Verhoeven, 51–73. Charlottesville: The University Press of Virginia, 2000.

Langley, Batty. *New Principles of Gardening*. London: A. Bettesworth and J. Batley, 1728.

Laurence, Anne. *Women in England, 1500–1760: A Social History*. London: Weidenfeld and Nicolson, 1994.

Leach, Neal, ed. *Rethinking Architecture*. New York: Routledge, 1997.

Lee, Sophia. *The Recess, or a Tale of Other Times*. Edited by April Alliston. Lexington: University Press of Kentucky, 2000.

Lees-Milne, James. *English Country Houses: Baroque, 1685–1715*. Feltham: Country Life Books, 1970.

Lefebvre, Henri. *The Production of Space*. Translated by Donald Nicholson-Smith. Malden, MA: Blackwell, 1991.

Levy, Anita. "Reproductive Urges: Literacy, Sexuality, and Eighteenth-Century Englishness." In *Inventing Maternity: Politics, Science, and Literature 1650–1865*, edited by Susan Greenfield and Carol Barash, 193–214. Lexington: University Press of Kentucky, 1999.

Lew, Joseph W. "Lady Mary's Portable Seraglio." *Eighteenth-Century Studies* 24 (1991): 432–50.

Lewis, Reina. *Rethinking Orientalism: Women, Travel, and the Ottoman Harem.* New Brunswick, NJ: Rutgers University Press, 2004.

Lindee, M. Susan. "The American Career of Jane Marcet's Conversations on Chemistry, 1806–1853." *Isis* 82, no. 1 (1991): 8–23.

Lippard, Lucy. *The Lure of the Local: Senses of Place in a Multicentered Society.* New York: New Press, 1997.

London, April. "Placing the Female: The Metonymic Garden in Amatory and Pious Narrative, 1700–1740." In *Fetter'd or Free? British Women Novelists, 1670–1815*, edited by Mary Anne Schofield and Cecilia Macheski, 101–23. Athens: Ohio University Press, 1986.

Long, Edward. *The History of Jamaica. Or, General Survey of the Antient and Modern State of that Island.* Vol. 2. London, 1774.

Lowe, Lisa. *Critical Terrains: French and British Orientalisms.* Ithaca: Cornell University Press, 1991.

Lowenthal, Cynthia. *Lady Mary and the Eighteenth-Century Familiar Letter.* Athens: University of Georgia Press, 1993.

Lynch, Dierdre Shauna. "The (Dis)locations of Romantic Nationalism: Shelley, Staël and the Home-Schooling of Monsters." In *The Literary Channel: The Inter-National Invention of the Novel*, edited by Margaret Cohen and Carolyn Dever, 194–224. Princeton: Princeton University Press, 2002.

Macdonald, Joyce. *Women and Race in Early Modern Texts.* Cambridge: Cambridge University Press, 2002.

Major, Philip, ed. *Literatures of Exile in the English Revolution and Its Aftermath, 1640–1690.* Burlington, VT: Ashgate, 2010.

Makowiecka, Maria Hanna. *The Theme of "Departure" in Women's Travel Narratives, 1600–1900: Taking Leave from Oneself.* Lewiston: The Edwin Mellen Press, 2007.

Mallinson, Jean. "Anne Finch: A Woman Poet and the Tradition." In *Gender at Work: Four Women Writers of the Eighteenth Century*, edited by Anne Messenger, 37–76. Detroit: Wayne State University Press, 1990.

Manley, Delarivier. *The Physician's Stratagem.* In *The Power of Love in Seven Novels.* London, 1720.

Marcet, Jane. *Conversations on Chemistry.* 5th ed. Vol 1. London: Longman, Hurst, Rees, Orme, and Brown, 1817.

———. *Conversations on Natural Philosophy.* 4th ed. London: Longman, Hurst, Rees, Orme, Brown, and Green, 1824.

Markley, A. A. "Charlotte Smith, the Godwin Circle, and the Proliferation of Speakers in *The Young Philosopher*." In *Charlotte Smith in British Romanticism*, edited by Jacqueline Labbe, 87–99. London: Pickering & Chatto, 2008.

Massey, Doreen. *Space, Place and Gender.* Minneapolis: University of Minnesota Press, 1994.

Maunu, Leanne. "Home is Where the Heart Is: National Identity and Expatriation in Charlotte Smith's *The Young Philosopher.*" *European Romantic Review* 15, no. 1 (March 2004): 51–71.

May, Jon. "Globalization and the Politics of Place: Place and Identity in an Inner London Neighbourhood." *Transactions of the Institute of British Geographers*, n.s., 21, no. 1 (1996): 194–215.

McDowell, Linda. *Gender, Identity and Place: Understanding Feminist Geographies*. Minneapolis: University of Minnesota Press, 1999.

McDowell, Linda and Jenny Sharp, eds. *Space, Gender, Knowledge: Readings in Feminist Geography*. New York: J. Wiley, 1997.

McGovern, Barbara. *Anne Finch and Her Poetry: A Critical Biography.* Athens: University of Georgia Press, 1992.

McKeon, Michael. *The Secret History of Domesticity: Public, Private, and the Division of Knowledge.* Baltimore: The Johns Hopkins University Press, 2006.

Mellor, Anne K. *Romanticism and Gender.* New York: Routledge, 1993.

———. "Women's Political Poetry." In *Mothers of the Nation: Women's Political Writing in England, 1780–1830.* Bloomington: Indiana University Press, 2002.

Mellor, Mary. *Feminism and Ecology.* New York: New York University Press, 1997.

Melman, Billie. *Women's Orients: English Women and the Middle East, 1718–1918.* Ann Arbor: The University of Michigan Press, 1992.

Mendelson, Sara, and Patricia Crawford. *Women in Early Modern England, 1550–1720.* Oxford: Clarendon Press, 1998.

Mies, Maria, and Vandana Shiva. *Ecofeminism.* London: Zed Books, 1993.

Mikhail, Alan. "An Irrigated Empire: The View from Ottoman Fayyum." *International Journal of Middle East Studies* 42 (2010): 569–90.

Miller, Shannon. *Engendering the Fall: John Milton and Seventeenth-Century Women Writers.* Philadelphia: University of Pennsylvania Press, 2008.

Mills, Sara. "Gender and Colonial Space." *Gender, Place and Culture: A Journal of Feminist Geography* 3 (1996): 125–48.

Milton, John. *Paradise Lost: An Authoritative Text, Sources and Background, Criticism.* Edited by Gordon Teskey. New York: W. W. Norton, 2005.

Montagu, Lady Mary Wortley. *Turkish Embassy Letters.* Edited by Anita Desai. Athens: University of Georgia Press, 1993.

Monteith, Kathleen E. A. and Glen Richards, eds. *Jamaica in Slavery and Freedom: History, Heritage and Culture.* Barbados: University of the West Indies Press, 2002.

Moore, Lisa L. "Queer Gardens: Mary Delany's Flowers and Friendships." *Eighteenth-Century Studies* 39, no. 1 (Fall 2005): 49–70.

More, Hannah. "The Slave Trade." London, 1788. <http://www.brycchancarey.com/slavery/morepoems.htm>.

Moretti, Franco. *Atlas of the European Novel, 1800–1900.* London: Verso, 1998.

Morgan, Kenneth. *The Bright-Meyler Papers: A Bristol West-Indian Connection 1732–1837.* Oxford: Oxford University Press, 2007.

Morgan, Philip D. "The Caribbean Islands in Atlantic Context, circa 1500–1800." In *The Global Eighteenth Century,* edited by Felicity Nussbaum, 52–64. Baltimore: The Johns Hopkins University Press, 2003.

Munroe, Jennifer. *Gender and the Garden in Early Modern English Literature.* Burlington, VT: Ashgate, 2008.

Murdoch, Scott. *The Terror of the Sea? Scottish Maritime Warfare, 1513–1713.* Boston: Brill, 2010.

Myers, Katherine. "Visual Fields: Theories of Perception and the Landscape Garden." In *Experiencing the Garden in the Eighteenth Century*, edited by Martin Calder, 13–36. Oxford: Peter Lang, 2006.

Neeley, Kathryn A. *Mary Somerville: Science, Illumination, and the Female Mind.* Cambridge: Cambridge University Press, 2001.

Nelson, Sarah, ed. *Hortense Mancini and Marie Mancini: Memoirs*. Chicago: University of Chicago Press, 2008.

Newton, Isaac. *Correspondence.* Edited by H. W. Turnbull. Cambridge: Cambridge University Press for the Royal Society, 1959.

Nicolay, Nicholas. "The Navigations, Peregrinations and Voyages, Made into Turkie." In *Race in Early Modern England: A Documentary Companion*, edited by Ania Loomba and Jonathan Burton, 115–19. New York: Palgrave, 2007.

Nussbaum, Felicity, ed. *The Global Eighteenth Century*. Baltimore: The Johns Hopkins University Press, 2003.

——. *Torrid Zones: Maternity, Sexuality, and Empire in Eighteenth-Century English Narratives.* Baltimore: The Johns Hopkins University Press, 1995.

——. "Women and Race: 'a difference of complexion'". In *Women and Literature in Britain 1700–1800*, edited by Vivien Jones, 69–88. Cambridge: Cambridge University Press, 2000..

O'Brien, Karen. *Women and Enlightenment in Eighteenth-Century Britain*. New York: Cambridge University Press, 2009.

O'Donnell, Mary Ann. *An Annotated Bibliography of Primary and Secondary Sources.* 2nd ed. Burlington, VT: Ashgate, 2004.

Ogborn, Miles. *Spaces of Modernity: London's Geographies, 1680–1780*. New York: Guilford Press, 1998.

Ogborn, Miles and Charles Withers. "Travel, Trade, and Empire: Knowing other Places, 1660–1800." In *A Concise Companion to The Restoration and Eighteenth Century*, edited by Cynthia Wall, 13–35. Malden, MA: Blackwell, 2005.

Ogborn, Miles and Charles Withers, eds. *Georgian Geographies: Essays on Space, Place and Landscape in the Eighteenth Century.* Manchester: Manchester University Press, 2004.

Ogilvie, Marilyn Bailey. "Caroline Herschel's Contributions to Astronomy." *Annals of Science* 32 (1975): 149–61.

Oldmixon, John. *The British Empire in America*. Vols 1 and 2. London: J. Brotherton, J. Clarke, A. Ward, J. Clarke, C. Hitch, J. Osbourn, E. Wicksteed, et al., 1741.

Opie, Amelia. *Adeline Mowbray.* Edited by Shelly King and John B. Pierce. Oxford: Oxford University Press, 1999.

Palk, Deirdre. *Gender Crime and Judicial Discretion, 1780–1830.* Woodbridge: Boydell Press, 2006.

Paravisini-Gebert, Lizabeth, and Ivette Romero-Cesareo, eds. *Women at Sea: Travel Writing and the Limits of Caribbean Discourse.* New York: Palgrave Macmillan, 2001.

Patey, Douglas Lane. "Anne Finch, John Dyer, and the Georgic Syntax of Nature." In *Augustan Subjects: Essays in Honor of Martin C. Battestin,* edited by Albert J. Rivero, 29–46. Newark: University of Delaware Press, 1997.

Payne, William W. "Book Notes: A Popular History of Astronomy During the Nineteenth Century." *The Sidereal Messenger* 5 (1886): 158–60.

Peirce, Leslie P. *The Imperial Harem: Women and Sovereignty in the Ottoman Empire.* New York: Oxford University Press, 1993.

Perry, Ruth. *The Celebrated Mary Astell.* Chicago: University of Chicago Press, 1986.

Pile, Steve and Neidi Nast. *Places Through the Body.* New York: Routledge, 1998.

Pincus, Steven. *Protestantism and Patriotism: Ideologies and the Making of English Foreign Policy, 1650–1668.* Cambridge: Cambridge University Press, 1996.

[Pittis, William]. *The Jamaica Lady: or, the life of Bavia. Containing an account of her intrigues, cheats, amours in England, Jamaica, and the Royal Navy* London: Tho. Bickerton, 1720.

Plummer, Patricia. "'The free treatment of topics usually taboo'd': Glimpses of the Harem in Eighteenth-and Nineteenth-Century Literature and the Fine Arts." In *Word and Image in Colonial and Post Colonial Literatures and Cultures,* edited by Michael Meyer, 47–68. New York: Rodopi, 2009.

Pocock, Douglas C. D. *Humanistic Geography and Literature: Essays on the Experience of Place.* London: Croom Helm, 1981.

Pohl, Nicole. *Women, Space, and Utopia 1600–1800.* Burlington, VT: Ashgate, 2006.

Pohl, Nicole, and Brenda Tooley, eds. *Gender and Utopia in the Eighteenth Century: Essays in English and French Utopian Writing.* Burlington, VT: Ashgate, 2007.

Pope, Alexander. *The Correspondence of Alexander Pope.* Edited by George Sherburn. London: Oxford University Press, 1956.

———. *The Poems of Alexander Pope: A One Volume Edition of The Twickenham Pope.* Edited by John Butt. New Haven: Yale University Press, 1963.

Porter, Roy. *Flesh in the Age of Reason.* New York: W. W. Norton, 2003.

Potter, Elizabeth. *Gender and Boyle's Law of Gases.* Bloomington: Indiana University Press, 2001.

Potts, Denys. "The Duchess Mazarin and Saint-Évremond: The Final Journey." In Shifrin, *The Wandering Life I Led,* 170–72.

"The Practice of Lights: or an Excellent and Ancient Treatise of the Philosophers Stone" (1683). Rpt. in *Collectanea Chymica: A Collection of Ten Several Treatises in Chymistry, Concerning the Liquor Alkahest, the Mercury of Philosophers, and other Curiosities worthy the Perusal.* N. p. London: William Cooper, 1684.

Pratt, Mary Louise. *Imperial Eyes: Travel Writing and Transculturation.* New York: Routledge, 1992.

Pred, Allan. "Place as Historically Contingent Process: Structuration and the Time-Geography of Becoming Places." *Annals of the Association of American Geographers* 74, no. 2 (1984): 279–97.

Psalms." In *Holy Bible: King James Version.* Camden, NJ: Thomas Nelson, 1972.

Punter, David. *The Literature of Terror.* 2 vols. London: Longmans, 1980, rpt. 1996.

"Reviews of New Publications: 66. *The Wanderer; or Female Difficulties* ... ." *The Gentleman's Magazine* 84 (1814). Part 1: 579.

Reiss, Timothy J. *Mirages of the Selfe: Patterns of Personhood in Ancient and Early Modern Europe.* Stanford: Stanford University Press, 2003.

Rennhak, Katharina. "Tropes of Exile in the 1790s: English Women Writers and French Emigrants." *European Romantic Review* 17, no. 5 (December 2006): 575–92.

Rich, Adrienne. *Blood, Bread, and Poetry: Selected Prose 1979–1985.* New York: W. W. Norton, 1986.

Richardson, Samuel. *Pamela.* Edited by Thomas Keymer and Alice Wakley. Oxford: Oxford University Press, 2001.

Ridgway, Christopher and Robert Williams. *Sir John Vanbrugh and Landscape Architecture in Baroque England 1690–1730.* Thrupp, Gloucestershire: Sutton Publishing, 2000.

Risk Management Solutions. "The December 1703 Windstorm." <http://www.rms.com/publications/1703_windstorm.pdf>.

"Rochester's Farewel." *Poems on Affairs of State: from the time of Oliver Cromwell.* 5th ed. Vol. 1. London, 1703.

Rogers, Katherine M. "Romantic Aspirations, Restricted Possibilities: The Novels of Charlotte Smith." In *Re-Visioning Romanticism: British Women Writers, 1776–1837,* edited by Carol Shiner Wilson and Joel Haefner, 72–88. Philadelphia: University of Pennsylvania Press, 1994.

Rose, Gillian. *Feminism and Geography: the Limits of Geographical Knowledge.* Minneapolis: University of Minnesota Press, 1993.

Rosenthal, Laura J. "Eliza Haywood: Discrepant Cosmopolitanism and the Persistence of Romance." *Nineteenth-Century Gender Studies* 3, no. 2 (2007). www.ncgsjournal.com/issue32/rosenthal.htm.

———. *Infamous Commerce: Prostitution in Eighteenth-Century British Literature and Culture.* Ithaca: Cornell University Press, 2006.

———. "Owning *Oroonoko*: Behn, Southerne and the Contingencies of Property." *Renaissance Drama,* n.s., 23 (1992): 25–58.

Rowe, Elizabeth Singer. *Friendship in Death* 1728. New York: Garland, 1972.

Said, Edward. *Culture and Imperialism*. New York: Knopf, 1993.

———. *Orientalism*. New York: Pantheon, 1978.

———. *Out of Place*. New York: Vintage, 1999.

———. "Reflections on Exile." In *Reflections on Exile and Other Essays*. Cambridge, MA: Harvard University Press, 2000.

Salih, Sara. "*Camilla* and *The Wanderer*." In *The Cambridge Companion to Frances Burney*, edited by Peter Sabor, 39–53. Cambridge: Cambridge University Press, 2007.

Salvagio, Ruth. *Enlightened Absence: Neoclassical Configurations of the Feminine*. Urbana: University of Illinois Press, 1988.

Sandys, George. "Relation of a Journey." In *Race in Early Modern England: A Documentary Companion*, edited by Ania Loomba and Jonathan Burton, 191–96. New York: Palgrave, 2007.

Saxton, Kirsten T. *Narratives of Women and Murder in England, 1680–1760: Deadly Plots*. Burlington, VT: Ashgate, 2009.

Schiebinger, Londa. "Maria Winkelmann at the Berlin Academy." *Isis* 78 (1987): 174–200.

Secor, Anna. "Islamism, Democracy, and the Political Production of the Headscarf Issue in Turkey." In *Geographies of Muslim Women*, edited by Ghazi-Walid Falah and Caroline Nagel, 203–25. New York: The Guilford Press, 2005.

Shadwell, Thomas. *The Virtuoso*. London: Henry Herringman, 1676.

Shanahan, John. "Ben Jonson's *The Alchemist* and Early Modern Laboratory Space." *JEMCS* (Spring/Summer 2008): 35–66.

Shapin, Steven and Simon Schaffer. *Leviathan and the Air Pump: Hobbes, Boyle, and the Experimental Life. Including and Translation of Thomas Hobbes, "Dialogus Physicus de Natura Aeris," by Simon Shaffer*. Princeton: Princeton University Press, 1985.

Shifrin, Susan. "'Subdued by a Famous Roman Dame': Picturing Foreignness, Notoriety, and Prerogative in the Portraits of Hortense Mancini, Duchess Mazarin." In *Politics, Transgression, and Representation at the Court of Charles II*, edited by Julia Alexander and Catharine MacLeod, 141–74. New Haven, CT: The Yale Center for British Art, 2007.

———, ed. *"The Wandering Life I Led": Essays on Hortense Mancini, Duchess Mazarin and Early Modern Women's Border-Crossings*. Newcastle-upon-Tyne: Cambridge Scholars Publishing, 2009.

Shifrin, Susan and Andrew R. Walkling. "'Iddylle En Musique': Performative Hybridity and the Duchess Mazarin as Visual, Textual, and Musical Icon." In Shifrin, *"The Wandering Life I Led"*, 48–99.

Shteir, Ann B. *Cultivating Women, Cultivating Science*. Baltimore: The Johns Hopkins University Press, 1996.

———. "Elegant Recreations? Configuring Science Writing for Women." In *Victorian Science in Context*, edited by Bernard Lightman, 236–55. Chicago: University of Chicago Press, 1997.

Simpson, David. "Raymond Williams: Feelings for Structures, Voicing 'History.'" *Social Text* 30 (1992): 2–26.

Smith, Charlotte. *The Banished Man*. In *The Works of Charlotte Smith*, Vol. 7, edited by M. O. Grenby. London: Pickering & Chatto, 2006.

———. *Emmeline, the Orphan of the Castle*. Edited by Loraine Fletcher. Peterborough: Broadview Press, 2003.

———. *The Poems of Charlotte Smith*. Edited by Stuart Curran. New York: Oxford University Press, 1993.

———. *The Young Philosopher*. Edited by Elizabeth Kraft. Lexington: University Press of Kentucky, 1999.

Smith, Edgar C. "Some Notable Women of Science." *Nature* 127 (1931): 976–77.

Smurzlo, Karyna. *The Novel's Seductions: Staël's "Corinne" in Critical Inquiry*. Lewisburg: Bucknell University Press, 1999.

Soja, Edward. *Postmodern Geographies: The Reassertion of Space in Critical Social Theory*. New York: Verso, 1989.

South, James. "Gold Medal to Miss Herschel." *Monthly Notices of the Royal Astronomical Society* 1 (1828): 62–64.

Southerne, Thomas. *Oroonoko: A Tragedy* (1696). In *The Works of Thomas Southerne*. Edited by Robert Jordan and Harold Love. Vol. 2. Oxford: Clarendon Press, 1988.

Spain, Daphne. *Gendered Spaces*. Chapel Hill: University of North Carolina Press, 1992.

Spengemann, William C. "The Earliest American Novel: Aphra Behn's *Oroonoko*." *Nineteenth-Century Fiction* 38, no. 4 (1984): 384–414.

Spivak, Gayatri Charkravorty. *A Critique of Postcolonial Reason*. Cambridge, MA: Harvard University Press, 1997.

Staël, Germaine, Madame de. *Corinne ou l'Italie*. Edited by Simone Balayé. Paris: Gallimard, 1985.

———. "De la littérature considérée dans ses rapports avec les institutions sociales." In *Oeuvres complètes de Mme. De Staël*. Vol. 13. Brussels: Auguste Wahlen et cie, 1820.

———. "Dix années d'exil." In *Oeuvres complètes de Mme. De Staël*. Vol. 15. Brussels: Auguste Wahlen et cie, 1820.

Streatfield, David. "Art and Nature in the English Landscape Garden: Design, Theory, and Practice, 1700–1818." In *Landscape Gardens and Literature of Eighteenth-Century England: Papers Read at a Clark Library Seminar, 18 March 1978*, 1–72. Los Angeles: William Andrews Clark Memorial Library, University of California Press, 1981.

Summerson, John. *Architecture in Britain 1530–1830*. Harmondsworth: Penguin, 1969.

Sypher, Wiley. *Guinea's Captive Kings: British Anti-Slavery Literature of the Eighteenth Century*. New York: Octagon, 1969.

Tayebi, Kandi. "Undermining the Eighteenth-Century Pastoral: Rewriting the Poet's Relationship to Nature in Charlotte Smith's Poetry." *European Romantic Review* 15, no. 1 (March 2004): 131–50.

Taylor, Charles. *Sources of the Self: The Making of the Modern Identity.* Cambridge, MA: Harvard University Press, 1989.

Taylor, Clare. "The Journal of an Absentee Proprietor, Nathanial Phillips of Slebech." *Journal of Caribbean History* XVIII (1984): 67–82.

Telescope, Tom. *The Newtonian System of Philosophy, A New and Improved Edition.* Philadelphia: Jacob Johnson, 1803.

Tinker, Chauncey. *The Salon and English Letters: Chapters on the Interrelations of Literature and Society in the Age of Johnson.* New York: Gordian Press, 1967.

Todd, Janet. *The Secret Life of Aphra Behn.* London: Pandora, 2000.

Trumpener, Katie. *Bardic Nationalism: The Romantic Novel and the British Empire.* Princeton: Princeton University Press, 1997.

Turner, Katherine. *British Travel Writers in Europe, 1750–1800: Authorship, Gender, and National Identity.* Burlington, VT: Ashgate, 2002.

Ty, Eleanor. *Unsex'd Revolutionaries: Five Women Novelists of the 1790s.* Toronto: University of Toronto Press, 1993.

Van Helmont, Jean Baptiste. "Praecipiolum: or the immature mineral-electrum. The first metal, which is the minera of mercury." In *Collectanea Chymica: A Collection of Ten Several Treatises in Chymistry, Concerning the Liquor Alkahest, the Mercury of Philosophers, and other Curiosities worthy the Perusal,* n.p. London: William Cooper, 1684.

Vickery, Amanda. *The Gentleman's Daughter: Women's Lives in Georgian England.* New Haven: Yale University Press, 1998.

———. "Golden Age to Separate Spheres? A Review of the Categories and Chronology of English Women's History." In *Women's Work: The English Experience, 1630–1914,* edited by Pamela Sharpe, 294–332. Auckland: Arnold, 1998.

Vieira, M. Fatima. "The Concept of Utopia." In *The Cambridge Companion to Utopian Literature,* edited by Gregory Claes, 3–27. Cambridge: Cambridge University Press, 2010.

Wahrman, Dror. *The Making of the Modern Self: Identity and Culture in Eighteenth-Century England.* New Haven: Yale University Press, 2004.

Wall, Cynthia. *The Literary and Cultural Spaces of Restoration London.* New York: Cambridge University Press, 1998.

Wallace, Elizabeth Kowaleski. "Transnationalism and Performance in 'Biyi Bandele's *Oroonoko*." *PMLA* 119, no. 2 (March 2004): 265–81.

Walton, John K. *The English Seaside Resort: A Social History 1750–1914.* Leicester: Leicester University Press; New York: St. Martin's Press, 1983.

Ward, Edward. "A Trip to Jamaica." In *Caribbeana: An Anthology of English Literature of the West Indies 1657–1777,* edited by Thomas W. Krise, 78–92. Chicago: University of Chicago Press, 1999.

Warton, Thomas. *The Poems on Various Subjects, of Thomas Warton.* London, 1791.

Watkin, David. *The English Vision: The Picturesque in Architecture, Landscape, and Garden Design.* New York: Harper & Row, 1982.

Watson, Tim. *Caribbean Culture and British Fiction in the Atlantic World, 1780–1870.* Cambridge: Cambridge University Press, 2008.

Watt, Ian. *The Rise of the Novel: Studies in Defoe, Richardson and Fielding.* London: Chatto & Windus, 1957.

Weil, Rachel. *Political Passions: Gender, the Family, and Political Argument in England, 1680–1714.* New York: Manchester University Press, 1999.

Weitzman, Arthur J. "Voyeurism and Aesthetics in the Turkish Bath: Lady Mary's School of Female Beauty." *Comparative Literature Studies* 39 (2002): 347–59.

Wheeler, Roxann. *The Complexion of Race: Categories of Difference in Eighteenth-Century British Culture.* Philadelphia: University of Pennsylvania Press, 2000.

Willard, Thomas. "Ovid and the Alchemists." In *Metamorphosis: The Changing Face of Ovid in Medieval and Early Modern Europe*, edited by Alison Keith and Steven Rupp, 151–64. Toronto: Center for Reformation and Renaissance Studies, 2007.

The William and Mary Quarterly 69, no. 1 (January 2012).

Williams, H. Noel. *Rival Sultanas: Nell Gwyn, Louise de Kèroualle, and Hortense Mancini.* London: Hutchinson & Co., 1915.

Williams, Raymond. *Politics and Letters: Interviews with New Left Review.* New York: Schocken Books, 1979.

Wilson, John Harold. *Court Satires of the Restoration.* Columbus: Ohio State University Press, 1976.

Wilson, Kathleen. *The Island Race: Englishness, Empire, and Gender in the Eighteenth Century.* London: Routledge, 2003.

———. *A New Imperial History: Culture Identity and Modernity in Britain and the Empire, 1660-1840.* Cambridge: Cambridge University Press, 2004.

Withers, Charles W. J. "Place and the 'Spatial Turn' in Geography and in History." *Journal of the History of Ideas* 70, no. 4 (2009): 637–65.

———. "Where Was the Atlantic Enlightenment? Questions of Geography." In *The Atlantic Enlightenment*, edited by Susan Manning and Francis Cogliano, 37–60. Aldershot: Ashgate, 2008.

Wordsworth, William. "Essay, Supplementary to the Preface (1815)." In *William Wordsworth*, edited by Stephen Gill, 640–42. London: Oxford, 1984.

Yeğenoğlu, Meyda. *Colonial Fantasies: Towards a Feminist Reading of Orientalism.* New York: Cambridge University Press, 1998.

Zinsser, Judith P. "Translating Newton's 'Principia': The Marquise de Châtelet's Revisions and Additions for Audience." *Notes and Records of the Royal Society of London* 55, no. 2 (2001): 227–45.

Index

Abolitionist movement 21, 30
Adeline Mowbray (Opie) 43
aesthetics 4, 6, 32, 58, 160, 190, 202
Africa 20, 22, 23–4, 32; *see also* slavery
Alchemist, The (Jonson) 165, 168–9
alchemy 15, 165–77
    domestic conventions and 170–72
    marriage and 175–7
    sociability and 172–5
Alliston, April 90
amatory fiction 14, 133–46
America 19, 115
Amerindian 27
Anatomy of Melancholy, The (Burton) 55
Anderson, Benedict 9
Anderson, Perry 93
architecture
    functionalistic division of 148–51, 157,
        158–9
    of gardens 134, 139
"Architecture, Authority, and the Female
        Gaze: Planning and Representation
        in the Early Modern Country
        House" (Friedman) 148–9, 158
Arnold, Christoph 67
Ashmole, Elias 169
associative public sphere 166, 168
Astell, Mary 128, 129
*Astronomical and Geographical Class
        Book for Schools, An* (Bryan) 74
astronomy 12, 67–71, 72, 73, 74, 77, 81, 82
Atlantic Enlightenment 20–21, 22, 23, 29, 32
Atlas of the European Novel (Moretti) 93, 95
attachment 21–2
Aubin, Penelope 143–4
Austen, Jane 145

Babha, Homi 8
Bachelard, Gaston 6
Bandele, 'Biyi 22, 32

Banished Man, The (Smith) 15, 179–93
Beach, Adam 24
Beachy Head (Smith) 206
"Beautiful Young Nymph" (Swift) 33
Beggs, Courtney 12, 13, 117
Behn, Aphra 10, 19, 20, 22, 25–30, 137
    Dutch Lover, The 168, 176
    History of the Nun, The 126
    Oroonoko 19–32
    Widow Ranter, The 28
Belinda (Inchbald) 43
Bell, Joseph 189
Benítez-Rojo, Antonio 28
Bergren, Anne 162
Bertha's Visit to Her Uncle in England
        (Marcet) 81
Binhammer, Katherine 185
Blake, Rev. J. L. 78
Bloodless Revolution *see* Glorious
        Revolution
bodies 3, 30, 53, 59
Bohls, Elizabeth A. 35
borderlands 12–13
borders 1, 5, 8, 12–13, 93, 110, 120n; *see
        also* coastline
botany 73, 81, 141
Bourdieu, Pierre 127
Boyle, Robert 166, 168, 169–70, 171, 172,
        173, 174, 175–6
Brady, Mary Pat 4
Braithwait, Edward 34–5
Brakenburgh, Richard 168
Brewer, Daniel 7
Britain *see* England
British colonies *see* Jamaica; Surinam
British Garden, The (Murray) 73
Brück, Mary T. 74, 80
Bryan, Margaret 67, 73, 74–7, 78, 79
    *Astronomical and Geographical Class
        Book for Schools, An* 74